The Routledge
Dictionary of Judaism

Compiled by two internationally renowned experts, and with over 600 wide-ranging and informative entries, this dictionary provides the reader with an invaluable reference aid to all areas of the religion.

It covers:

- Different forms of the religion, such as Orthodox, Reform, Conservative, and New Age Judaism, and its history from the formative age to the present day
- Its institutions, religious practices, and life-cycle rites such as Berit Milah, Bar Mitzvah and Bat Mitzvah
- Key texts and people, including the oral and written Torah, Moses, the Prophets, Abraham Joshua Heschel, Martin Buber
- Holy days and festivals including Sabbath, Passover, Hanukkah, Sukkot, and holy objects such as the Shofar, Lulab, Tefillin
- Theological terms, doctrine, and philosophy including entries on Purity and Pollution, Kavvanah, and the Judaism of Holocaust and Redemption

Jacob Neusner is Research Professor of Religion and Theology at Bard College, Annandale-on-Hudson, New York. **Alan J. Avery-Peck** is Kraft-Hiatt Professor of Judaic Studies and Chair of the Department of Religious Studies at the College of the Holy Cross, Worcester, Massachusetts.

Other titles by the authors
Dictionary of Judaism in the Biblical Period, from 450 B.C. to 600 A.D. (Macmillan Publishing Co., N.Y., 1995)
The Encylopaedia of Judaism (E.J. Brill, Leiden, Boston and Köln; and Continuum International Publishing, New York and London, 2000)
The Blackwell Companion to Judaism (Blackwell Publishers, Oxford, 2000)
The Blackwell Reader in Judaism (Blackwell Publishers, Oxford, 2001)

The Routledge
Dictionary of Judaism

Jacob Neusner
and
Alan J. Avery-Peck

Routledge
Taylor & Francis Group

NEW YORK AND LONDON

First published 2004
by Routledge
29 West 35th Street, New York, NY 10001

Simultaneously published in the UK
by Routledge
11 New Fetter Lane, London EC4P 4EE

Routledge is an imprint of the Taylor & Francis Group

© 2004 Jacob Neusner and Alan J. Avery-Peck
Illustrations © 2004 Suzanne Neusner
Typeset in Times by HWA Text and Data Management, Tunbridge Wells
Printed and bound in Great Britain by MPG Books Ltd, Bodmin, Cornwall

Library of Congress Cataloging in Publication Data
Neusner, Jacob, 1932–
   The Routledge dictionary of Judaism / Jacob Neusner & Alan J. Avery-Peck.
     p. cm. – (The Routledge dictionaries)
   1. Judaism–Dictionaries. I. Avery-Peck, Alan J. (Alan Jeffery), 1953–
    II. Title. III. Series.
   BM50.N47 2003
   296´.03–dc21   2003007260

British Library Cataloguing in Publication Data
A catalogue record for this book is available from the British Library

ISBN 0–415–30264–1

Preface

This dictionary addresses the religion that finds in the Torah—God's revelation to Moses at Mount Sinai—the full and complete account of what God wants from humanity. In the perspective of this religion, of Judaism, God's presence is located especially in Israel, the people who know God, and who, forming God's kingdom in the Torah, stand in a covenanted relationship with God. By "Israel" Judaism thus means the people that came into being at Sinai by accepting the Torah; they are the heirs and descendants of the patriarchs and matriarchs, of Abraham and Sarah, Isaac and Rebecca, Jacob and Leah and Rachel. Israel, the people, and Judaism, their religion, as they are referred to here, thus represent supernatural categories, not to be confused with the ethnic group, the Jewish people and its culture, or with the nation-state, the State of Israel. In these pages, we speak of the "Israel" of the liturgy and holy books of the religion, Judaism.

When the sources of Judaism refer to the religion they represent, they use the word "Torah." By this they mean, first of all, the Pentateuch or the Five Books of Moses (Genesis, Exodus, Leviticus, Numbers, and Deuteronomy). With this term, they also refer to the Prophets—Joshua, Judges, Samuel, Kings, Isaiah, Jeremiah, Ezekiel, and the Twelve Minor Prophets—which, like the books of the Pentateuch, are read within the synagogue liturgy. A third part of the Torah is the Writings (Ketubim), consisting of Psalms and Proverbs, Job and Chronicles. In addition to these books, comprising the Torah in written form and corresponding to what Christians refer to as "the Old Testament," Judaism affirms as part of the Torah an oral tradition, transmitted not in writing but in memory, in oral form, from master to disciple, from Moses on down into the early centuries of the Common Era. The Oral Torah today is contained in the writings of Talmudic Judaism: the Mishnah, Tosefta, the Jerusalem and Babylonian Talmud, and the Midrash compilations.

"Judaism" thus is the religion of Torah, both the Pentateuch revealed by God to Moses at Mount Sinai in written form and the teachings given by God to Moses that were not written down but were orally formulated and transmitted in a chain of tradition. This means that, from the viewpoint of Judaism, when the Torah, oral and written, is properly explained, people who practice Judaism—the people of Israel—know what God has to say to them and what He wants them to do. Judaism thus is the account of the way of life and world view of Israel, the holy people, as set forth by God to Moses at Mount Sinai in the Torah, the whole Torah, part oral and part written.

What we aim to define

In this dictionary, we define the vocabulary in Hebrew and in English that conveys the details of the Torah, the religion the world calls "Judaism." In presenting these definitions, we address an audience of students in the academic study of religion, including theology, and of lay readers with an interest in Judaism. For these groups we offer definitions—some brief, some elaborate—of the key terms of Judaism that they are likely to encounter in their reading. That is a practical goal, but it is an important one, because Judaism encompasses beliefs and behaviors, narrative and theology, a vast library of holy books, a cadre of holy persons. Its way of life defines holy days and holy places, permitted and forbidden actions. Vast encyclopedias, in many volumes, do not succeed in encompassing all that is to be known about Judaism, with its history extending back for nearly four millennia, its geography covering much of the globe, its canon encompassing entire libraries of writings, and its ethnic foundations dispersed through much of the world.

Guided by our experience of the focus of interest of our audience, we have chosen to emphasize—though hardly to limit ourselves to—the classical or formative age of Judaism. That is the period that produced Scripture and the texts of Rabbinic Judaism that serve as the foundation for all later Judaic systems. While covering a range of data that extends to the present day, including modern Judaic figures and movements, we emphasize the universal and classical, those books, concepts, and institutions characteristic of Judaism in its formative age.

This emphasis represents a judgment on what our readers are likely to want to know, and it affects the proportion and detail of coverage, not inclusion or exclusion. What are the specific types of data we deem to require definition here? Our list of words for inclusion covers these areas: literature; persons; forms and history; institutions; practices and life-cycle rites, both public and private; theological terms and categories that pertain to the Judaic understanding of existence; Judaic symbols; places; times; calendars, holy days and holy places; purity and pollution; objects, gestures and clothing; and the like. Responding to what we deem required, entries are of varied length, some discursive, some brief, as the item in hand requires.

Still, this is a general dictionary, not an encyclopedia of all conceivable facts pertaining to the Jews and Judaism. Thus we do not offer extensive articles, complete with critical bibliographies. We provide, rather, a convenient, ready reference to guide reading in Judaism in the setting of the study of religion.

Transliteration and abbreviations

'Aleph	'	Mem	m
Bet	b	Nun	n
Gimel	g	Samekh	s
Daled	d	'ayin	'
Hé	h	Peh	p
Vav	v	Saddi	ṣ
Ziyyan	z	Quf	q
Het	ḥ	Resh	r
Tet	t	Shin	sh
Yud	y	Sin	s
Khaf	kh	Tav	t
Lamed	l		

For cases in which Hebrew terms do not have a standard English spelling, we use a simple system of transliteration. We represent Hebrew letters by the Roman counterparts indicated in the table and reproduce words as pronounced in Israeli Hebrew. Except in cases in which notation of an aleph or ayyin is necessary for proper pronunciation, these letters are only indicated by the corresponding vowel.

We try to find neutral language to refer to matters that elicit strong, partisan response, in politics or in theology. So far as possible, outside of translations, we use gender-neutral language. In referring to B.C.E. and C.E., rather than B.C. and A.D., we have selected language that avoids theological assertions. Depending on the context, we refer to the Holy Land as either "the land of Israel," as it was known to Judaism through all time, or "Palestine," the name given to the country by the Romans later on. Where either phrase is used, we intend no political statement of any kind. "Palestine" is a necessary geographical term in some contexts, "land of Israel" a required theological term in others.

<table>
<tr><td>Jacob Neusner</td><td>Alan J. Avery-Peck</td></tr>
<tr><td>Bard College</td><td>College of the Holy Cross</td></tr>
</table>

A

Ab Fifth month of the Jewish year, July-August, in which the fast of the Ninth of Ab (Tisha beAb – see AB, NINTH OF) falls.

Ab, Ninth of (Hebrew: *Tisha beAb*) Day of mourning for the destruction of the Jerusalem Temple in 586 B.C.E. and again in 70 C.E. and for other occasions of destruction and loss of life in the history of Judaism. The month of Ab falls in late July, early August. The Ninth of Ab is marked with a 24-hour fast and other symbols of grief, including prohibitions against bathing and sexual relations. The day's liturgy includes the dirge-like chanting of the Book of Lamentations, which tells the story of the Temple's destruction. In the synagogue, the ark curtain is removed, the sanctuary is dimly lit, and congregants sit on the floor or on low benches, all signs of mourning.

Ab Bet Din Within Talmudic Judaism, judge of a court; second in charge of the principal court; second to the patriarch (Hebrew: *nasi*) in Mishnah Abot Chap. 1 (see ABOT).

Abodah Zarah (Lit.: "alien form of divine worship") Mishnah tractate devoted to idolatry. Supplies rules and regulations to carry out the fundamental biblical commandments about the destruction of idols and all things having to do with idolatry, with special reference to commercial relationships, matters pertaining to idols, and the prohibition on drinking wine, some of which has served as a libation to an idol. What a gentile is not likely to use for the worship of an idol is not going to be prohibited. What may serve not as part of idolatry but as an appurtenance thereto is

prohibited for Israelite use but permitted for Israelite commerce. What serves for idolatry is prohibited for use and for benefit. Certain further assumptions about gentiles, not pertinent specifically to idolatry, are expressed. Gentiles are assumed routinely to practice idolatry, bloodshed, and fornication, without limit or restriction. Jews may not sell to gentiles bears, lions, or anything that is a public danger. They do not help them build a basilica, scaffold, stadium or judges' tribunal. They do not make ornaments for an idol, sell them produce that is not yet harvested, or sell them land in the Holy Land. These things belonging to gentiles are prohibited, and the prohibition concerning them extends to deriving any benefit from them at all: wine, vinegar, earthenware that absorbs wine, and hides pierced at the heart. Both versions of the Talmud address this tractate.

Abot (Hebrew: "The Fathers") Attached to, but not part of, the MISHNAH, Abot, also known as Pirqei Abot, that is, "Sayings of the Fathers," consists of five chapters of wise sayings. These comprise mainly a handbook for disciples of sages, especially those involved in administration of the law. The sayings are assigned to named authorities, and their topics, over all, derive from the realm of wisdom: right conduct with God, society, self. While the sayings cover miscellaneous topics, the list coheres as a whole because everything on it is part of a chain of transmission—tradition—beginning with Moses on Sinai. So one sentence joins the next because all the sentences enjoy the same status, that imparted by the Torah. The topical program is also cogent, with its recurrent emphasis on Torah study and the social, intellectual, and personal virtues required for Torah study.

Always published with the Mishnah but autonomous of that document's literary and programmatic attributes, Abot cites authorities of the generation generally assumed to have flourished after the completion of the Mishnah. It hence may have been written ca. 250 C.E., though this is only a guess.

While separate from the Mishnah in literary form, Abot's proposition and message form the keystone and centerpiece of the Mishnaic literature. The document serves as the Mishnah's first and most important apologetic, stating in abstract terms the ideals for the virtuous life that are set forth by the Mishnah's sages and that animate the Mishnah's laws. Abot's presentation of sayings of sages extending from Sinai to figures named in the Mishnah links the Mishnah to Sinai. The claim is that, because of the authorities cited in its pages, the Mishnah constitutes part of the "Torah revealed to Moses at Sinai." This is expressed in Abot's opening sentence: "Moses received the Torah at Sinai and handed it on to Joshua, Joshua to elders, and elders to prophets. And prophets handed it on to the men of the Great Assembly" (Haknesset Ha-Gadol). They said three things: Be prudent in judgment. Raise up many disciples. Make a fence for the Torah."

The verbs, "receive ... hand on ...," in Hebrew yield the words *qabbalah*, tradition, and *masoret,* also tradition. The theological proposition that validates the Mishnah thus is that the Torah is a matter of tradition. The tradition goes from master to disciple, Moses to Joshua and so on to the authorities of the Mishnah itself, found later in the list. That fact forms an implicit claim that part of the Torah was, and is, orally formulated and orally transmitted, and that the Mishnah's authorities stand in the tradition of Sinai, so that the Mishnah, too, forms part of the TORAH of Sinai. This position is a different approach to claiming divine authority from that taken in other ancient texts, for instance, by PSEUDEPIGRAPHIC writers, who imitate the style of Scripture or who claim to speak within the same gift of revelation as Moses. It is one thing to say one's holy book is Scripture because it is like Scripture or to claim that the author of the holy book has a revelation independent of that of Moses. These two positions concede to the Torah of Moses priority over their own holy books. Abot makes no such concession in alleging that the Mishnah is part of the Torah of Moses. It appeals to the highest possible authority in the Israelite framework, claiming the most one can claim in behalf of a book that, in fact, bears the names of men who lived fifty years before the apologists themselves. Abot's apologia for the Mishnah, rather, rests upon the persons of the sages themselves: incarnations of the Torah of Sinai in the here-and-now.

Abot deRabbi Natan (Hebrew: "The Fathers according to Rabbi Nathan") An amplification of Mishnah Tractate ABOT, which, in 250 C.E., delivered its message through aphorisms assigned to named sages. A few centuries later—the date is indeterminate but ca. 500—Abot deRabbi Natan, a vast secondary expansion of that tractate, endowed those anonymous names with flesh-and-blood-form, recasting the tractate by adding a sizable number of narratives. The authorship of Abot deRabbi Natan thus contributed in a systematic and orderly manner the color and life of biography to the named but faceless sages of Mishnah Tractate Abot.

Abot deRabbi Natan presents an ideal of the sage as a model for the everyday life of the individual, who must study the Torah and also work and, through the good life, prepare now for life after death. But Abot deRabbi Natan has a different conception of the sage and of the value and meaning of the study of the Torah, and also has selected a new medium for the expression of its distinctive conception. For here, the sage is not a judge and teacher alone but also a supernatural figure. Now, study of the Torah in preference to making a living promises freedom from the conditions of natural life. And, finally, Israel as the holy people takes center-stage.

Abraham   Viewed in Judaism, Christianity, and Islam as the first monotheist. With his wife, Sarah, he was the progenitor of Israel, the community formed by those who abandon idolatry and instead worship the one God. Abraham was called by God to leave his country of origin and journey to the Holy Land, which God promised to his descendants (Genesis 12:1ff.). Abraham and Sarah obeyed and with them monotheism began in humanity. God made himself known to Abraham step by step through a series of trials; at each point, Abraham withstood the test and showed himself faithful.

Adam   The first man, created by God on the sixth day of creation, according to the narrative of Genesis 1:1–2:3. Formed of the earth (*adamah* in Hebrew), Adam was made in God's image: "Let us make man in our image, after our likeness, and let him have dominion over the fish of the sea and the birds of the air and the cattle. ... So God created man in his own image, in the image of God he created him; male and female he created them" (Genesis 1:26–27). EVE, the first woman, was created out

of Adam's rib. Adam and Eve were given the Garden of Eden as their domain and were to live there forever, never having to do servile labor and never having to die. They were given the fruit of all the trees of the garden but one. But they disobeyed the one commandment that God gave them, which was not to eat of the fruit of the tree of the knowledge of good and evil, "for in the day that you eat of it, you shall die" (Genesis 2:16–17). Inveigled by the serpent, Adam and Eve ate that fruit. As a result, they were driven from Paradise, and Adam was punished, "In the sweat of your face you shall eat bread till you return to the ground, for out of it you were taken; you are dust and to dust you shall return" (Genesis 3:19).

Adar   Twelfth month in the Jewish year, February-March; contains 29 days in ordinary years, 30 days in leap years and includes the festival of Purim and four special Sabbaths: Sheqalim, Zakhor, Parah, and HaHodesh.

Adar, Seventh of   Date traditionally believed to be the anniversary of the birth and the death of Moses.

Adar Sheni   Intercalated twenty-nine day month, added in leap years to keep the lunar and solar calendars synchronized. Adar Sheni is added in the third, sixth, eighth, eleventh, fourteenth, seventeenth and nineteenth years of the nineteen-year Jewish calendar cycle (*mahzor*).

Adon Olam   Synagogue hymn, "Lord of the World," used to conclude most worship services. It contains the dogmas of divine unity, timelessness, and providence.

Adoption   Not recognized in talmudic law, which holds that a child's status derives from the natural relationship to the parent and cannot be altered or artificially created; still, within Talmudic law, one may assume responsibility for a child's person and estate as a guardian. An adopted child of gentile origin converts to Judaism (see GER) upon reaching the age of maturity, twelve for females, thirteen for males. Adopted babies are immersed on the stipulation that, upon reaching maturity, they will freely opt to convert to Judaism. So too, an adopted male infant is circumcised on the stipulation that, upon reaching maturity, he will confirm that it is his will to enter Israel.

Adultery   Sexual relations between a married woman and a man not her husband; according to Scripture, both parties are liable to the death penalty. In the case of insufficient evidence, the wife may be subjected to the ordeal of the bitter water described at Numbers 5:12–31 (see SOTAH).

Afikoman   The middle piece of three pieces of MATZAH (unleavened bread) placed on the SEDER plate at the PASSOVER table; the middle piece is divided into two, the larger part of which is called afikoman, meaning either post-prandial entertainment or desert. Its consumption marks the end of the Passover meal.

Agency   (Hebrew: *Shelihut*) The theory that a second party may legally act in behalf of a person, as if the principal had done the action; a person's agent is equivalent to the person, and one is bound by what the agent does as though having done it himself; but agency does not pertain to transgression, and if the agent does not carry out instructions, the sender is not accountable for the deed. An agent may serve to effect a betrothal or a divorce.

Aggadah   Literally: telling, narration; generally: lore, theology, fable, biblical exegesis, ethics; exposition of theological and ethical topics; exegesis of non-legal passages of Scripture. By "Aggadah" in Hebrew is meant "narrative," ordinarily, narrative based upon, or in response to, Scripture.

Agunah   (Hebrew: "abandoned woman") A woman who is not free to remarry, who is held to be in a marital relationship even though her husband may be dead, his whereabouts are unknown, or, although they are separated, he will not provide her a writ of divorce. In light of the existing marriage, she cannot enter into a new one. The problem of the Agunah arises because, in Jewish law, only the husband can provide a writ of divorce; if he is unavailable or unwilling to do so, the woman has no recourse. Absence of proof of the husband's death may also impose the status of Agunah on the widow. In modern Judaism, Orthodoxy and the Conservative movement continue to require a Jewish writ of divorce (see GET) alongside a civil proceeding before a rabbi will officiate at a woman's remarriage. The problem of the Agunah accordingly continues to arise among adherents of these modes of Jewish observance. The Reform movement requires only civil divorce, which may be initiated by either party to the marriage. Within REFORM JUDAISM, the problem of the Agunah accordingly ceases to arise at all.

Ahab, King   King of ancient Israel, criticized by the prophet Elijah for worshipping Baal, the fertility god of the land rather than the Lord (1 Kings 17–18). The Rabbinic tradition represents Ahab as an enemy of Israel, seeking to wipe out the knowledge of God set forth in Torah study.

Akkum   Abbreviation of the first letters of the words in Hebrew for "worshippers of stars and planets," stands for pagans or idolaters.

Alenu (Hebrew: "Let us [praise him, Lord over all the world]") A prayer found at the conclusion of every synagogue service, comprising at the moment of the congregation's departure a self-conscious rehearsal of Israel's election and peoplehood. As the community goes forth, they look forward to the day on which all humanity will acknowledge God as ruler of the world and author of creation. In this prayer, therefore, Judaism asks for the end of idolatry and the beginning of universal worship of the one true God. The prayer thus sets forth the eschatological aspiration of Israelite monotheism. The unique, the particular, attest to divine sovereignty, pertinent to all people, all groups.

Aliyah (Hebrew: "going up") "Ascent" in particular to the Land of Israel or, from within the Land, ascent to Jerusalem, as an act of pilgrimage. In the synagogue, the term refers to the honor of "ascending" to the Torah, that is, of participating in the worship service by reciting the blessings that introduce and conclude each section of the Torah lection or by being of some other service to the Torah: opening or closing the ark, carrying, lifting, or dressing the scroll. In contemporary parlance the term Aliyah also refers to permanent immigration to the state of Israel.

In classical Judaism, pilgrimage to the Jerusalem Temple was required three times yearly, on the festivals of PASSOVER, SUKKOT, and SHABU'OT, when all Israel was called to appear before God, to keep a feast to the Lord, and to rejoice (Exodus 23:17, Deuteronomy 16:15, and Deuteronomy 16:17). Aliyah thus formed the concrete occasion for Israel's most immediate and tangible encounter with God.

In Mishnah tractate Ḥagigah, the pilgrimage is given concreteness through law. The Mishnah takes up the pilgrims' complementary obligations of sacrifice and cultic purity. The Israelite is to be seen in the Temple court on the feast with a whole offering (birds or cattle; "None shall appear before me empty," Exodus 23:15). Keeping the feast, furthermore, means presenting a peace offering when one makes his appearance on the first festival day of the feast. The duty of rejoicing involves a peace offering in addition to the festal peace offering: "the peace offering of rejoicing in the feast," in line with Deuteronomy 27:7: "And you shall sacrifice peace offerings and shall eat thereof and you shall rejoice before the Lord your God."

Am Ha'Areṣ (Hebrew: "people of the land") In Rabbinic usage: a boor, unlearned, not a disciple of the sages. The opposite of a Ḥaber, who is an associate of a Pharisaic circle, one who is lettered in the Torah.

Amalek Blood-enemy of Israel (Exodus 17:8–16), he comes to symbolize implacable foes through all time; described as irreconcilable enemy, ancestor of all later enemies; in Talmudic Judaism, often identified with Rome.

Amidah See SHEMONEH ESREH.

Amora Rabbinical teacher in the Land of Israel and Babylonia in Talmudic times (ca. 200–600 C.E.). The Amoraim (pl.) are the principal authorities of the two versions of the TALMUD and the primary commentators on the MISHNAH, TOSEFTA, and other pre-Talmudic legal traditions. The term "Amoraic" designates a statement or text that derives from the period and authority of the Amoraim.

Amos The first prophet of ancient Israel from the 8th century B.C.E. whose actual words we possess, Amos directed a call for justice not only to the king, as Nathan did to David and Elijah to Ahab, but to the rulers and the upper classes in general. He criticized the sacrificial service cult but saw God standing by the altar. He criticized the shrines that ignored social oppression.

Analogical-Contrastive Thinking   A mode of reasoning, characteristic of Rabbinic legal texts, that holds that if things are alike, they follow the same rule, but if they are not alike, they follow opposite rules from one another. While never identified in itself, this mode of thought is common in the formation of the rules of the MISHNAH at its earliest layers (ca. 10–200 C.E.).

Ancient Israel   In the context of the religion, Judaism, the term refers to the people called by God to carry out God's will for Creation. In ancient times, from ca. 1400 B.C.E. onward, as portrayed by the Hebrew Scriptures, the people Israel all are children of the same forebears, ABRAHAM and SARAH. People join the family by accepting the God of Abraham, and converts to Judaism are called "children of Abraham and Sarah." The people-family took shape in response to God's call to Abraham and his blessing accorded to his son ISAAC and to Isaac's son JACOB and their family. That people was promised a land, called the Land of Israel, where they would realize the promise of Creation that the world would be perfect and build a paradise. But because they did not keep God's instruction, contained in the Torah, God's teaching to Moses at Sinai, they lost the Land, as Adam had lost Eden. But the Torah contains the promise that, when the people Israel realize the imperatives of the Torah, they will recover the Land and restore Eden.

Anti-Semitism   Historical Christian doctrine of Jew-hatred and of contempt for Judaism, the religion. In common usage, the term also encompasses the racist anti-Semitism of the German Nazis and of some Islamic extremists, from which phenomena it rightly should be distinguished. In the early centuries C.E., the doctrine developed that "the Jews killed Christ" (that is, "deicide") and that the guilt for that act is inherited by all Jews from then on. Further, the Church put forth the claim that it represented "the true Israel," heir to the divine promises, and that the Jews, Christ-killers, were rejected by God and were not really, or no longer, "the true Israel" of whom the Hebrew Scriptures spoke. The Jews, furthermore, no longer had the valid Torah of Sinai since, in light of the doctrine of the oral Torah, they now followed a false revelation, having forged new documents attributed to Moses but never revealed by him. The promises of the prophets, ISAIAH, JEREMIAH, Ezekiel, all were fully kept in the return to Zion of the sixth century B.C.E., and the Jews no longer had a future; they would never return to Jerusalem and recover their country, the land of Israel. Christian anti-Semitism further maintained that Jews were extravagant gluttons and dissolute, depraved and wanton, and that they were to be kept alive only to bear witness to the truth of Christianity. At the second coming, the Jews too would convert to Christ.

This doctrine of hatred for the Jews and contempt for Judaism formed the foundation for modern racist anti-Semitism, which imputed to Jews on a racial, genetic basis the same evil qualities that Christianity had assigned to them on an inherited basis; the difference was that Christianity held that Jews could atone for their sins and crimes by conversion to Christianity, while modern racist anti-Semitism holds that there is no remedy for the Jews' condition. Christian anti-Semitism thus held that Jews might live, just not as Jews, while racist anti-Semitism holds that Jews should not live at all.

Apikoros (Hebrew: *Epicurus*) Unbelief or, generally, belief in hedonism; one who denies the Torah, rejects the commandments; does not respect the sages.

Apocrypha Jewish writings composed circa 250 B.C.E.-100 C.E. and found in the Greek translation of the Bible (Septuagint) but not incorporated in the biblical canon set out by the rabbis of the first centuries C.E. These books accordingly are included in the Roman Catholic and Greek Orthodox Bibles but are not accepted as authoritative by Jews and so are not included in Jewish printings of Scripture. The Apocrypha encompasses 1 Esdras, 2 Esdras (not found in the Septuagint but included in most editions of the Apocrypha), Tobit, Judith, Rest of Esther, the Wisdom of Solomon, Ecclesiasticus, Additions to Jeremiah (Baruch, the Letter of Jeremiah), Additions to Daniel (the Prayer of Azariah, the Song of the Three Children, Susanna, Bel and the Dragon), the Prayer of Manasseh, and 1 and 2 Maccabees.

The conception of the Apocrypha as a distinct compendium derives from the Church father Jerome, who, in the fourth century C.E., included these books as a separate collection at the end of his Latin translation of Scripture. In 1546, the Council of Trent declared all these books, except for 1 and 2 Esdras, to be part of the so-called Old Testament. The Roman Catholic Church subsequently distinguished these works, referred to as "deuterocanonical," from the books of the Hebrew Bible, referred to as "protocanonical." In contrast to the Roman Catholic Church, Protestant Reformers did not accord the Apocrypha canonical status. Within English-speaking countries, the Protestant practice has been not to include these books in editions of authorized translations.

Flourishing interest in the study of ancient Judaism in the past decades has led to increased inclusion of the Apocrypha within editions of the Bible and to its study as a valuable resource for understanding ancient Judaism and the Jewish origins of Christianity.

Apostate See MESHUMAD.

Aqedah (Hebrew: "The binding [of Isaac]") The biblical account of how ABRAHAM bound ISAAC to an altar and was prepared to offer him up as a sacrifice (Genesis 21–22), read during synagogue worship on Rosh Hashanah. In the biblical account, God tested Abraham's faith by commanding him to bring Isaac to Mount Moriah and to offer him up as a sacrifice. This Abraham was ready to do, and it was only at the last moment, with Abraham's hand raised, the knife poised for the slaughter, that God called Abraham and told him not to offer his son but to present, instead, a ram caught by its horns in a nearby bush. The appropriateness of this account to the High Holidays, at which time it is read during synagogue worship, is revealed in the Rabbinic reading of the story, which depicts the ram sacrificed in place of Isaac as a paradigm for Israelite life: "The Holy One, blessed be he, showed Abraham a ram tearing itself out of one thicket and getting caught in another, over and over again. He said to him, 'So will your children be trapped by sins and entangled among troubles, but in the end they will be redeemed through the horn of a ram [sounded on the New Year].' Then 'the Lord will appear over them, and his arrow go forth like lightning; [the Lord God will sound the trumpet, and march forth in the whirlwinds of the south. The Lord of hosts will protect them'] (Zechariah 9:14–15). That is in line with the following verse of Scripture: 'And in that day [of salvation] a great trumpet will be blown' (Isaiah 27:13)]" (Pesiqta deRab Kahana XXIII:X).

Aqiba One of the most important Rabbinic authorities, active in the late first and early second centuries C.E., between the two Jewish wars with Rome; his full name is Aqiba b. Joseph. In the MISHNAH and TOSEFTA far more legal statements are ascribed to Aqiba than to any other authority of his generation or to almost any later authority. He also is known for his unique approach to interpreting Scripture. He held that, as a divine book, the Bible contains no redundancies and that every element of the text, including spelling and orthographic characteristics, has meaning and purpose. In line with this thinking, Aqiba even found meaning in the accusative particle ("*et*"), which introduces a direct object but which generally is held to have no semantic significance.

Aqiba's importance in early Rabbinic law is reflected by a statement in the Tosefta that he "arranged laws" and by midrashic references to the "Great Mishnah-compilation" of Aqiba (and of several other early authorities). Scholars have taken these statements to mean that Aqiba organized a collection of Tannaitic (see TANNA) law that served as a source for the final version of the MISHNAH. This view of Aqiba's role in Tannaitic law is represented in the Talmud's statement that all anonymous rules in the MISHNAH, TOSEFTA, SIFRA, and SIFRE reflect Aqiba's legal perspective. While reflecting Aqiba's centrality as a Tannaitic authority, this statement clearly is not in any way literally true.

Early Rabbinic sources only preserve Aqiba's legal pronouncements. Later texts add a great deal of information about his life. Born into a humble family, in his youth, Aqiba reportedly was unlearned and an enemy of scholars. He worked as a shepherd for Kalba Savua, the wealthiest man in Jerusalem. Aqiba's interest in study of Torah began when, against her father's wishes, Kalba Savua's daughter Rachel agreed to marry him if he would devote himself to study. To fulfill her request, Aqiba reportedly left Rachel for a total of 24 years, eventually returning, according to the Talmudic story, with 12,000 of his own students. Aqiba ultimately headed his own academy in Bene Beraq. According to the Talmud, unlike his Rabbinic colleagues, Aqiba enthusiastically welcomed the Bar Kokhba revolt and saw in Bar Kokhba the long-awaited messiah. For continuing publicly to teach Torah, Aqiba was imprisoned by the Romans and, after a long stay in prison, was tortured to death.

Arakhin MISHNAH tractate on the topic of Leviticus 27:1–8, vows of the value of a person (chaps. 1–6); Leviticus 27:16–25, dedication to the Temple, and redemption from the Temple of a field one has inherited (chaps. 7–8); Leviticus 27:28–29, the devoted thing (chap. 8); Leviticus 25:25–34, the sale of a house in a walled city and how it is redeemed (chap. 9). All may pledge the value of another or have their own value pledged by others; there is a difference between pledging a valuation, which is fixed, and pledging the worth or price, which is determined by the market; pledges are collected from those who promise a valuation. A field that one has inherited reverts at the Jubilee; if its value is pledged to the Temple, one redeems it proportionate to the years the Temple will hold it; if the field is not redeemed when the Jubilee comes, the priests take it and pay for it. The tractate is ignored by both versions of the TALMUD.

Aramaic A language widely spoken in the middle of the 1st millennium B.C.E. It was originally spoken by the Aramaeans, who spread it throughout the Assyrian Empire, which they served as scribes, so that their language was widely used in official business throughout the Assyrian empire. The Babylonian Empire, from 612 B.C.E., made Aramaic the official language of government, and that status was maintained in Persian times, from the sixth through the third century B.C.E. There was an official Aramaic, along with local dialects. Aramaic was replaced by Greek as the official language of state when Alexander the Great conquered Persia in 330 B.C.E. An eastern dialect, Babylonian Aramaic, was spoken by the Jews of Babylonia and is used extensively in the TALMUD of Babylonia, a commentary to the MISHNAH that exercised, and still exercises, great influence in Judaism. Biblical Aramaic is represented by parts of Ezra and Daniel. Jesus spoke Aramaic. Galilean Aramaic was used by Jews in the Galilee from the third to the seventh century C.E., and it is represented by the Talmud of the Land of Israel and certain Midrash compilations, GENESIS RABBAH in particular.

Arba Kossot (Hebrew: "Four Cups") The four cups of wine drunk during the Passover SEDER, one at the start, with the QIDDUSH; one at the end of the narrative; one at the end of the Grace after Meals; and the fourth at the end of the liturgy of the seder. The drinking of four cups of wine at the seder is associated with God's four promises of redemption at Exodus 6:6–7: "I will *bring you out* from under the burdens of the Egyptians, and *I will deliver you* from their bondage, and *I will redeem you* with an outstretched arm and with great acts of judgment, and *I will take you for my people....*"

Arba'ah Turim (Hebrew: "Four Towers")

Comprehensive code of public and private law compiled by Jacob ben Asher (1270?-1340), based on the legal decisions of his father and of MAIMONIDES. The code is in four sections: 1) *Oraḥ Ḥayyim*, on laws relating to prayer, 2) *Yoreh De'ah*, on personal conduct, 3) *Eben Ha'ezer*, on family law and personal status, and 4) *Ḥoshen Mishpat*, on civil law. The Arba'ah Turim was universally accepted as authoritative. Joseph Karo's (see KARO, JOSEPH) commentary on it, the *Beit Yosef*, served, in turn, as the foundation for classical Judaism's best known law code, Karo's *Shulḥan Arukh*. From its completion and up to the publication of the *Shulḥan Arukh*, the Arba'ah Turim was the standard code of law within both Ashkenazic and Sephardic communities.

Ark of the Covenant A box associated with the Lord's presence (Exodus 25:10–22, Deuteronomy 10:1–5). It was kept first in the tabernacle, the holy place that accompanied the Israelites in the wilderness during their forty years of wandering in the desert after the Exodus and before the conquest of the land of Israel, then in Solomon's temple. The ark was regarded as the footstool of the deity, who was invisible. It contained the testimony or the tablets of the Ten Commandments. It disappeared—no one knows how—and is not included in the list of what Nebuchadnezzar took to Babylon, which spelled out the objects the Babylonians took from the Temple; omission from the list suggests that the object was no longer available, since, if it had been, it would have been taken along (2 Kings 25:13–17).

Arvit See MA'ARIV.

Asarah Batlanim (Hebrew: "ten unoccupied men") Ten men free of all other obligations, available for the study of the Torah and recitation of prayers in a quorum (*minyan*). A town was considered large if it had ten such persons.

Asarah BeTebet   Fast day on the tenth of TEBET, commemorating the beginning of Nebuchadnezzer's siege of Jerusalem in 588 B.C.E., an event that anticipated the destruction of the Temple two years later, in 586 B.C.E. Like other minor fasts, the fast of Tebet lasts only from dawn to dusk. Unlike the fasts of Tisha beAb (see AB, NINTH OF) and YOM KIPPUR, it does not begin with sunset on the preceding evening.

Asceticism   Abstaining from pleasures of this world; common, especially in classical Judaism, in the form of fasting, e.g., in times of crisis, along with prayers for rain, divine grace; may also involve abstaining from wine, sexual relations; expresses fear of sin, penance for sin. See NAZIRITE.

Aseret HaDibrot (Hebrew: "Ten Words") See TEN COMMANDMENTS.

Ashkenazim   Jews from Christian Europe, in contrast to Jews from Islamic Mediterranean countries, who are referred to as SEPHARDIM. The name Ashkenaz derives from Genesis 10:3, the name of the eldest son of Gomer, son of Japheth. This name became identified with Germany. Ashkenazic Jewry originated in Speyer, Worms, and Mayence in the tenth century and gradually moved eastward into Germany and Bohemia, then Poland, Lithuania, White Russia, and elsewhere in Eastern Europe. The principal cultural divisions of Jews throughout the world, especially in the State of Israel, are between Ashkenazic and Sephardic Jews, each group, in the State of Israel, having its own chief rabbi. The religious systems of Ashkenazic and Sephardic Judaism are the same in their main features, but liturgical detail and religious custom distinguish one from the other. For instance, Sephardic Jews eat rice on Passover, Ashkenazim do not. The vast majority of American, Canadian, and British Jews are Ashkenazim.

Ashrei   (Hebrew: "Happy are they") The title given to Psalm 145, of which Ashrei is the first word, read in morning and afternoon worship.

Assimilation   Taking on the traits of a culture different from the one in which a person is born. In the framework of Judaism: modifying distinctive practices of Judaism to accommodate the circumstances of life among gentiles. "Assimilated Jews" are persons of Jewish ethnic origin who do not choose to take on the differentiating traits of Jewish ethnicity, culture, or religion, as diverse contexts define those traits.

Astrology   Belief in the influence of stars and planets on human life; prognostication based on stars and planets; a pseudo-science widely affirmed by the sages of classical Judaism but also denied as a force in Israel's history or in individual Jews' lives. The word for guiding star is *mazal* (planet), and the blessing, *mazal tov*, commonly translated as "good luck," means, "under a propitious star."

Atonement   (Hebrew: *kapparah*) The forgiving of sin by God. God offers atonement to those who engage in acts of repentance, a process designated by the Hebrew term "*teshuvah*," which means, literally, "return" and refers to the individual's break from sinful conduct and return to proper behavior before God. Judaism thus sees the process of repentance, rather than God's offering of atonement, as central to religious and social life. Repentance is listed as one of the seven things God made before creation (Babylonian Talmud Nedarim 39b), and it is seen as an action equivalent to the rebuilding of the Jerusalem Temple and the restoration of the sacrificial cult (Babylonian Talmud Sanhedrin 43b), the highest goals of orthodox Jewish religious life. Repentance is viewed as the most direct and efficacious manner of placating God and assuring God's continued protection.

In light of this, even the Day of Atonement (YOM KIPPUR), the occasion on which God annually judges and forgives the people, is significant, primarily in that it leads people to focus upon the process through which they must repent and correct their ways. On Yom Kippur, God is believed to grant forgiveness only to those who have already repented; a simple profession of faith or promise to behave correctly in the future is not sufficient (Mishnah Yoma 8:8).

Judaism holds that forgiveness is available to all who repent and that the hand of God is continually stretched out to those who seek atonement (Babylonian Talmud, Pesaḥim 119a). Moreover, recognizing the dramatic change of behavior and intense commitment to God's will that stand behind true repentance, Judaism praises those who have sinned and repented even beyond those who have never sinned: "In a place in which those who repent stand, those who are completely righteous cannot stand" (Babylonian Talmud Berakhot 34b).

In Jewish thought, repentance is always possible, even on the day of death. The only requirement is that the desire to repent be serious and that the individual forsake his or her sinful ways. By contrast, one who continually repents but then sins again is not granted God's forgiveness, even on the Day of Atonement (Mishnah Yoma 8:9). Atonement is not achieved through the pronouncing of a linguistic formula or through simple participation in a rite of expiation. It depends, rather, upon a true commitment to changing one's life, turning from sin, and engaging in proper behavior before God.

Azazel   The place to which the scapegoat of Leviticus 16:8–10 is sent. On the Day of Atonement, described at Leviticus 16, when a rite of sacrifice atones for sin, the high priest puts lots on two goats, one for the Lord, the other for Azazel. The goat designated "for the Lord' is presented as a sin offering. The goat "for Azazel" is sent off to the wilderness for Azazel. The term was later identified with Azazel, one of the two heads of the rebellious angels in 1 Enoch 6–16, a book in the PSEUDEPIGRAPHA of the Hebrew Scriptures. Azazel then occurs as the principal demon in the "Apocalypse of Abraham," a writing added in later times to the Hebrew Scriptures. In popular Hebrew, another word for hell or the underworld.

B

B.C.E. Abbreviation for "before the Common Era," more appropriate in many contexts than B.C., that is "before Christ."

Ba'al (Hebrew: "Master") Canaanite fertility god, also called "prince," "lord of the earth," "lord of rain and dew," "storm god" ("He who rides on the clouds") or "lord of the heavens." In Scripture, frequently the god to whom apostate Israelites are said to have adhered.

Ba'al Kore' (Hebrew, literally: "the one who reads") In synagogue worship, the individual responsible for the public chanting of the pentateuchal lection, from a Torah scroll, according to its traditional cantillation, which takes place on Mondays, Thursdays, Sabbaths, and festivals.

Baal Shem Tov (Hebrew: "Master of the Good Name") Designation for Israel b. Eliezer, founder of Hasidism (ca. 1700–1760), often referred by the acronym "Besht." Early in his life a popular healer, from the 1730s onward he undertook travels and attracted to himself circles of followers in Podolia (Ukraine), Poland and Lithuania, and elsewhere. When he died, in 1760, he left disciples who organized the Hasidic movement in southeastern Poland and Lithuania.

Ba'al Teshuvah (Hebrew: "one who repents") One who reverts to Judaism from a position of indifference or hostility; a formerly-secular and non-observant Jew who undertakes some type of religious observance, adopts a religious viewpoint, and moves into the religious and theological framework of Judaism. The pattern of reversion might bring a Reform Jew into a Conservative Rabbinical seminary, or a Conservative Jew into an Orthodox Yeshiva. Sometimes reversion may mean that a formerly indifferent ("assimilated") Jew discovers his or her Jewishness and determines to engage with the organized Jewish community. Reversion comes about for some in a personal crisis, for others in an event involving the state of Israel. In general, the pattern of reversion is marked by the movement from the life of an isolated individual to participation in a Jewish social entity ("the community" in one or another definition). In this way, personal and private religiosity or utter secularity lose their hold, and public and social religiosity take over. This pattern of reversion now encompasses large numbers of Jews who have adopted a profoundly religious and supernatural view of Israel, as God's people, and of themselves as well, and so have adopted the way of life of the received Judaism of the dual Torah or of one of its continuators, whether Reform, Orthodox, or Conservative. The single most striking trait of the contemporary Judaic religious world, in all its diversity, is the return to Judaism of formerly secular Jews, on the one side, or the movement from less rigorous to more complete observance of the holy way of life, on the other.

Baba Qamma, Baba Meşia, Baba Batra (Aramaic: "the first/middle/last gate") Mishnah tractate on civil law, comprising thirty chapters devoted to torts and damages. Baba Qamma addresses damages for chattels, that is, one's property, animate and inanimate (1:1–6:6), and persons (7:1–10:10). Baba Meşia proceeds to the disposition of disputed property, 1:1–2:11, conflicting claims on lost objects, returning an object to the original owner; rules covering bailment, 3:1–12; then illicit commercial transactions, 4:1–5:11, such as overcharging, false advertising, and usury, which is strictly forbidden. Now the exposition shifts to normal relationships, e.g., hiring workers, rentals, and bailments in which no tort is involved, 6:1–8:3. Rules on real estate run from Baba Meşia 8:4–10:6 and Baba Batra 1:1–5:5; these chapters attend to landlord–tenant relationships, including relationships with a tenant-farmer and sharecropper; paying workers promptly; rules governing joint holders of common property; not infringing upon the property rights of others; establishing title to a field through usucaptions ("squatter's rights"); transferring real estate and movables through sale of real estate. Baba Batra 5:6–7:4 deals with licit commercial transactions, covering conditions for the irrevocable transfer of goods, the point at which a sale is final; unstated stipulations in commercial transactions. Finally, the discussion turns to inheritances, wills, and other commercial and legal documents (8:1–10:8), e.g., writs of debt and the like. Both versions of the Talmud devote important and lengthy expositions to these subjects.

Babylon, Babylonia Babylon, the city, and Babylonia, the region, were located where the Tigris and Euphrates rivers come close together, the area around present day Baghdad, in Iraq. Babylonia was the empire that conquered Judea in 586 B.C.E. and sent the Jews into exile. Jews remained in Babylonia from 586 to 1952 C.E., when most left for Israel and the West.

BaMidbar (Hebrew: In the Wilderness.) Hebrew title of the fourth book of Moses, Numbers, which tells the story of Israel's wandering in the wilderness between Egypt and the land of Israel.

Bar Mitzvah (Mişva) A male (*bar* = son) who is required to keep the religious imperatives, or commandments (mitzvah = commandment, plural, mitzvot), of the Torah. Entry into this age of responsibility is at thirteen years. A male who is a bar mitzvah and so responsible for himself in keeping the imperatives of the Torah may be called to read from the Torah in public worship and may lead the assembly of worshippers in their public prayer. Because he is subject to the commandments, he also may act as an agent to carry out the responsibilities of others who are subject to them, should they designate him to do so. The youth's entry into the status of bar mitzvah is commonly celebrated in synagogue worship and through family festivities. In common parlance, the term Bar Mitzvah thus is used also to refer to the ceremonies marking a thirteen-year-old boy's entry into Jewish adulthood, that is, the synagogue worship service in which the child is called to the Torah for the first time and the associated family celebrations. In the case of a female, the term BAT MITZVAH (*bat* = daughter) is used and her initiation may take place as early as twelve years of age.

Baraita A teaching cited in the name of a Tannaitic authority (see TANNA) or formulated as a Tannaitic rule but not found in the Mishnah; hence "external" to the Mishnah but authoritative.

Barekhu "Praise" or "Bless," the opening word for the call to public worship, "*Barekhu et Hashem Hamevorakh,*" "Blessed is the Lord, who is to be blessed."

Barukh (Hebrew: "blessed") Opening word of blessing-formula, *Barukh atah* ..., "blessed are You ...." generally followed by a description of the category of action to follow, e.g., "who has sanctified us by His commandments and commanded us to…" do such and so.

Basar BeHalab   (Hebrew: "meat with milk") A forbidden mixture, as indicated by Scripture's statement: "You shall not seethe a kid in the mother's milk" (Exodus 23:19, 34:26, Deuteronomy 14:21). In Judaism, this prohibition is taken to mean that all cooking of meat and milk together or eating them together is forbidden; milk extends to all dairy products. See DIETARY LAWS.

Bat Mitzvah (Miṣva)   A female (*bat* = daughter) who is responsible for keeping the religious imperatives, or commandments (*mitzvah* = commandment, plural, *mitzvot*), of the Torah. In classical Judaism, entry into this age of responsibility for a girl was at twelve years; in contemporary times, especially in the Reform and Conservative movements, it is reckoned at thirteen, the same as for a boy. Today, too, the girl's entry into the status of bat mitzvah is celebrated in synagogue worship and through family festivities, just as is the case for a boy. The first such Bat Mitzvah ceremony took place in 1922 in the US. It was introduced by Mordecai Kaplan, founder of RECONSTRUCTIONIST JUDAISM, to mark the coming of age of his eldest daughter, Judith. Today, Bat Mitzvah ceremonies take place in Reform, Reconstructionist, Conservative, and some Orthodox synagogues (see BAR MITZVAH).

Bat Qol   In Talmudic literature, a voice not identified as belonging to a human being, emanating from heaven, announcing an opinion; this replaced prophecy as a means of heavenly community with human beings. Yet the heavenly echo bore no weighty authority, and sages did not expect that further Torah revelations would be conveyed to them through that medium. When—the story is told—a heavenly echo announced, for example, "the decided law accords with Rabbi X," his opponent, Rabbi Y, stood up and proclaimed, "The Torah is not in heaven," meaning that the sages who have mastered the Torah-traditions are free through their processes of learning and reasoning to determine what the Torah requires, and further supernatural intervention is unwelcome and, moreover, not to be heeded.

Bathsheba   Wife of the Israelite general, Uriah, whom David (see DAVID, KING), the king of Israel, took as his mistress while her husband was away at war (2 Samuel 11–12). David further arranged for her husband to die in battle. He then married her. She was the mother of Solomon (see SOLOMON, KING), who succeeded David as king of Israel.

Bavli   The Babylonian Talmud; see TALMUD.

Beersheba   A city northeast of the contemporary Beer Sheva in the Negeb. It is mentioned in connection with the wanderings of the patriarch, Abraham, in ancient times. It was destroyed and the area was not occupied until ca. 400 B.C.E., when the Persians built a fortress on the site.

Bekhorot   Mishnah tractate devoted to rules on the firstborn of man, who was to be redeemed for five sheqels (*pidyon haben* (Numbers 18:16); of a clean beast, e.g., flock or herd, to be given to the priest; and of an unclean beast, e.g., an ass (Exodus 13:13), redeemed in exchange for a lamb, or destroyed. The firstborn of an ass is dealt with at chap. 1, clean cattle, in 2–7, and man in chap. 8. Issues raised are secondary to the scriptural laws on the same subject, e.g., the status of an unborn offspring of the ass of a gentile, purchased by an Israelite; a cow that born an offspring like an ass; other matters that are subject to doubt. Since a firstling beast may be slaughtered when it is blemished, the process of examining the firstling, the blemishes taken into account, and the like, are set forth. The firstborn of man may or may not receive the inheritance of the first born. The rules on tithing cattle are set forth in chap. 9: the tithe is given both in the Holy Land and abroad, the extent of the herd that is tithed, and how the tithing is carried out. The Babylonian Talmud provides a commentary to this tractate.

Benei Yisrael (Hebrew: "Children of Israel") Children of the patriarchs, Abraham, Isaac, and Jacob who is also known as Israel, and their wives and concubines; then, all those who, through the Torah, know, worship, and serve the one true God. Among the children of Israel are counted, also, not only heirs born to the faith but those who by choice or conversion have accepted God's rule in the Torah and so make themselves part of Israel. "Israel" in ancient Judaism should not be confused with the contemporary state of Israel; the word in the sources of Judaism refers only to the holy people, children of Abraham, Isaac, and Jacob, subject to the Torah and God's dominion. See ISRAEL.

Berakhah Hebrew for a benediction, blessing, or praise (see BARUKH).

Berakhot (Hebrew: "Blessings") Mishnah tractate concerning blessings, benedictions, recitation of the Shema, the Amidah, Grace after Meals, and blessings for special occasions. The tractate sets forth the liturgy governing everyday life at home: reciting the SHEMA (chaps. 1–3), reciting the Prayer (*Amidah*, chaps. 4–5) (see SHEMONEH ESREH); the various blessings recited before eating different kinds of food and the Grace after Meals and its protocol (chaps. 6–8), and blessings said on other occasions, besides eating food, as well as personal prayers (chap. 9). Both the Jerusalem Talmud and the Babylonian Talmud (see TALMUD) provide commentaries to this tractate.

Bereshit (Hebrew: "In the beginning") The Hebrew title of the first book of the Five Books of Moses, Genesis. See GENESIS.

Berit (Hebrew: "covenant") A treaty, contract, or agreement. The covenants between the Lord and the Israelites were treaties between unequal parties. The Lord, the superior party, grants the Israelites the covenant of his own volition. His side requires that he protect the people and provide for them a land and a succession. The Israelite's side is to carry out the treaty's stipulations. The Lord makes the covenant irrevocable. The supreme covenant is the one with Moses, who met God face to face. See COVENANTAL NOMISM.

Berit Milah (Hebrew: "Covenant of Circumcision") The physical expression of the covenant between God and Israel carried out through the religious rite of circumcision of a male child; removal of the foreskin of the penis.

Circumcision takes place on the eighth day after birth, traditionally in the presence of a quorum (*minyan*) of ten adult males. Very commonly, it is done in the home, not in the hospital, among relatives and friends. There is nothing private nor merely surgical about the operation. The practice found sometimes today of only having a surgical operation in no way carries out the rite of circumcision, for what matters in the Berit Milah is not primarily the physical act of circumcision but the story contained in the ritual formula. This story transforms the birth of a child to an individual couple into a metaphor for something more, a simile of something that transcends. The tale tells how God sees the family beyond time, joined by blood not of pedigree but through circumcision, genealogy framed by fifty generations of loyalty to the covenant in blood and birth from the union of the womb of a Jewish woman with the circumcised penis of her husband: this is the fruit of the womb.

Berkovits, Eliezer (1908–)   Orthodox rabbi and theologian, best known for his approach to the problem of explaining the Holocaust in light of the Jewish (and Christian) concept that God acts in history to champion the good and protect the innocent. Contrary to this idea, the Holocaust suggests either that such a God does not exist at all, that God does not have the powers ascribed to him, or that the Jews somehow sinned and therefore deserved punishment. Berkovits responds by arguing that to use the Holocaust as proof against God's existence vulgarizes the deathcamps. People must, rather, continue to reason and wrestle with God, like Abraham and Job, who similarly confronted God and the question of God's justice.

Berkovits rejects radical theological approaches that use the Holocaust to prove that there is neither justice nor judge, that the universe is indifferent to human suffering. He holds instead that the presence in the death-camps of people who died with dignity, who faced death heroically, who refused to give in to the evil around them, and who, despite all, affirmed their belief in God proves God's existence and power. The resolve of those in the camps to fulfill religious commandments and to abide by religious law despite degradation, misery, and death confirms the transcendental meaning of existence, proving that God was present.

How, then, to comprehend God's silence in allowing the killing? Berkovits refers to the biblical and post-biblical Jewish concept of *El Mistater*, the God who hides. He holds that, while different in magnitude from previous catastrophes of Jewish history, the Holocaust raises the same theological question as those events, of why God appears hidden to the innocent who call upon him for salvation.

God's choice to remain hidden, in Berkovits's view, is not the result of God's inability to help or of God's indifference. It is, rather, a consequence of God's desire to allow for human freedom and free will, which are possible only if God renounces his own power to control history. By remaining silent, God gives people the choice of being righteous or evil. Only by allowing this choice—and so creating the possibility of evil—does God create the possibility for evil's opposites—peace, goodness, and love. God, in this view, is all good, and from God's good comes people's capacity to strive for good. But God's approach to human freedom also grants human beings the capacity to fall short of the divine ideal, since human freedom cannot be restricted even by God.

Berkovits's theology reveals a twofold dichotomy within the divine, who is seen to be both present and absent. God is present without being manifest (e.g., in the actions of the good in the face of evil), and absent without being completely inaccessible (e.g., God allows evil to happen but assures it will not ultimately triumph). This latter point is supported for Berkovits by the creation, seemingly in response to the Holocaust, of the State of Israel. Berkovits sees in this proof that God's hiddenness is not absolute, that when human evil becomes too overwhelming, God reveals himself and takes action.

Beṣah (Heb: "egg") Mishnah tractate, also called *Yom Tov* (festival) on the rules for preparing food on a festival day, when cooking, but not working, is permitted (Exodus 12:16). The problem for the tractate thus is to define what acts involved in the preparation of food are to be deemed cooking and which are merely work. In its answer, Beṣah states that food for use on the festival must be designated for that purpose, in fact or at least potentially, prior to the festival day, and that the preparation must be done in some manner different from the way in which food is prepared on secular days. A distinction further is drawn between actually preparing food and acts of labor not directly pertaining to the actual preparation but relevant thereto. Both versions of the Talmud provide commentaries on this tractate.

Bet Am (Hebrew: "house of people") An early term for synagogue.

Bet Din Jewish court of law judging civil, criminal, and religious cases according to *halakhah*.

Bet HaMiqdash The Temple, that is, the building in Jerusalem in which sacrifices were offered. The first Temple was built by Solomon and dedicated ca. 900 B.C.E. It was destroyed by the Babylonians in 586 B.C.E. The second Temple was ordered to be rebuilt by the Persian emperor, Cyrus (Koresh), after he conquered the Babylonians, ca. 530. The main work of rebuilding the Temple was accomplished by Nehemiah, under the direction of the scribe Ezra, in ca. 450 B.C.E. It was destroyed by the Romans in 70 C.E. In 135, the Romans forbade Jews from reentering Jerusalem and praying at the ruins of the Temple. The Western Wall ("wailing wall") survived and became accessible to Jews once more in 1967.

The Temple marked the point of the convergence of lines of historical, social, and political order and God as ruler on earth, corresponding to the rules of nature and of God as creator in heaven. Assembling within its walls, the priesthood, Levites, and Israelites, men, women, and children, upper as well as lower castes, embodied in one place and at one time the people of ISRAEL as a whole, symbolizing the social order, honoring the political structure, and celebrating the regularity of nature. The people of Israel came together there as pilgrims, offered up to God what the Torah defined as appropriate service, in the smoke of burning meat, grain, and other offerings. Looking backward, the assembly of Israel before God celebrated its very formation in the Exodus from Egypt. Looking forward, the nation prayed for the prosperity brought by rain in the autumnal season and for safe passage through the dry season to come. In the rites in the Temple, Israel fulfilled its obligations under the covenant and, confronting God there, maintained its hope in the continuing blessing that represented God's promise in return. It is for this reason that, almost 2000 years since the destruction of the Temple, Jewish liturgy continues to look forward to the rebuilding of the Temple and the reestablishment of the cult, symbols of the messianic perfection of Israel's relationship with God, and the fulfillment of God's promises to His holy people.

Bet Midrash House of study; space set aside for study of the Torah; more generally: a school for Torah study.

Bimah Platform, the place from which worship is led in synagogue.

Binyan Ab Mikkatub Eḥad A principle of Scripture interpretation used in the Midrashic literature that maintains that one may use a single verse of Scripture to establish a generative analogy, if the same phrase occurs in said verse and in a number of parallels; in that case, the rule that is found in one verse applies to all verses in which the same phrase is found.

Binyan Ab Mishene Ketubbim   A principle of Scripture interpretation used in the Midrashic literature that maintains that one may use two verses of Scripture to establish a generative analogy, if the same phrase occurs in two verses of Scripture and in a number of parallels. In that case, the rule that is found in one verse applies to all verses in which the same phrase is found.

Birkat HaMazon   (Hebrew: "The blessing upon food," "Grace after Meals") The blessing of thanks recited after eating food, which, along with the blessings recited prior to eating, transforms the act of nourishment into a direct encounter with God, deemed to provide the food that is eaten, and a reprise of Israel's condition in time and eternity.

The Grace is in four principal paragraphs, moving from the here-and-now to the time to come, from the meal just eaten to the Messianic banquet. It starts with the ordinary and says what is required, which is, thanks for a real meal in today's world:

> Blessed art Thou, Lord our God, king of the universe, who nourishes all the world by His goodness, in grace, in mercy, and in compassion. He gives bread to all living things, for His mercy is everlasting. And because of His great goodness we have never lacked, and so may we never lack, sustenance—for the sake of His great name. For He nourishes and feeds everyone, is good to all, and provides food for each one of the creatures He created. Blessed art Thou, O Lord, who feeds everyone.

The first of the four principal paragraphs leaves those present where they were: at the table at which they ate the meal. Then comes the narrative that defines the context of a meal:

> We thank Thee, Lord our God, for having given our fathers as a heritage a pleasant, a good, and spacious land; for having taken us out of the land of Egypt, for having redeemed us from the house of bondage; for Thy covenant, which Thou hast set as a seal in our flesh, for Thy Torah which Thou has taught us, for Thy statutes which Thou hast made known to us, for the life of grace and mercy Thou hast graciously bestowed upon us, and for the nourishment with which Thou dost nourish us and feed us always, every day, in every season, and every hour.
>
> For all these things, Lord our God, we thank and praise Thee; may Thy praises continually be in the mouth of every living thing, as it is written, "And thou shalt eat and be satisfied, and bless the Lord thy God for the good land which He hath given thee." Blessed art Thou, O Lord, for the land and its food.

The entire sacred history of Israel comes into play, from the Exodus from Egypt to circumcision. All are invoked for a single occasion, a meal, which marks a human experience that has changed one's condition from hunger to satisfaction. The occasion points toward the end as well:

> O Lord our God, have pity on Thy people Israel, on Thy city Jerusalem, on Zion the place of Thy glory, on the royal house of David Thy Messiah, and on the great and holy house which is called by Thy name. Our God, our Father, feed us and speed us, nourish us and make us flourish, unstintingly,

O Lord our God, speedily free us from all distress.

And let us not, O Lord our God, find ourselves in need of gifts from flesh and blood, or of a loan from anyone save from Thy full, generous, abundant, wide-open hand; so we may never be humiliated, or put to shame.

O rebuild Jerusalem, the holy city, speedily in our day. Blessed art Thou, Lord, who in mercy will rebuild Jerusalem. Amen.

The climax refers to Jerusalem, Zion, David, the Messiah, the Temple—where God was sustained in times past; then dependence on God alone, not on mortals; and the rebuilding of Jerusalem. All of these closely-related symbols invoke the single consideration of time at its end: the coming of the Messiah and the conclusion of history as we now know it. The opening Psalms have prepared us for this appeal to the end-time: exile on weekdays, return to Zion on Sabbaths and holy days.

Blessed art Thou, O Lord our God, king of the Universe, Thou God, who art our Father, our powerful king, our creator and redeemer, who made us, our Holy One, the Holy One of Jacob, our shepherd, shepherd of Israel, the good king, who visits His goodness upon all; for every single day He has brought good, He does bring good, He will bring good upon us; He has rewarded us, does reward, and will always reward us, with grace, mercy and compassion, amplitude, deliverance and prosperity, blessing and salvation, comfort, and a living, sustenance, pity and peace, and all good—let us not want any manner of good whatever.

The fourth and concluding paragraph of the Grace after Meals—more is added for special occasions—returns us to the point at which we began: thanking God for food. Of the four paragraphs, the first and the fourth, which multiplies prayers for future grace alongside thanks for goodness now received, begin and end in the here and now. The two in the middle invoke a different mode of being altogether.

Birkat Kohanim   The priestly blessing, Numbers 6:22–27: "The Lord bless you and keep you, the Lord deal kindly with you and show you grace, the Lord make His face to shine upon you and grant you peace." The priests are admonished, "Thus they will link My name with the people of Israel and I will bless them." Individuals of priestly descent continue today to use this formulation to bless worshippers in the synagogue during festival prayers (see DUKHAN). The priestly blessing also commonly is used by parents to bless their children on the eve of the SABBATH.

Blasphemy   In classical Judaism, uttering the tetragrammaton—the four letter name of God—after prior warning not to do so. That narrow definition occurs at Mishnah Sanhedrin 7:5. A broader definition, encompassing those who have no portion in the world to come, occurs at Mishnah Sanhedrin 10:1 and covers, further, "(1) He who says, the resurrection of the dead is a teaching which does not derive from the Torah, (2) and the Torah does not come from Heaven, and (3) an Epicurean (see APIKOROS). R. Aqiba says, 'Also: (4) He who reads in heretical books, and (5) he who whispers over a wound and says, 'I will put none of the diseases upon you which I have put on the Egyptians, for I am the Lord who heals you' (Exodus 15:26). Abba Saul says, 'Also: (6) He who pronounces the divine name as it is spelled out.' "

Buber, Martin (1878–1965)   Foremost modern Jewish theologian, philosopher, and Zionist thinker; born in Vienna, the grandson of Solomon Buber, an important scholar of Midrashic and other Jewish literatures. He studied at the universities of Vienna, Leipzig, Zurich, and Berlin, under the philosophers Wilhelm Dilthey and Georg Simmel. As a young student, he joined the wing of the Zionist movement that advocated the renewal of Jewish culture (Blau-Weiss). In opposition to Theodor Herzl's political Zionism, Buber thus focused upon education rather than political action. As a Hebrew humanist, he additionally called for peaceful coexistence with the Arabs. Buber was appointed to a professorship at the University of Frankfurt in 1925, but when the Nazis came to power he received an appointment at the Hebrew University of Jerusalem where, in 1938, he became a professor of social philosophy .

At age 26, Buber became interested in Hasidic thought, and he was subsequently responsible for bringing Hasidism to the attention of young German intellectuals, who had previously scorned it as the product of ignorant Eastern European Jewish peasants. HASIDISM had a profound impact on Buber's thought, and he credited it as being the inspiration for his theories of spirituality, community, and dialogue. Indeed, Buber's work created a new system of Jewish religious belief, referred to as neo-Hasidism. Buber also wrote about utopian socialism, education, Zionism, and respect for the Palestinian Arabs; with Franz Rosenzweig, he translated the Hebrew Bible into German.

Buber is known today for his theological writings, which propose a dialogue-theory in which all relationships, including those between people and God, can be classified as I-Thou or I-It. This theory has been influential in Christian as well as Jewish theological thinking.

Burning Bush   The bush from which God first appeared to Moses, at Exodus 3:1–10. Appearing as a flame within a bush that was not itself consumed, God charged Moses with leading the Israelite people out from Egyptian bondage. In Jewish iconography, the burning bush represents either the presence of God or the eternal nature of the Jewish people and the SINAI covenant.

C

C.E. In dates, abbreviation for "common era;" used instead of A.D. in most non-Christian writings.

Canaanites The people originally resident in the land God had in mind for ISRAEL. They polluted the land, so were "vomited out" (Leviticus 18:25) of it, and their land was turned over to the people Israel, who held it on condition that they not pollute it.

Candelabrum See MENORAH.

Canon *"Torah Shelemah,"* the whole Torah, that is, God's revelation made manifest in the Torah. Rabbinic Judaism appeals to the story that at Sinai God revealed revelation, or "Torah," to Moses in two media. One was in writing, hence "the written Torah," *Torah shebikhtab,* corresponding to the Hebrew Bible ("Old Testament"). The other medium for revelation was through oral formulation and oral transmission, hence "the oral Torah," *Torah she be'al peh,* the memorized Torah. The literature of Rabbinic Judaism therefore takes its place as a component of the Torah, part of God's revelation to Israel, and hence part of the canon that comprises all of the texts deemed by Judaism to be revealed and holy.

A simple definition of "the canon" of Judaism follows. In addition to the written part of the Torah possessed by all Israel, the canon of Judaism encompasses the Rabbinic literature, that is, the corpus of writing produced in the first seven centuries C.E. by sages who claimed to stand in the chain of tradition from Sinai and uniquely to possess the oral part of the Torah. Among the many, diverse documents produced by Jews in the first seven centuries of C.E., only a small group cohere and form the distinctive part of the canon called "Rabbinic literature." Three traits distinguish this literature from all other Jewish (ethnic) and Judaic (religious) writing of that age.

1 These writings of law and exegesis, revered as holy books, copiously cite the Hebrew Scriptures of ancient Israel ("Written Torah").
2 They acknowledge the authority, and even the existence, of no other Judaic (or gentile) books except the ancient Israelite Scriptures.
3 These writings ubiquitously cite sayings attributed to named authorities, unique to those books themselves, most of them bearing the title "rabbi."

Other writings of Jews, e.g., JOSEPHUS, to begin with do not claim to set forth religious systems or to form holy books. Other Judaic writings ordinarily qualify under the first plank of the definition, and the same is to be said for Christian counterparts. The second element in the definition excludes all Christian documents. The third dismisses all writings of all Judaisms other than the one of the dual Torah. Other Judaic writings cite Scriptural heroes or refer to a particular authority; none except those of this Judaism sets forth, as does every Rabbinic document, extensive accounts of what a large number of diverse authorities say, let alone disputes among them.

Any book out of Judaic antiquity that exhibits these three traits—focus upon law and exegesis of the Hebrew Scriptures, exclusion of all prior tradition except for Scripture, and appealing to named sages called rabbis—falls into the category of Rabbinic literature and hence of the canon of Judaism. All other Jewish writings exhibit the first trait, in varying proportions, and some the second as well, but none all three. These other writings accordingly are not deemed part of the canon of Judaism.

Cantor   (Hebrew: *ḥazan*) The clerical officiant who chants the liturgy in the synagogue. In Talmudic times, the title *ḥazan* referred to a community leader in general; in early medieval times it came to connote a permanent prayer leader, the need for which developed as the liturgical tradition became more complex and as the public's knowledge of Hebrew declined. Since the *ḥazan* represented the community in prayer, the position was viewed as extremely important and often was held by highly regarded rabbis. From the earliest period, a chief qualifications of the *ḥazan* was a pleasant voice. This aspect of the position grew in importance in the nineteenth and twentieth centuries, as the cantorial repertoire was increasingly influenced by European musical trends. In this period, cantors gained high regard for their vocal skills as well as for their piety and Jewish knowledge.

Today, individuals trained in schools of sacred music at the seminaries of the Reform, Conservative, and Orthodox movements are invested as cantors. ("Investment" of a cantor is parallel to "ordination" of a rabbi.) Judaism, however, does not require that its liturgy be chanted by such a cantor. Accordingly, within all three movements, liturgical rites are frequently chanted by lay leaders or by professionals who have not received formal training. Such individuals are referred to as *ḥazan*, *shaliaḥ ṣibbur* (literally, "representative of the community"), or, in the Reform movement in particular, as "cantorial soloist;" by contrast, in Reform, the English title "cantor" is normally reserved for those who have been invested by a seminary.

In traditional forms of Judaism, only men are permitted to lead the congregation in prayer. Today, in Reform, Conservative, and Reconstructionist synagogues, women as well may receive this honor.

Carmel   Mountain in the northwest of the land of Israel, on which the city of Haifa is built. Mount Carmel is noteworthy because there Elijah confronted the priests of Ba'al, that is, those that made offerings to Ba'al rather than to the Lord (1 Kings 18). It divides the plain of Esdraelon and the Galilee to the east and north from the coastal plain to the south.

Central Conference of American Rabbis   (CCAR) In the U.S.A., the national association of Reform rabbis, established by Isaac Mayer Wise in 1889.

Chief Rabbinate   Office still existing today in the United Kingdom, the State of Israel, and several other countries that continues the ancient Jewish practice of assigning religious authority—whether over a region, country, or all Jewry—to a single individual. In medieval Spain, the office was called *rab de la corte*, reflecting the individual's role as a liaison between the Jewish community and the royal court, which often had a role in designating an individual for this office in the first place. In the Ottoman Empire, and in some Sephardic communities, the chief rabbi is called *ḥakham bashi*, or *ḥakham* (meaning "chief sage" and in France *grand rabbin*.

Chronicles, Book of   Part of the sequence of the biblical books, comprising Ezra and Nehemiah, and 1–2 Chronicles, that surveys the history of Israel from Adam to Ezra and Nehemiah themselves. The unknown author lived probably at ca. 350–300 B.C.E. The book starts with genealogies from Adam to King Saul (see SAUL, KING) (1 Chronicles 1–2), the death of Saul and the reign of David (see DAVID, KING) (1 Chronicles 10–29) and Solomon (see SOLOMON, KING) (2 Chronicles 1–9), the division of the monarchy into northern and southern kingdoms to the end of the exile of the Israelites from the land of Israel, ca. 530 B.C.E., when the Persians permitted them to return to the Land (2 Chronicles 10–36). In 1–2 Chronicles, the books of Samuel and Kings appear as a source but have been revised. David is glorified and idealized; he is credited with organizing the Temple service. Solomon is treated very favorably as well. The focus is on the southern kingdom of Judah, rule by the house of David, and the Temple of Jerusalem. The genealogies make the point that the true Israel was realized in David's kingdom.

Circumcision   See BERIT MILAH.

Cohen   See KOHEN.

Confirmation   Within the movements of contemporary Judaism, a ceremony in which students who complete a program of Judaic studies declare their commitment to live as Jews and to follow the precepts of Judaism. Parallel to the Christian confirmation rite, in which the relationship with God established by baptism is confirmed, early nineteenth-century reformers adopted this communal ceremony to provide young adults with an opportunity to make a public declaration of their adherence to the Jewish faith. Within early Reform, confirmation often entirely replaced the BAR MITZVAH celebration. By the mid-twentieth century, however, as Reform re-adopted the Bar and Bat Mitzvah ceremonies, confirmation became a separate ritual entirely. Found now in the Conservative movement and some Orthodox synagogues as well, confirmation generally involves older students, ages 16–17, who have completed a synagogue's program of post-Bar or Bat Mitzvah Judaic study. Confirmation ceremonies generally are held on the festival of SHABU'OT, appropriate as the holiday that celebrates the revelation at SINAI and marks Jews' annual reaffirmation of their commitment to and responsibilities under the Torah.

Conservative Judaism   A movement in modern Judaism occupying the middle position between the ritual and theological liberalism of Reform and the traditionalism of Orthodoxy. Conservative Judaism's centrism emerges from the movement's distinctive ideology. It differs from Reform, but is similar to Orthodoxy, in insisting on the continuing authority of Jewish law (*halakhah*). At the same time, contrary to Orthodox views, Conservative Judaism stresses the extent to which *halakhah* has always been subject to historical development and so appropriately continues to change today. According to the Conservative movement, Jewish law thus is obligatory—a traditionalistic perspective—while the form it takes is subject to the needs and understandings of each age—a liberal approach.

The Conservative movement has its foundations in the "positive-historical school" that developed in Germany in the nineteenth century under the leadership of Zechariah Frankel. Positive-historical ideology held that critical evaluation is necessary and appropriate in order to derive an accurate picture of the true theology and precepts of Judaism. At the same time, this approach maintained that the central practices of Judaism, codified by their acceptance by the Jewish people over time, continue to demand strict observance, no matter what their actual historical origins. In this, we see again the uniting of the Reform perspective, with its interest in critical evaluation, with the Orthodox view of the authority of tradition.

The positive-historical school's centrist attitude toward Jewish belief and practice evolved into a powerful religious movement only in the United States. There, beginning in the 1880s, the masses of newly arriving Jewish immigrants formed a natural constituency for a "conservative" approach to Jewish practice. While most of these Eastern European immigrants were no longer under the spell of Orthodoxy, they found Reform, a product of the German Jews who had arrived before them, to be distant from the Judaism they recognized as authentic. They found in the Conservative movement an environment that felt Jewishly legitimate but that, allowing for the introduction of many changes, was comfortable to increasingly assimilated Americans, for whom Judaism would not control every aspect of life. This melding of traditionalism and change allowed Conservative Judaism to become, until the last years of the twentieth century, the largest branch of American Judaism.

The nascent Conservative movement in the United States was particularly shaped by Solomon Schechter, an acclaimed rabbi and scholar brought to America in 1901 to lead the movement's foundering Jewish Theological Seminary, which had been created in 1887. Schechter introduced the concept of "Catholic (in the sense of 'universal') Israel," which asserted that, alongside tradition, the legitimate content of Jewish thought and practice is determined by what the Jewish people as a whole believe and do. This idea appropriately defined Conservative Judaism in the early

parts of the twentieth century, when support for Jewish dietary laws, observance of the Sabbath, and the desire to maintain the traditional structure of Jewish prayer was common among those who identified themselves as Conservative. Thus, Conservative Judaism retained truly traditional sensibilities as regards these Judaic practices even as its congregations adopted mixed seating and the use of English readings during worship, refined the dietary laws to make observance of Kashrut more compatible with a modern lifestyle, and altered Sabbath law so as to allow the use of electricity and, notably, to permit driving to synagogue worship on Sabbaths and festivals. Over time, the movement has also taken a wholly egalitarian stance, allowing full participation of women in all aspects of synagogue life and ritual and, since 1984, ordaining women as rabbis.

Still, as the twentieth century progressed, the idea that the actual practices of Jewish people can define what is authentically Judaic, or even that the practices of its members can be used to demarcate Conservatism as a distinctive approach, has became increasingly difficult to maintain. Along with this, the question of what traditions one must observe in order to be deemed a Conservative Jew has become vexing. In general, Conservative Jews continue to desire a more traditional synagogue experience than exists within Reform, and they expect that their rabbis and cantors will observe the laws of traditional Judaism. But recent studies show that only 24 percent of members of Conservative synagogues keep kosher homes (a much smaller number observes kashrut outside of the home) and that only 37 percent light Sabbath candles, the most basic indicator of even a modicum of Sabbath observance. The percentage that regularly attends synagogue worship is low, close to that found in the Reform movement. The result is that, at the beginning of the twenty-first century, observers have adroitly defined the Conservative synagogue as a congregation of Reform Jews led by an Orthodox rabbi. This leaves open the most basic question of how, in the future, Conservative Judaism will maintain the sense of obligation to Jewish tradition on which it was founded, while at the same time retaining the commitment of Jews who decreasingly consider Jewish practice a necessary and meaningful aspect of religious life.

The Conservative movement today is represented by a range of institutions. Chief among them are the Jewish Theological Seminary and the newer Ziegler School of Rabbinic Studies at the University of Judaism in Los Angeles, where rabbis of the movement are trained; the Rabbinical Assembly, which is the central organization of Conservative rabbis and the law committee of which defines the movement's stance on specific issues of Jewish law and practice; the United Synagogue, which is the umbrella organization of affiliated congregations; United Synagogue Youth, the movement's youth movement; Women's League for Conservative Judaism; and the Federation of Jewish Men's Clubs. The movement's theology has most recently been set out in Robert Gordis, ed., *Emet Ve-Emunah: Statement of Principles of Conservative Judaism* (New York, 1988).

Conversos   Also known as Marranos (Spanish: "swine"), Jews forcibly converted to Christianity in Spain from 1391 to 1492, who secretly continued to practice Judaism; the Conversos remained a distinct group within Spanish society. The Jews of Portugal were forcibly baptized in 1497, and many followed suit. Conversos practiced Christianity outwardly and Judaism in secret. Many ultimately escaped from Spain and Portugal and reverted to Judaism; they were accepted by other Jews, not as apostates but as forced converts. The Inquisition, founded in 1480, exercised jurisdiction over Conversos, not over professing Jews. For four hundred years, the Inquisition in Spain and Portugal as well as in the Western Hemisphere pursued the Conversos, who ultimately ceased to exist as a distinct group. The Jewish communities of the Western hemisphere derived from Conversos who escaped from Spanish and Portuguese colonies to Dutch and British ones. Known by their family origin in Judaism, however many generations earlier, Conversos preserved certain Judaic practices and customs, e.g., lighting candles at dusk on Friday evening and fasting on the Day of Atonement.

Convert   See GER.

Covenantal Nomism   The doctrine that ISRAEL is subject to a covenanted relationship with God, which is carried out by obedience to the teachings of the Torah, including its laws. The covenant between God and Israel is contained in the Torah revealed by God to Moses at Mount Sinai. The piety of Israel, defined by the Torah, in concrete ways served to carry out the requirements of the covenant. Covenantal nomism, is thus life under the laws of the Torah, lived so as to fulfill Israel's covenant with God.

Creed   A concise, formal statement of a religion's fundamental beliefs, largely absent from Judaism, which has always focused as much upon correct forms of behavior as upon correct belief. Accordingly, neither the Hebrew Bible nor the Talmudic literature present encompassing credal statements. Only in the tenth century, in response to internal pressure from the Karaite movement (see KARAITES) and corresponding to theological discussions then occurring within Islam, did Jewish thinkers begin to formulate statements on Jewish belief. Referred to as "obligations of the heart" (*hovot haLevavot*), "primary principles" (*hathalot*), "cornerstones" (*pinot*), and, most frequently, "foundational beliefs" (*iqqarim*), these creeds attempted comprehensively to express the content of Jewish belief.

Although not the earliest such formulation, the thirteen principles of Maimonides (1135–1204) are among the best known and most important of all Jewish creeds. Presented in the context of his commentary to Mishnah Sanhedrin Chapter 10, Maimonides' principles define the "APIKOROS" who, according to the Mishnah, has no share in the world to come. In the Thirteen Principles, MAIMONIDES accordingly proposed to delineate the beliefs that are necessary and sufficient to assure an individual's salvation. According to Maimonides, these beliefs are 1) that God exists and 2) is uniquely unitary; 3) God is not corporeal and cannot be accurately described in anthropomorphic terms; 4) God is eternal and 5) alone is to be worshipped; 6) God designated prophets, 7) the greatest of whom was Moses, who 8) received the entire Torah; 9) the Torah cannot be abrogated or in any way altered; 10) God knows people's deeds and 11) rewards or punishes them as appropriate; 12) the messiah will come, and 13) the dead will be resurrected.

Maimonides' thirteen principles became central in Judaism when, by about 1300, they were formulated as a hymn ("*Yigdal*"), which appears in almost all forms of the Jewish daily liturgy. By the mid-sixteenth century, these principles circulated in a clearly credal formulation,

introduced with the statement, "I believe with perfect faith that ...."

Among the major critics of Maimonides' formulation, Ḥasdai Crescas (d. 1412) had the most enduring impact on the later development of Jewish creeds. Crescas defined the formulation of a creed as a philosophical task, involving the logical ordering of beliefs so that basic axioms could yield secondary conceptions. Crescas additionally introduced the notion of intentionality, defining a heretic not by what he believes but by the perceived source of his belief. A heretic holds beliefs, whether right or wrong, that he views as independent of the teachings of the Torah. According to Crescas, but contrary to Maimonides, one who understands his beliefs to derive from the Torah cannot be called a heretic, even if those beliefs are, in fact, false.

At the foundation of Crescas' creed are the notions of God's 1) existence, 2) unity, and 3) incorporeality. Six pillars stand on these root principles: 1) God's knowledge of people's deeds, 2) divine providence, 3) God's omnipotence, 4) the appointment of prophets, 5) free will, and 6) the role of the Torah in assuring eternal happiness. These pillars lead to eight additional beliefs that Crescas sees as characteristic of Judaism but not fundamental: 1) God's creation of the world, 2) human immortality, 3) divine retribution, 4) resurrection, 5) the immutability of the Torah, 6) that Moses was the greatest prophet, 7) the divine origin of priestly instruction, and 8) the coming of the messiah.

Isaac Abravanel (1437–1508) devoted an entire treatise to the formulations of Jewish belief of Maimonides, Crescas, and Joseph Albo (ca. 1380–ca. 1440). While raising numerous objections to Maimonides' Thirteen Principles, Abravanel ultimately allied himself with

Maimonides, defining heresy, for instance, on the basis of the content of one's belief, without regard for the perceived source of the specific beliefs. But Abravanel broadly rejected the claim that any narrow selection of beliefs can accurately encompass the content of Judaism. Since the Torah was divinely revealed, everything it contains must be accepted; no hierarchy of belief is possible. The rejection of any Jewish belief is heresy and denies the individual a place in the world to come.

The modern period in the formulation of Jewish creeds was heralded by Moses Mendelssohn (1729–1786), who argued that Judaism, unlike Christianity, contains no dogmas. Judaism's truths, rather, are identical with the eternal truths discoverable through reason, independent of revelation. These truths are 1) that God, who created and rules all things, is one; 2) that God knows all and metes out rewards and punishment through natural and supernatural means; and 3) that God made his will known through Scripture. In Mendelssohn's view, these truths, which represent the content of all natural religions, are to be distinguished from Judaism's ritual laws, the only part of Judaism that depends upon revelation rather than reason.

Affected by Kant's critique of rational religion, later Jewish thinkers largely rejected Mendelssohn's approach. Reformers, in particular, have worked to offer clear guidance regarding the essential beliefs that derive from the writings of Judaism. By defining what Jews must believe, the reformers countered traditional Judaism, which focused rather upon the rituals that Jews must practice. For these thinkers, however, the concept that Judaism is an evolving religion has led to only broadly defined tenets, e.g., in the Reform movement's PITTSBURGH PLATFORM (1885), which defines Judaism as "ethical monotheism." This approach stands in contrast to that of orthodox thinkers, who continue to define Judaism through its ritual. This is exemplified in the writing of Samson Raphael Hirsch (1808–1888) (see HIRSCH, SAMPSON RAPHAEL), the first spokesman for a modern orthodoxy, who proposed that "the catechism of the Jew is his calendar."

Cultic Purity   (Hebrew: *Tahor/Tamé*; "clean/unclean") The concept that a person or object can be in a status that precludes contact with the Temple or cult. Uncleanness ("ritual impurity") is transferred to other persons or objects in a variety of ways, including contact, supporting the weight of an unclean object, or being under the same roof with it. The state of uncleanness is unrelated to any tangible condition, e.g., being physically dirty, but is corrected primarily through bathing ("ablution"), which renders the individual clean ("pure"). (See PURIFICATION, RITES OF.)

In ancient Judaism, cultic purity was important when Israelites entered the Temple of Jerusalem and, by analogy, in certain other transactions, e.g., eating or procreation. "Purity" referred to the removal of all marks of uncleanness as defined by the Torah, e.g., the uncleanness imparted by the corpse or things like the corpse. Priests and Levites were required to attain a state of cultic purity in order to enter the holy places of the Temple and perform Temple rites. All Israelites, not only the priestly castes, who entered the Temple were required to undergo a rite of purification from the effects of uncleanness that accumulate over time. In particular, on the three Pilgrim Festivals, PASSOVER, SHABU'OT, and Tabernacles (see SUKKOT), ordinary Israelites—not priests, not Levites—went to the Temple to offer the festival sacrifices and so undertook the condition of cultic cleanness, just like the Temple priests and Levites.

Beginning at the end of the Second Temple Period, the PHARISEES, followed in the first centuries C.E. by the Mishnah's rabbis, extended Scripture's notion that purity matters primarily in the Temple. They held that all food should be eaten in cleanness, as though it were a sacrifice on the Temple altar. Numerous laws make clear the practical implications the rabbis understood these matters to have. Since Scripture holds that cleanliness is comparable to holiness, the Rabbinic perspective intended in a concrete manner to transform the entire people of Israel into a holy nation of priests. Within Orthodox Judaism until the present day, rules for cultic purity continue to be followed, represented, in particular, in the practice of the ritual washing of hands before meals and in the observance of menstrual taboos.

D

Dabbar Melamed Me'inyano   A principle of exegesis of Scripture found in the Midrashic literature that holds that the meaning of a verse of Scripture may be established by the context in which the verse occurs.

Darkhei HaAmori   (Hebrew: "Ways of the Amorites") Practices deemed by Talmudic Judaism to be superstitious and forbidden, e.g., use of charms or good luck talismen.

David, King   The second king of Israel, after Saul. The prophet SAMUEL selected David when Saul (see SAUL, KING), whom he had originally anointed, did not fully carry out God's commandments. David greatly expanded the monarchy founded by Saul at the initiative of Samuel. The extensive account of his life is found at 2 Samuel 17–24 and 1 Kings 1–2. According to these texts, he embodied the ideal king, and his descendant would be the anointed one, the Messiah of the house of David, assigned the task of ingathering the exiles and inaugurating the life of the world to come. Thus the royal family inaugurated by David and continued by his son, Solomon, is supposed at the end of time to produce the anointed king, the Messiah.

Dayyan   (Hebrew: "judge") A member of a Rabbinic court; a judge in cases of Jewish law.

Dead Sea Scrolls   A library of writings, hitherto unknown, of an ancient community of Judaism, found after World War II near Qumran, in the land of Israel.

Decalogue   See TEN COMMANDMENTS.

Demai   Mishnah tractate on produce concerning tithes. The tractate defines the items subject to tithing as doubtfully tithed produce, indicates how doubtfully-tithed produce is handled and used; legislates for commercial and commensal relations between those who are trustworthy in tithing and outsiders; provides details of the tithing procedure; delineates to what extent, in a case of shared ownership of produce, one owner is responsible for tithing the portion that he gives to the other owner. The tractate is analyzed by the Jerusalem TALMUD.

Derekh Eretz   (Hebrew: "way of the land") Normal custom, correct conduct; good manners, courtesy, etiquette. Also: mode of earning a living; job, career, profession. Within classical Judaism, disciples of sages are expected to master both Torah-learning and derekh eretz, meaning, study the Torah and also earn a living. They also are supposed to show derekh eretz to masters, meaning, to treat teachers with dignity; and all Israel are expected to display derekh eretz, meaning, courtesy, to all persons they meet.

Deuteronomy   (Hebrew: *Devarim*) The fifth book of the Pentateuch, organized as an address by Moses to the people of Israel before they entered the Promised Land. The address reviews Israel's past, goes over the laws Moses gave the people at Mount Sinai, and emphasizes that keeping the laws is necessary for the welfare of the people of Israel in the land of Israel. "Deuteronomy" means "repetition of the law." After a prologue, chaps. 5–11 present an introductory speech by Moses; 12–26, the reiteration of the laws, and the conclusion, the blessings, and curses that attend upon keeping or violating the law. The main point is that faithfulness to the Lord and obedience to the commandments bring blessing, while worship of foreign gods and violation of the law bring a curse; and the only place for worshipping the Lord is God's chosen place, understood to refer to Jerusalem.

Diaspora   Dispersion, exile of Jews from the land of Israel; Jews who live outside the holy land. See GALUT.

Dibbuk   (Hebrew: "adhesion") According to QABBALAH, the soul of a deceased sinner that transmigrates into the body of a living person.

Dietary Laws   Referred to as kashrut, the rules about foods that a Jew may or may not eat, a status determined both by the nature of the foodstuff and the manner in which it is prepared. Food that is permissible is referred to as "kosher," meaning "fit" or "proper;" what is impermissible is called *treif*, literally "torn" or "unfit." The rules of kashrut derive from the Torah, which permits for consumption only fish that have fins and scales and animals that part the hoof and chew the cud (e.g., sheep, cows, but not camels, pigs) (Leviticus 11:3). To yield permissible meat, animals must be slaughtered according to a fixed, humane method (Hebrew: *shehitah*), which is accompanied by a blessing on the part of the specially trained slaughterer (*shohet*). The Torah furthermore prohibits shellfish, worms, snails, flesh torn from a living animal, etc. Blood may not be consumed and so must be drained from meat before the meat may be eaten (Leviticus 17:10) . Any mixture of meat and milk is forbidden, whether the items are actually cooked together or simply served together at the same meal; after eating meat, one may not eat dairy products for a period of time (one to six hours, depending on custom). Fish and what is neither dairy nor meat products are considered neutral (*pareve*) and may be prepared and eaten with either meat or dairy foods. In order to prevent the mixing of meat and dairy products, observant Jews maintain separate dishes and utensils for preparing and serving meat and milk meals. See also BASAR BEHALAB, SHEHITAH.

Dina DeMalkhuta Dina   (Aramaic: "The law of the land is the law [that is, is binding].") The principle that Jews are subject to the civil law wherever they live; gentile governments are valid, so long as they are bound by traits of justice and equity. Attributed to Samuel, principal authority of the Babylonian Talmud, the principle of "dina demalkhuta dina" maintains that gentile governments are legitimate, their taxes to be paid, their laws to be obeyed. The application of this principle means that civil marriage and divorce of Jews outside Israel is recognized under Israeli law.

Divorce   See GERUSHIN.

Dogma   See CREED.

Dukhan   Platform, on which, in the Temple, Levites sang Psalms while the animal sacrifices were offered; priests stood there to recite the priestly benediction. The term now is used in English as a verb; "to dukhan" refers to the priests' blessing of the synagogue congregation with the words of the priestly benediction.

E

Eber Min HaHai Hebrew: "limb cut from a living animal;" may not be eaten, because the practice of cutting limbs from living beasts violates the requirement of humanity to animals (*Ṣar ba'alei ḥayyim*).

Edom In Scripture, a kingdom in Transjordan, neighbor to the land of Israel; enemy of ancient Israel.

Eduyyot (Hebrew: "testimonies") Mishnah tractate formed out of collections of testimonies in the names of major authorities: SHAMMAI, HILLEL, and their Houses (chap. 1); authorities of Yavneh (chaps. 2–3); the Houses of Hillel and Shammai, with the House of Hillel in the more stringent position (chaps. 4–5); authorities of Yavneh (chaps. 6–7); finally, a unit organized around the use of a common literary form (chap. 8). Every statement in the tractate has a primary location in some other Mishnah tractate, from which it is quoted here.

Eglah Arupah In Scripture, the rite of breaking a heifer's neck in atonement for the neglect of a corpse, Deuteronomy 21:1–9.

Eighteen Benedictions See SHEMON-EH ESREH.

El See ELOHIM.

El Malé Raḥamim (Hebrew: "God full of compassion") Funeral dirge; prayer for the deceased chanted on memorial occasions and at funerals. The text is as follows:

O God, full of compassion and exalted in the heights, grant perfect peace in Your sheltering presence, among the holy and pure, to the soul of the deceased, who has gone to his eternal home. Master of mercy, we beseech You, remember all the worthy and righteous deeds that he performed in the land of the living. May his soul be bound up in the bond of life. The Lord is his portion. May he rest in peace. And let us say, Amen.

Eliezer ben Hyrcanus Mishnah sage, end of the first century C.E., disciple of Yohanan ben Zakkai; along with Joshua ben Hananiah, he smuggled Yohanan out of besieged Jerusalem in the time of the Roman siege of 70 C.E. and brought him to the Roman commander, Vespasian, who allowed the Rabbinic sages to continue their work of Torah study. A principal sage in the foundation of the Mishnah.

Elijah Prophet in Judea in the time of Ahab, eighth century (1 Kings 17:19, 2 Kings 1–2). He is supposed to return at the end of history to announce the coming of the Messiah (Malachi 4:5–6). Miracle-stories are told about Elijah in 1–2 Kings. He is held in Rabbinic sources to be coming to settle moot legal questions, and he was further expected to reveal the coming of the Messiah.

Elohim (Hebrew: "God") A plural Hebrew word for God (singular: *Eloha*), one of the most frequent titles in the Hebrew Bible for the God of the Israelites, but also used to refer to pagan gods. This word is distinct from the Tetragrammaton (YHWH), which is usually translated "Lord."

Judaism knows God through the Torah, where God makes himself known to humanity. The Torah's single most important teaching about God, who creates the world, gives the Torah, and redeems humanity at the end of days, is that humanity is like God, so Genesis 1:26: "Let us make man in our image, after our likeness." God and the human being are images of one another. That is why the angels could not discern any physical difference whatever between man—Adam— and God (Genesis Rabbah VIII:X). The task of the Judaic statement of monotheism is to mediate between the paradox that God and humanity correspond by reason of Adam's and Eve's being created in God's image.

The Hebrew Scriptures portray God in richly personal terms, God feels and thinks in ways analogous to humanity. Thus God wants, cares, demands, regrets, says, and does—just like human beings. In the written Torah, God is not merely a collection of abstract theological attributes, nor a mere person to be revered and feared. God is not a composite of regularities but a very specific, highly particular personality, whom people can know, envision, engage, persuade, impress. Rabbinic sages painted this portrait of a personality by making up narratives in which God figures like other (incarnate) heroes.

ISRAEL, the holy people, meets God in the Torah at SINAI, when God—not Moses—proclaims, "The Lord, the Lord! a God compassionate and gracious, slow to anger, abounding in kindness and faithfulness, extending kindness to the thousandth generation, forgiving iniquity, transgression, and sin" (Exodus 34:6). Thus God reveals himself to humanity through Israel, beginning with Abraham. It is because God wants to be known and makes himself known that Israel claims to know God, and the Torah contains that knowledge that God wishes to impart to humanity. For those who practice Judaism, the encounter

with God takes place in the Torah, hence, in the study of the Torah. The place and time for meeting God is not only at prayer, but in the holy circle of sage and disciples, and it is in books that portray God's self-revelation to Moses at the burning bush (Exodus 3) or in the still small voice ELIJAH heard.

Judaism in its formative sources portrays God in four ways: as premise, presence, person, and personality:

1 God as premise occurs when sages reach a particular decision because they believe that God created the world and revealed the Torah. Thus a particular proposition appeals to God as premise of all being, e.g., author and authority of the Torah. Things are decided one way, rather than some other, on that basis. The conviction of the givenness of God who created the world and gave the Torah stands at the foundation of all forms of Judaism before modern times.

2 God as presence involves the sages' referring to God as part of a situation in the here and now. When sages speak of an ox goring another ox, they do not appeal to God to reach a decision and do not suggest that God, in particular, has witnessed the event and plans to intervene. But when they speak of a wife being accused of unfaithfulness to her husband, they expect God to intervene in the required ordeal of the bitter waters and so declare the decision for the case at hand. In the instance of the goring ox, God is a premise of discourse, having revealed in the Torah the rule governing such a case. In the case of the accused wife, God is not only premise but present in the discourse and in making a decision. God thus constitutes a person in certain settings, not in others.

3 One may readily envisage God as premise without invoking a notion of the particular traits or personality of God. So too, in the case of God as presence, no aspect of the case at hand demands that we specify particular attitudes or traits of character to be imputed to God. But there is a setting in which God is held always to know and pay attention to specific cases, and that involves God as a "you," that is, as a person. For example, all discourse concerning liturgy understands that God also hears prayer, so that God is not only a presence but a person who responds to what is said, requiring certain attitudes and rejecting others. God further is not only present but a participant when the Torah is studied among disciples of sages.

4 God emerges as a vivid and highly distinctive personality, actor, protagonist, partner in dialogue, hero. In references to God as a personality, God is given corporeal traits. God looks like God in particular, just as each person exhibits distinctive physical traits. Also in matters of heart, mind, and spirit, well-limned individual traits of personality and action alike endow God with a particularity as can be identified in each individual human being. When God is given attitudes but no active role in discourse, referred to but not invoked as part of a statement, God serves as person. When God participates as a hero and protagonist in a narrative, God gains traits of personality and emerges as God like humanity: God incarnate.

Despite such endowing of God with personality, and despite the fact that humanity is made in God's image, nonetheless, God is wholly other, and human beings cannot hope to understand everything God does. Their task is to remain silent in the face of the awesome mystery represented by God. This is illustrated in the following Talmudic story (Bavli Menahot 29b):

A Said R. Judah said Rab, "When Moses went up to the height, he found the Holy One, blessed be He, sitting and tying crowns to the letters [of the Torah]."

B "He said to Him, 'Lord of the universe, why is this necessary?'

C "He said to him, 'There is a man who will arrive at the end of many generations, and Aqiba b. Joseph is his name, who will interpret on the basis of each point of the crowns heaps and heaps of laws.'

D "He said to Him, 'Lord of the universe, show him to me.'

E "He said to him, 'Turn around.'

F "[Moses] went and took his seat at the end of eight rows, but he could not understand what the people were saying. He felt weak. When discourse came to a certain matter, one of [Aqiba's] disciples said to him, 'My lord, how do you know this?'

G "[Aqiba] said to him, 'It is a law revealed by God to Moses at Mount Sinai.'

H "Moses' spirits were restored.

I "He turned back and returned to the Holy One, blessed be He. He said to Him, 'Lord of the universe, now if you have such a man available, how can you give the Torah through me?'

J "He said to him, 'Be silent. That is how I have decided matters.'

K "He said to Him, 'Lord of the universe, You have now shown me his mastery of the Torah. Now show me his reward.'

L "He said to him, 'Turn around.'

M "He turned around and saw people weighing out his flesh in the butcher-shop.

N "He said to Him, 'Lord of the universe, such is his mastery of Torah, and such is his reward?'

O "He said to him, 'Be silent. That is how I have decided matters.'"

Humans are like God, possessing free will, but humans are not God. God does what He likes, with whom He likes. In the end, the Torah requires acceptance of God's decrees, whatever they are, when the undeserving receive glory, when the accomplished come to nothing.

Elul Counting from Nisan, the sixth month of the Jewish year, August-September, season for repentance prior to the New Year, at the beginning of the next month, Tishrei.

Emancipation In the context of Judaism, the bestowing upon Jews the rights and duties of citizenship; a political process, commencing with the French Revolution, 1789, by which Jews ceased to form autonomous, self-governing communities within a larger empire and were changed into undifferentiated citizens. This was part of a larger movement of emancipation of serfs, women, slaves, Catholics (in Protestant countries, for instance, Great Britain), and the political change produced important results for Judaism. While Emancipation left Jews, like non-Jews, subject to and equal before the law, Judaism in its classical formulation had rested on the premise that the Jews were governed only by God's law and formed God's people. The conflicting political premises of the nation-state and the Torah scarcely permitted reconciliation. The result was the emergence of new Judaic systems— REFORM JUDAISM, Liberal Judaism, ORTHODOX JUDAISM, Positive Historical Judaism (in the U.S.A.: CONSERVATIVE JUDAISM)—each of them alleging that they formed the natural next step in the

unfolding of "the tradition," meaning the Judaic system of the dual Torah, written and oral.

Emancipation developed in three periods. In the first, 1740–1789, ending with the French Revolution, advocates of the Jews' emancipation maintained that religious intolerance accounted for the low caste-status assigned to the Jews. Liberating the Jews would mark another stage in overcoming religious intolerance. During this period, the original ideas of Reform Judaism came to expression, although the important changes in religious doctrine and practice were realized only in the earlier part of the nineteenth century. In the second period, 1789–1878, from the French revolution to the Congress of Berlin, the French revolution brought Jews political rights in France, Belgium, Netherlands, Italy, Germany, and Austria-Hungary. As Germany and Italy attained unification and Hungary independence, the Jews were accorded the rights and duties of citizenship.

During this second period, Reform Judaism reached its first stage of development, beginning in Germany. It made possible for Jews to hold together the two things they deemed inseparable: their desire to remain Jewish and their wish to be one with their "fellow citizens." By the middle of the nineteenth century, Reform had reached full expression and had won the support of a sizable part of German Jewry. In reaction against Reform, Orthodoxy came into existence. But Orthodoxy no less than Reform asked how "Judaism" could co-exist with "German-ness," meaning citizenship in an undifferentiated republic of citizens. (See also WISSENSCHAFT DES JUDENTUMS.) A centrist position, mediating between Reform and Orthodoxy, was worked out by theologians in what was then called the Historical School, and what, in twentieth-century America, took the name of Conservative Judaism. The period from the French Revolution to the Congress of Berlin therefore saw the full efflorescence of all of the Judaisms of political modernization.

In the third period, 1878 to 1933, from the Congress of Berlin to the rise of the Nazis to power in Germany, anti-Semitism as a political and social movement attained power. Jews began to realize that Jewish civic and political equality did not automatically bring social recognition or acceptance. The Jews continued to form a separate group; they were racially "inferior." The impact of the new racism would be felt in the twentieth century, with the response of the Judaisms of that period forming a final chapter in the legacy of Emancipation.

Enoch   Also referred to as the Ethiopic Book of Enoch, a writing attributed to Enoch, surviving in the Ethiopic language only. Enoch was the seventh descendant from the generation of Adam (Genesis 5:21–24). He lived for 365 years, and at the end of his life on earth, he did not die but "walked with God." He spent time with the angels during and after his stay on earth. The Ethiopic Apocalypse of Enoch, 1 Enoch, contains a collection of revelations ascribed to him. It was originally written in Aramaic and then translated into Greek and from Greek into Ethiopic. The work focuses on Enoch's walking with God as a heavenly journey. It further contains an elaboration of Genesis 6:1–5, the mating of the watchers (sons of God) and mortal women, which produced a race of giants who devastated the earth and brought on the flood of the period of Noah.

Eretz Yisrael   (Hebrew: "Land of Israel") The territory that, in the narrative of Genesis, God promised to Abraham and gave to the people of Israel on condition that they keep the covenant. Originally the land of Canaan, the land of Israel was transferred by God to the people of Israel as the location for the formation of the kingdom of priests and the holy people that Israel undertook to form when it accepted God's dominion in the Torah.

The question of the borders of the Land at various points in the history of Judaism is moot; for Judaism, the religion, what matters is the holiness of the Land, which is enhanced when the Land is occupied by the Holy People. The union of Land and People marked Israel's attainment of Eden when Joshua led Israel into the Land. That union would have stood for ever, had Israel not sinned. Sinning, Israel lost the Land. The restoration for good will take place, classical Judaism teaches, when Israel has repented its sin, atoned, and attained reconciliation with God. Then the Messiah will gather in the exiles of Israel and restore the People of Israel to the Land of Israel, the new Eden of the world to come. At that time, humanity at large will acknowledge the unity of God and enter into the condition of Israel too. So the Land in concrete and in theological terms defines a principal component of classical Judaism.

The only territories differentiated in world geography are the Land of Israel and, therein, the only city that is differentiated from all other cities is Jerusalem. These are heavily differentiated, e.g., as to levels of sanctification, while no other territory or city in the world is differentiated in any way at all. These are holy, and no other territory or city is holy, just as Holy Israel is different in genus from all other social entities in humanity.

Erev   Evening, sunset, beginning of a new day, as in Genesis 1:5: "And there was evening, and there was morning, a first day." Within the Jewish reckoning of time, the new day begins in the evening. Accordingly, Sabbaths and other holidays always are considered to start at sundown of the evening before the day of their principal celebration.

Erub   A symbolic fence that creates an area of shared domain much larger than the actual area in which any individual or family dwells. An erub, which may encompass an entire neighborhood or even a town, thus creates a large area within which it is permitted to carry objects on the Sabbath day, on which Scripture prohibits one to carry outside of his or her "domain."

Erub Tabshilin   1) A portion of food set aside prior to the Sabbath as a symbolic meal shared by the householders who dwell around a shared courtyard. The presence of this shared meal causes their domains to be treated as blended into a single domain for purposes of carrying on the Sabbath, on which Scripture restricts one to carrying only within his or her "domain."

2) In an instance in which the Sabbath follows immediately after the conclusion of a festival, a portion of food set out before the beginning of the festival symbolizing the beginning of the preparation of meals for the Sabbath. Foods may subsequently be prepared on the festival day for Sabbath use. In the absence of an Erub Tabshilin, only food intended for consumption on the festival itself may be prepared on that day.

Erubin   Mishnah tractate on the limits on carrying and traveling on the Sabbath established in Scripture and how they are observed. It concerns the provision of a common outer boundary to unite private domains into a single shared territory (ERUB); and the provision of a common, communal meal for the same purpose

(ERUB TABSHILIN). A treatment of this tractate is found in both the Jerusalem and Babylonian Talmuds.

Erusin   In Jewish marriage, the rite of betrothal, in which the woman is sanctified, or designated as holy, to a particular man. This is followed by the *nissuin*, in which the union is consecrated. In ancient times, these ceremonies were often separated by as much as a year. Today they are included within a single wedding rite. See HUPPAH.

Essenes   Sect in ancient Judaism, one of the three best-known groups, alongside the PHARISEES and SADDUCEES; flourished from the second century B.C.E. to the latter part of the first century C.E. The Essenes formed monastic communities that generally excluded women; they held property in common; daily life was regulated by officials. They were few in number. They were meticulous in their observance, with special attention to the Sabbath and to cultic purity. They believed in immortality and divine recompense for sin, but, like the Sadducees, denied bodily resurrection, which the Pharisees affirmed. They lived ascetic lives of manual labor and kept the Sabbath through prayer throughout the day. Some maintain that the Dead Sea library, the scrolls found at Qumran beginning in 1947 that revealed a whole new set of writings of Judaism, derives from a community of Essenes.

Esther   Heroine who saved the Israelites in the Persian empire from destruction by the vizier, Haman. The biblical Book of Esther recounts her story; that book, written on a parchment scroll, is read on PURIM, which celebrates Esther's heroism and the Jews' victory over Haman.

Esther Rabbah Midrashic commentary

on the Book of Esther. The commentary's primary message, found in its first part, is that the nations are swine, their rulers are fools, and Israel is subjugated to them only because of its own sins. But just as God saved Israel in the past, so the salvation that Israel can attain will recapitulate the former ones. The work thus sets forth a proposition entirely familiar from the books of Deuteronomy through Kings and much of the prophetic literature: sin accounts for the people of Israel's subjugation. Atonement will lead to God's salvation and the restoration of Israel to its land and intended stature.

Eternal light (Hebrew: *Ner Tamid*) In the synagogue, a light burning perpetually before the ark in which the Torah scrolls are kept. The *Ner Tamid* symbolizes the candelabrum that burned continually in the wilderness tabernacle and later in the Jerusalem Temple (see Exodus 27:20, Leviticus 24:2). In synagogues today, the *Ner Tamid* is normally an electric bulb placed in a decorative housing and suspended before the ark. Oil lamps and candles may also be used.

Etrog Citron, a type of citrus fruit resembling a lemon, one of four species carried in synagogue on SUKKOT, from Leviticus 23:40, "fruit of a goodly tree."

Etz Hayyim Torah Commentary Edition of the Pentateuch designed for use within Conservative synagogues, published in 2001. Alongside the Hebrew text and English translation, it contains three levels of commentary, 1) a statement of the simple meaning of each biblical passage, 2) a reflection on the religious significance of the material, and 3) discussions of the ramifications of the Bible's statements for later Jewish law and practice.

Eve (Hebrew: *Havah*) Woman, counterpart to ADAM, Man, in the creation narrative of Genesis. God created Man and Woman in his image (Genesis 1:27): "Male and female he created them." He created woman because, "It is not good for man to be alone, I will make a fitting helper for him" (Genesis 2:18). "So the Lord God cast a deep sleep upon the man … and he took one of his ribs and closed up the flesh at that spot. And the Lord God fashioned the rib that he had taken from the man into woman, and he brought her to the man" (Genesis 2:21–22).

Exilarch (Aramaic: *Resh Galuta*; "head of the exile") Head of the Jewish community in Babylonia in talmudic and medieval times. Recognized by the government as ethnarch, ruler of the ethnic group. Parallel to the Patriarch, recognized as the governor of the Jewish community of the land of Israel by the Roman government, pagan, then Christian, until the early fifth century.

Exodus, Book of The second book of the Five Books of Moses (Pentateuch). Exodus tells the story of the Egyptian bondage and the exodus of the Israelites from Egypt and their journey to Mount SINAI, led by Moses (chaps. 1–18). The second half records the covenant between ISRAEL and God at SINAI and sets out the laws that would order Israel's life, with extensive attention (chaps. 29–40) to the building of the altar of the tabernacle in the wilderness, where God would be worshipped through animal offerings, and the dedication of the priesthood to divine service.

F

Fackenheim, Emil (1916–) German-born rabbi, theologian, and religious existentialist; best known for his view that the Holocaust represents a new revelation, through which God presented a 614th commandment forbidding Jews to cease practicing Judaism, which would have the impact of handing Hitler a posthumous victory. Fackenheim rejects interpretations that deem the Holocaust the result of Jews' sin and, in general, repudiates the idea that any "explanation" of the Holocaust is possible. Instead he employs a model of dialogical revelation, similar to that proposed by Martin Buber, in which revelation is the personal encounter of an I with the Eternal Thou (God).

Fackenheim insists that, despite their outrage at God and humankind, Jews must continue to believe. God, he argues, is always present in history, even if we cannot understand what God is doing or why he allows suffering to occur. Most important, Fackenheim asserts that, from the death camps, as from Sinai, God commanded Israel, imparting what he terms the "614th commandment," which imposed upon the Jewish people a sacred obligation to survive. In the face of the death camps, Jewish existence itself becomes a holy act. Under this new commandment, Jews are forbidden to despair of redemption or to become cynical about the world and humanity. Such cynicism is an abdication of responsibility for the repair of the world and results in the delivery of the world into the hands of Nazism. Most important, in the face of the Holocaust, Jews are "forbidden to despair of the God of Israel, lest Judaism perish." The voice that speaks from Auschwitz demands that no Jew reject his faith. To do so is to contribute to the demise of the Jewish people and religion, so as to participate in the accomplishment of the work Hitler himself could not complete.

In his depiction of a God who speaks from Auschwitz, Fackenheim invests the age-old Jewish will for survival with transcendental importance. Insofar as the Nazis wished to eradicate Jews from the earth, Jews are commanded to withstand annihilation. Paradoxically, in this approach, Hitler, rather than the Torah revealed at Sinai, makes it incumbent upon Jews after the Holocaust to remain Jewish and to observe the teachings of Judaism. To accept the religion and precepts of the God of Sinai is to deny the evil desired by Hitler. But, conversely, to reject the God of Sinai or to deny one's standing as a Jew—no matter what one's reason for doing to—is to affirm Hitler's plan and program. This, of course, no Jew can do.

Falashas (Amharic: "exiles") Jewish ethnic group originating in Ethiopia that follows a form of Judaism based upon the Bible, certain books of the Apocrypha, and other religious writings. Originally living in the provinces surrounding and to the north of Lake Tana, beginning in 1975 members of the group came to Israel, where a large community of Ethiopian Jews now resides.

Ethiopian Jewish tradition traces the group's origin to dignitaries from Jerusalem who accompanied the Queen of Sheba back to Ethiopia after her visit with Solomon (1 Kings 10). Ethnographers hold that the group descends from the

Agau tribes and was converted by Jews in southern Arabia or permanently living in Ethiopia before the fourth century, when the Askum dynasty converted to Christianity. The Falashas' numbers may have been augmented by Jewish captives brought to the area in 525 C.E.

Despite religious persecution, loss of their original political independence, and the partial success of nineteenth-century Protestant missionaries, the Ethiopian Jews have maintained their religious and social distinctiveness. Their religion is based primarily upon Scripture, which they have in the Ge'ez translation used by the Ethiopian church. The Falashas believe that there is one God, who chose Israel, and whose Messiah will lead the people back to the Holy Land. They observe the Pentateuchal laws concerning clean and unclean animals and other matters of ritual purity. They wash their hands before eating and recite blessings before and after meals. Boys are circumcised on the eighth day. The Falashas observe the Sabbath and other festivals, including a variation of the fast of Ab, but excluding PURIM and HANUKKAH. Burial is on the day of death and is followed by seven days of mourning (see SHIVA).

Religious life centers on the *mesgid* (synagogue), which is divided into two halls. One of these, the "holy of holies," contains a handwritten parchment Pentateuch, bound as a book. Only the priest and *dabtara* (religious teacher) may enter this room. An altar in the synagogue's courtyard is used for the Passover sacrifice. Prayers are recited in Ge'ez, the traditional literary language of Ethiopia.

Several of the Ethiopian Jews' religious observances do not derive from Judaism. While their priests (*kessim*) claim Aaronide descent, upon ordination by the high priest, any educated man can assume priestly functions. Apparently because of contact with

Christianity, the Falashas also have monks and nuns, who live in monasteries or in seclusion outside of the villages. Circumcision of females was traditionally practiced, as in many parts of Africa. The Falashas share the Ethiopian belief in spirits, and they make and use various amulets, charms, and incantations.

After the state of Israel declared its independence in 1948, enactment of the Law of Return, which gives every Jew the right to Israeli citizenship, led the Israeli rabbinate to consider whether or not the Falashas were Jews. An affirmative answer in 1975 led to a program of bringing Ethiopian Jews to Israel. By 1981, 1400 Falashas had reached Israel. In 1984–1985, a secret Israeli airlift codenamed Operation Moses brought about 8000 Falashas to Israel. In 1989, an estimated 12,000 to 17,000 remained in Ethiopia, subjected to conditions of famine and anti-Semitism. They were left behind when Operation Moses became widely publicized and was halted by the Ethiopian government. As late as 1989, attempts to secure their release were unsuccessful.

In Israel, the Ethiopian Jewish community has been economically successful but has engaged in a continuing struggle for acceptance by Israel's orthodox rabbinate. Despite the earlier determination that Falashas are Jews, the rabbinate wishes formally to convert them to Judaism. The Israeli rabbinate and, therefore, the Interior Ministry refuse to recognize marriages performed by the Falasha priests. This struggle has created significant strife within the Ethiopian Jewish community itself, with factions arguing for and against accommodation of the Israeli orthodoxy.

Fast Days (Hebrew: *Tzom, Ta'anit*) In Judaism, fasting is practiced as an aspect of repentance, as a sign of mourning, or to request divine assistance. Two annual fasts are observed for a full twenty-four hours, from sundown to sundown: the penitential fast of the Day of Atonement (YOM KIPPUR) and the fast of the Ninth of Ab (Tisha beAb – see AB, NINTH OF), which commemorates the destructions of the First and Second Temples in Jerusalem. Other fasts are observed from sunrise to sunset. These include the fast of the seventeenth of Tammuz, which recalls the breaching of the walls of Jerusalem prior to the Temple's destruction, the FAST OF GEDALIAH, on the third of Tishrei, which marks the events described at 2 Kings 25:22–25, the FAST OF ESTHER (see Esther 4:16), and the FAST OF THE FIRST BORN, which precedes PASSOVER. Private fasting is not common in Judaism, with such fasts observed primarily to mark the anniversary of a near-relative's death, on one's wedding day (if it does not fall on the first of the month), prior to the ceremony, and by those who are present when a Torah scroll is dropped.

Fast of Esther   The fast recorded in the biblical Book of Esther (4:16), by which ESTHER prepared herself to approach King Ahasuerus. This fast still is commonly observed among traditional Jews on the thirteenth of Adar, the day preceding Purim. Like all minor fasts, it takes place from dawn to dusk rather than beginning at sundown on the preceding evening.

Fast of Gedaliah   A day of fasting observed by traditional Jews on the third of Tishrei, commemorating the assassination of Gedaliah and his associates in Mitzpeh (2 Kings 25, Jeremiah 40).

Fast of the First Born   (Hebrew: *Tzom Bekhorot*) The day of fasting observed by traditional Jews on the thirteenth of Nisan, the day preceding the beginning of Passover, commemorating the release of first born Jewish males from the plague of the death of the first born that struck Egypt. The fast of the first born may be concluded in the morning hours when those fasting gather to witness an individual's completion of the study of a Rabbinic treatise. All present at such an occasion are commanded to participate in a celebratory feast, which overrides the obligations of the fast.

Fetus   Human being in the womb of the mother, regarded after forty days from conception as possessing a soul; abortion for any purpose other than saving the life of the mother is not permitted; until the baby is born, the life of the mother takes precedence over life of the embryo; once the baby is born, the baby's life takes precedence. A guardian can be appointed to protect the rights of the embryo.

Fringes   See ṢIṢIT.

G

Gabai A functionary in the synagogue (usually translated as warden) who assures that individuals are assigned to and called up to the podium for the performance of specific aspects of the worship, e.g., reciting the blessings before and after the reading of each Torah lection. While the Torah is being read during worship, a Gabai is stationed at each side of the podium to follow along with the reader and to assure that no errors are made in the reading.

Gabriel One of four holy angels who stand in God's presence. The name Gabriel means, "power of God" or "man of God." He is mentioned along with Michael and Raphael. In the biblical book of Daniel 8–9 he is God's messenger to Daniel, explaining divine mysteries.

Galut (Hebrew: "Exile") In classical Judaism, the separation between God and humanity, a theological, not political or cultural, concept. The initial condition of Exile pertains to Adam and Eve, who are sent out of Paradise (Eden) by reason of sin. Comparable to Adam and Eve, the people of Israel goes into exile from its Eden, which is the land of Israel, for the same reason. That exile took place in 586 B.C.E., when the Babylonians conquered Jerusalem, destroyed the Temple built by Solomon (see SOLOMON, KING) centuries earlier, and took much of the Israelite population into Exile in Babylonia (see BABYLON, BABYLONIA). Three generations later, in ca. 530 B.C.E., the Persians conquered the Babylonians and restored ISRAEL to the land of Israel—thus, exile and return. Stories told by Judaism through the ages thus rework the theme of exile from God and return to God and to the condition God had had in mind in creation, which is to say, Paradise.

The Five Books of Moses, Genesis through Deuteronomy, finally promulgated in 450 B.C.E. at the climax of the process of restoration of Israel to its Temple and its Land, made the first and authoritative statement of exile and return. Israel could never take its existence as permanent and unconditional. Like Eden, the land of Israel is not a given but a gift; the promise of giving the Land to the people of Israel is conditional; the land is there to be lost, the people there to lose it and to cease to be—all because of what they do or do not do. The lessons drawn by Judaism from the conception of Galut are these: the life of the group is uncertain, subject to conditions and stipulations. But what actually did happen in that uncertain world—exile but then restoration—marked the group as special, different, select. That experience (in theological terms) rehearsed the conditional moral existence of sin and punishment, suffering and atonement and reconciliation, and (in social terms) the uncertain and always conditional national destiny of disintegration and renewal of the group.

Gan Eden (Hebrew: "Garden of Eden") Paradise, created by God as a residence for Adam and Eve, the first man and woman: "The Lord God planted a garden in the east of Eden, and placed there the man whom he had formed. And from the ground the Lord God caused to grow every tree that was pleasing to the sight and good for food, with the tree of life in the middle of the garden and the tree of knowledge of good and evil" (Genesis 2:8–9). God instructed Man and Woman to eat anything they wanted except for the fruit of the tree of the knowledge of good and evil (Genesis 2:17). They violated this restriction and for their disobedience were driven out of the Garden of Eden. In Judaism, "Gan Eden" is synonymous with life eternal and is used interchangeably with *olam haba*, meaning "world to come." See OLAM HABA.

Gaon   Eminence, excellency; title of head of Babylonian talmudic academies in the sixth–eleventh centuries; later used to refer to a distinguished talmudic scholar.

Gates of Prayer   Also called the *New Union Prayerbook*, a volume of weekday, Sabbath, and festival prayers developed by the Reform movement's Central Conference of American Rabbis for use in the Reform synagogue. First published in 1975, *Gates of Prayer* was the first completely new prayer book used in American Reform synagogues since the publication of the first Union Prayerbook in the late nineteenth century.

Geiger, Abraham (1810–1874)   The leading intellectual figure of Reform Judaism in the nineteenth century, who viewed Judaism as a constantly evolving organism. In accordance with this view, Geiger held that the changed conditions of modern society called for the continued evolution of Judaism, that it is the right and obligation of contemporary rabbis to adapt Jewish practice and thought to modern scientific knowledge and social and ethical sensibilities. Geiger thus recognized change itself as "traditional." Change represents the way things always were and so legitimately now goes forward. The Jews change, having moved from constituting a nation to a different classification of social entity. The messiah concept now addresses the whole

of humanity, not only speaking of national restoration. Revelation turns out to form a progressive, not a static, fact. In these ways Geiger—and, with him, Reform Judaism—appealed to history to validate his positions.

Geiger grew up in Frankfurt and undertook university studies at Heidelberg, then Bonn, with special interest in philosophy and Semitics. University study formed the exception, not the rule, for Jews. By definition, therefore, the change Geiger had to explain came about through a decision of the former generation, namely to give their son a secular education. Geiger thus explained the changes his parents already had made. Notably, among the intellectual leaders in Geiger's day, not only he, but his arch-opponent, Samson Raphael Hirsch, founder of Orthodox Judaism, also acquired a university education. So Orthodox Judaism too emerged as the result of changes brought about by the generation prior to the age of the founders.

In synagogue pulpits, Geiger was not always appreciated for either his flawless German or his questioning of routine. Most of his work, however, concerned not the local synagogue-community but the constituency of Judaic learning. He produced a periodical, the *Scientific Journal for Jewish Theology*, from 1835 onward, which was founded on the idea that knowledge of the historical facts would make it possible to determine the ways in which Judaism could appropriately be shaped so as to serve the needs of the contemporary community. Through systematic learning Judaism would undergo reform. Reform Judaism thus rested on deep foundations of historical scholarship (see WISSENSCHAFT DES JUDENTUMS).

Geiger had in mind to analyze the sources and evolution of Judaism. If science (used in its German sense of systematic learning) could uncover the sources of the Jewish "spirit," then, in Max Wiener's words, "the genius of his people and … its vocation" would serve "as a guide to the construction of a living present and future." Geiger's principle of Reform remained fixed. Reform had to emerge from *Wissenschaft*, "a term which he equated with the concept of the understanding of historical evolution." To him "Judaism in its ideal was religion per se, nothing but an expression of religious consciousness. Its outer shell was subject to change from one generation to another." All things emerge out of time and change. But when it comes time to trace the history of time and change, contemporary categories assuredly defined the inquiry. Thus Geiger produced, out of ancient times, portraits congruent to the issues of his own day.

Gelilah (Hebrew: "rolling") In the synagogue, the ritual of dressing the Torah scroll from which the weekly, Sabbath, or holiday lection has just been read. The scroll is tied shut, and its mantel and other adornments are replaced. The individual who performs the ritual of Gelilah is referred to as the Golel.

Gemara (Aramaic: "completion") Comments on and discussions of the Mishnah, found in the Jerusalem Talmud and the Babylonian Talmud. Together, the Mishnah and its commentary—the Gemara—are referred to as the TALMUD.

Gemilut Ḥasadim (Hebrew: "acts of lovingkindness") Supererogatory acts of humanity, over and above the religious duties of service to fellow human beings that the Torah requires. From the cessation of Temple sacrifices, such acts are deemed the counterpart to Temple sacrifices of atonement, in line with Hosea 6:6: "For I desire mercy, not sacrifice."

Genesis (Hebrew: *Bereshit*) The first book of the Five Books of Moses, which tells the story of the creation of the world and of the first generations of humankind, ten from Adam, the first human being, to Noah, the one righteous man of his generation, and ten from Noah to Abraham (Genesis 1–11). It proceeds to narrate the patriarchal story of the beginning of Israel as the family of the patriarchs, Abraham, Isaac, and Jacob (Genesis 12–38). The story of how the Israelites went down to Egypt in the time of Joseph, Jacob's eleventh son, who was especially favored by his father and was an object of jealousy for his brothers, fills out the remainder of the book (Genesis 39–50), including Jacob's final blessing of his twelve sons, the founders of the TWELVE TRIBES OF ISRAEL (Genesis 49).

Genesis Rabbah Completed in ca. 400–450 C.E., sometime after the Jerusalem Talmud, a verse-by-verse commentary that transforms the book of Genesis from a genealogy and family history of ABRAHAM, ISAAC, JACOB, and JOSEPH, into a book of the laws of history and rules for the salvation of Israel: the deeds of the founders are read as omens and signs for the final generations. In Genesis Rabbah, the entire narrative of Genesis is made to point toward the sacred history of the Jewish people: its slavery in Egypt and redemption; its coming Temple in Jerusalem; its exile and salvation at the end of time. In Genesis Rabbah's reading, Genesis proclaims the prophetic message that the world's creation commenced a single, straight line of significant events leading in the end to the salvation of Israel and, through Israel, of all humanity. The single most important proposition of Genesis Rabbah is that, in the story of the beginnings of creation, humanity, and Israel, we find the meaning and direction of the entire life of the Jewish people. The deeds of the founders supply signals for the children about what is going to come in the future. So the biography of Abraham, Isaac, and Jacob also constitutes a protracted account of the history of Israel later on.

Genesis Rabbah emerges from that momentous century in which the Roman Empire passed from pagan to Christian rule and in which Christianity adopted a policy of repression of paganism that rapidly engulfed Judaism as well. The issue confronting ISRAEL in the land of Israel therefore proved immediate: the meaning of the new and ominous turn of history, the implications of Christ's worldly triumph for the other-worldly and supernatural people, Israel, whom God chooses and loves. Genesis Rabbah addressed the circumstance of historical crisis and generated remarkable renewal, a rebirth of intellect in the encounter with Scripture, now in quest of the rules of salvation. So the book of Genesis, which portrays how all things had begun, would testify as well to the message and method of the end: the coming salvation of Israel.

The sages thus read Genesis as the history of the world with emphasis on Israel. So the lives portrayed, the domestic quarrels and petty conflicts with the neighbors, all serve to yield insight into what was to be. That is because the deeds of the patriarchs taught lessons on how the children were to act, and, it further followed, the lives of the patriarchs signaled the history of Israel. Israel constituted one extended family, and the metaphor of the family, serving the nation as it did, imparted to the stories of Genesis the character of a family record. History become genealogy conveyed the message of salvation. These propositions really laid down the same judgment, one for the individual and the family, the other for the community and

the nation, since there was no differentiating one from the other. Every detail of the narrative therefore served to prefigure what was to be, and Israel found itself, time and again, in the revealed facts of the history of the creation of the world, the decline of humanity down to the time of Noah, and, finally, its ascent to Abraham, Isaac, and Israel.

Geniza   A storehouse used by Jews to avoid otherwise discarding holy writings, especially texts that contain the name of God. The most important such storage place was uncovered in Fostat, near the old area of Cairo, in 1899 by Solomon Schechter and yielded documents dated from 640 to 1100 C.E. In the find were the lost Hebrew version of Ecclesiasticus, extracts from Aquila's Greek translation of the Scriptures, the Zadokite Fragments, and other important documents. The Cairo Geniza is the single most important source of documentary evidence on Judaism in medieval Islam.

Ger   Convert to Judaism; sometimes referred to as *Ger Ṣedeq*, a righteous proselyte, sincere convert. According to Judaism, in accepting the unity and sovereignty of God embodied in the Torah, the convert acquires a genealogy that explains his or her share in the God of Israel. The genealogy is via Abraham and Sarah, referred to as the convert's "parents," who, even before reaching the promised Land, had made converts in Haran (Genesis 12:5). The convert is equivalent to the native-born Israelite, for the "Israel" of which Judaism speaks encompasses all those who accept God's dominion and select for themselves a place in the family of Israel. Concretely, the convert receives a Hebrew name and, like a new-born son, a male convert is circumcised into the covenant of Abraham. Both the male and the female convert are immersed in water that has collected naturally, for example, a lake, river, ocean, or an immersion-pool (*miqveh*). Besides circumcision and immersion, there is a synagogue rite, in which a court of three rabbis questions the convert, who makes a Declaration of Faith. In some places, the language is as follows (Harlow, *Rabbi's Manual*, p. 78):

> I hereby declare my desire to accept the principles of the Jewish religion, to follow its practices and ceremonies, and to become a member of the Jewish people …. I pray that I may always remain conscious of the duties that are mine as a member of the House of Israel. I declare my determination to maintain a Jewish home. Should I be blessed with male children, I pledge to bring them into the Covenant of Abraham. I further pledge to rear all children with whom God may bless me in loyalty to the Jewish faith and its practices.
>
> "Hear O Israel, the Lord our God, the Lord is one …"

Gerushin The formal dissolution of matrimony through divorce. The husband alone has the legal right of divorce and, according to Talmudic law, can dissolve the marriage for any cause whatsoever, without the wife's needing to consent. Later Judaism restricted the husband's ability to divorce his wife, holding by the eleventh century that a divorce could be finalized only with the wife's consent. Similarly, the right of the wife to force her husband to grant her a divorce increasingly was recognized.

Judaism does not view divorce as a sin but, rather, as an agreement made by the involved parties concerning their personal status. Accordingly, Judaism sees no need to establish guilt, and the parties themselves must agree to the terms of the settlement, which only in the most extreme cases can be imposed by a religious court (*bet din*).

In Jewish law, the husband is explicitly granted the right to sue for divorce in a case in which the wife committed adultery or apostasy, acted immorally, refused sexual relations, was barren, had an incurable disease, or refused to live where he desired. Similarly, the wife's right to petition for divorce is recognized in cases in which the husband behaves immorally or cruelly, has a disease or disgusting occupation, is sterile, refuses to have sexual relations, becomes an apostate, fails to support the wife, or engages in crime. The court itself may impose a divorce when the partners are found to comprise a forbidden (e.g., incestuous) relationship, when the wife engaged in adultery and the husband refused to sue for divorce, or when health reasons make cohabitation dangerous. In contemporary Judaism, these lists of reasons are largely irrelevant; outside Israel, a Jewish divorce generally is carried out as a consequence of the completion of a civil divorce.

The divorce itself is effected through a bill of divorce, called a "*get*" or "*sefer keritot*" ("document of separation"). In light of the serious nature of divorce, forms of this document may not be mass produced or prepared ahead of time. Rather, each *get* must be individually prepared by a scribe at the request of the husband and for the wife he wishes to divorce.

In the Conservative and Orthodox movements, and in Israel, a Jew who has not received a Jewish divorce is not permitted to remarry in a religious ceremony, even if a civil divorce has been obtained. The Reform movement has dispensed with the process of gerushin, accepting the civil divorce as determinative of the status of the individuals. A husband may remarry immediately after a divorce, a wife must wait 90 days.

Get   A writ of divorce, required to dissolve a Jewish marriage. The *get* must be written at the express behest of the husband, who gives it to the wife. See GERUSHIN.

Ge'ulah   (Hebrew: "Redemption") God's salvation of humanity from the condition of sinfulness; the salvation of holy Israel from the condition of Exile and the restoration of humanity to Eden and of ISRAEL to the land of Israel.

Gezerah Shavah   A principle of Scripture interpretation that maintains that a verbal analogy is formed from one verse to another by means of finding the same words in both verses; the result is that a principle identified in the one verse governs in the other as well, by reason of the verbal analogy that has been established.

Ginzberg, Louis (1873–1953)   Scholar of Rabbinic literature, one of the theologian-historians who created CONSERVATIVE JUDAISM. He grew up in Lithuania and left for the U.S.A. in 1899. Ginzberg advocated religious practice for Conservative Judaism based on the inherited ideals of traditional Judaism while allowing diverse belief, including the ignoring of the creeds and theological canons of traditional Judaism. Ginzberg thus stressed that Judaism comprises a way of life rather than a theology.

Ginzberg's theory of the role of history in the formation of religion is expressed in the statement: "Fact, says a great thinker, is the ground of all that is divine in religion and religion can only be presented in history—in truth it must become a continuous and living history." This extreme statement of the positive-historical school will not have surprised the reformers of Ginzberg's day. It provides a guide to the character of Conservative Judaism in the context of the changes of the nineteenth and twentieth century. The appeal to fact in place of faith, the stress on practice to the subordination of belief—these form responses to the difficult situation of sensitive intellectuals brought up, like Ginzberg, in one world but living in another.

Ginzberg's scholarly work covered the classical documents of the oral Torah, with special interest in subjects not commonly emphasized in the centers of learning he had left. But while the subject changed, the mode of learning remained constant. Ginzberg's work emphasized massive erudition, collecting and arranging texts, together with episodic and ad hoc solutions to difficult problems of exegesis. But the work remained primarily textual and exegetical, and, when Ginzberg ventured into historical questions, the received mode of talmudic discourse—deductive reasoning, ad hoc arguments—predominated.

The claim to critical scholarship forms, for Conservative Judaism, the counterpart to Orthodoxy's appeal to the Torah as God's will. Much is made in the theologies of Conservative Judaism of historical fact, precedent, discovering the correct guidelines for historical change. But the essential mode of argument accords with the received patterns of thought of the Yeshiva-world from which Ginzberg took his leave. Talmudists such as Ginzberg, who acquired a university training, including an interest in history, and who also continued to study Talmudic materials, never fully overcame the intellectual habits ingrained from their beginnings in *Yeshivot*. Ginzberg is best known for his masterly work *Legends of the Jews* (1909), translated into English by Henrietta Szold (see SZOLD, HENRIETTA).

Gittin   Mishnah tractate on writs of divorce: how they are prepared and delivered (chaps. 1–3); the law of agency for receiving and handing the writ over (chaps. 6–7); stipulations and conditions in writs of divorce (chap. 7)); invalid writs of divorce by reason of improper delivery, improper preparation, improper stipulations, or invalid witnesses (chaps. 8–9). This tractate is commented on in both the Jerusalem Talmud and the Babylonian Talmud.

God   See ELOHIM.

Gog and Magog   In Ezekiel 38–39, the figure of Gog, a prince of the land of Magog, embodies Israel's enemy marching from the north, who will ravage ISRAEL before God destroys him. In the War Scroll from Qumran, Gog and his assembly will be chastised at the end of time. In Revelation 20:8, Magog is no longer a land but someone alongside Gog at the final battle, after Satan is loosed after a thousand years. They fight with Israel in the days of the Messiah.

Golah   The exile; anywhere Jews are located outside of the Holy Land. See GALUT.

Golem   A creature made in human form and brought to life by magical means, especially through the invocation of holy names. The golem is mentioned in the Talmud but becomes best known in medieval Jewish and non-Jewish folk literature, most famously in the eighteenth century tale that Rabbi Judah Loew b. Bezalel of Prague created a golem to protect the city's Jews from POGROMS but was forced to destroy it, by removing the holy name from its forehead, when it became uncontrollable.

Golus   Ashkenazic pronunciation of *Galut*. In this pronunciation, the term is used to refer to exile, life in the diaspora, discrimination, and humiliation. See GALUT.

Goy   (Hebrew: "nation;" plural: *goyim*) In the Bible, a synonym for " 'Am," nation. The people of Israel are referred to by it.

In classical Rabbinic writings, by contrast, "goy" refers to an idolater. In these writings, all of humanity is divided between Israel, defined as those who know God and accept the Torah, and gentiles, who worship idols. Idolaters die and do not rise from the dead. Israel is destined to rise from the grave and stand in judgment, with most of Israel promised eternal life in the restoration of the Garden of Eden, or Paradise, at the end of days. This is the difference—the only consequential distinction—between Israel and gentiles. In contemporary parlance, a derogatory term of reference for a gentile; the adjectival form, *goyish*, similarly distinguishes its referent in a negative way as unJewish.

H

Habad Hasidism A form of Hasidism founded by Shneur Zalman of Liady (1745–1813) that stresses not only ecstatic religious experience but also Torah study. The term Habad is an acronym for Hokhma, Binah, Da'at, the Hebrew terms for Wisdom, Understanding, Knowledge. The movement is also referred to as Lubavitch Hasidism. Many members of Habad Hasidism believe that their most recently deceased leader, Menachem Schneerson (1902–1994), known as the Lubavitcher Rebbe, is the Messiah and will rise from the dead to save the world.

Habdalah The rite that after sundown, at the end of the Sabbath or festival, marks the separation of the holy time of the Sabbath or festival to the secular or profane time of the everyday week. See QIDDUSH.

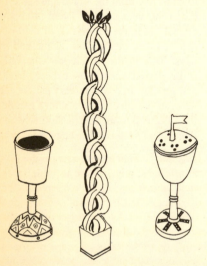

Habdalah Wine cup, braided candle and spice box used for Habdalah.

Haber An associate of a Pharisaic circle, one who is lettered in the Torah and who meticulously tithes and preserves cultic cleanness when eating ordinary food. The opposite of an 'Am Ha' Ares. In modern Hebrew it simply means a comrade or member of an organization.

Hadassah U.S. women's Zionist organization, the largest and most effective organization of Jewish activity in the world today; maintains health programs in the State of Israel and educational programs for its members in the diaspora, particularly North America. Hadassah was founded in 1912 by Henrietta Szold (see SZOLD, HENRIETTA).

Haftarah The prophetic lection that accompanies the reading of a passage of the Pentateuch iin the worship of the synagogue. Over a cycle of one year (in some places, three years), the entire Pentateuch is read as the climax of the Sabbath morning service. Each week the Haftarah, a selection of a passage in the prophets, often intersecting with a theme or event in the Pentateuchal lection, is read as well. Similarly on holidays, the prophetic Haftarah follows the reading of the section of the Torah appropriate to the particular occasion.

Hagar The Egyptian servant whom SARAH, wife of ABRAHAM, gave to Abraham as a concubine. She was the mother of ISHMAEL but was sent away at Sarah's insistence when Ishmael competed with ISAAC, Abraham's son by Sarah herself. Hagar's story is found at Genesis 16, 21:8–21, and 25:12.

Hagba'ah (Hebrew: "lifting") In

synagogue ritual, the act of lifting and displaying for the congregation the Torah scroll from which the weekly, Sabbath, or holiday lection has just been read. The ritual allows all members of the congregation to view the writing and express reverence for the scroll. As it is lifted, the congregation chants: "This is the Torah that Moses set before the people of Israel, from the mouth of God, through Moses."

Haggadah   The liturgical book containing the ritual for the SEDER held on PASSOVER eve. The Haggadah narrates the story of the Exodus from Egypt, illustrated through symbolic foods and embellished through a line-by-line interpretation of Deuteronomy 26:5–9.

The ritual found in the Haggadah is first referred to at Mishnah Pesahim Chapter 10, which describes a festival meal marked by a set order (Hebrew: *Seder*) of foods and a required liturgy. At the heart of the meal, there is an explanation of the significance of three foods (unleavened bread, bitter herbs, and the Passover burnt offering) and the recitation of psalms. In Talmudic times, this ceremony was expanded through the addition of a discussion of Israelite history leading up to and including captivity in Egypt. In later developments, continuing to the present, liturgical poems and other homilies have been added to the basic format set in the Talmudic period.

The body of the Haggadah begins by associating unleavened bread with "the bread of affliction" consumed by the Israelites in Egypt. This passage expresses the hope that all who participate in the Passover will, in the coming year, enjoy freedom in the land of Israel. Next comes a set of questions regarding the ways in which the night of the Passover seder differs from all other nights ("*Mah Nishtanah*," "The Four Questions," traditionally recited by the youngest child present). The answer to these questions, beginning in the passage *Avadim Hayinu* ("We were enslaved by Pharaoh"), introduces several stories regarding the obligation to recount the story of the Exodus and the recitation of that story itself. This recitation is introduced by Deuteronomy 26:5–8, interpreted in the Haggadah to mean "An Aramean would have destroyed my father" and embellished by homilies that focus upon the inability of the Egyptians to break the spirit of their Israelite captives. These passages expand as well upon the plagues and the dividing of the sea that allowed the Israelites to escape the pursuing Egyptians.

The actual Passover meal is introduced by a passage cited in the name of Rabban Gamaliel, who states that during that meal one must explain the significance of the Passover sacrifice, the bitter herbs, and the unleavened bread (see Exodus 12:8). The meal is followed by the usual grace and then a medieval exhortation, *Shefokh Hamatkha* ("Pour out your wrath"), comprised of Scriptural verses that urge God to take vengeance on nations that oppress the people of Israel and to bring ELIJAH the prophet, the precursor of the messiah. Recitation of psalms follows, and the Haggadah is concluded by a number of passages and songs that praise God as the source of all life. See PASSOVER.

Hagigah   Mishnah tractate on the festal offerings; pilgrims are to bring three such animal sacrifices: an appearance offering, which is a burnt offering and yields no food for the priest or the pilgrim; festal offering (hagigah proper), which is in the class of peace offerings and does yield meat; and peace offerings of rejoicing, which yield meat as well. The appearance offering is required at

Deuteronomy 16:14–17, the festal offering at Deuteronomy 16:15. The tractate describes the liability and cost of the appearance offering, festal offering, and peace offering of rejoicing (chaps. 1–2) and how these are presented on the Sabbath day (chap. 2); since these offerings bring common folk to the Temple, the rules of cultic cleanness as they affect ordinary folk and Holy Things of the cult are laid out (chaps. 2–3); first come gradations of strictness of rules of cultic cleanness, from the lowest, unconsecrated food eaten as within the rules of cleanness covering sacred food; then tithe and heave offering; then Holy Things (e.g., sacrifices, which yield meat for the priest and the pilgrim) and the rules of strict cleanness affecting these. See ALIYAH.

Halakhah (Hebrew: "Path") The legal content of the Talmudic, Midrashic, and later Rabbinic literatures, as distinguished from the Aggadah, or exegetical and homiletical materials. In common parlance, the term Halakhah denotes the sum total of Jewish law, defining thereby the Jewish way of life and encompassing matters ranging from religious ritual and ethics to rules regulating social interactions and business practices. The Halakhah directs how things are to be done rightly. It defines norms of conduct.

The Halakhah reaches its initial statement in the MISHNAH, ca. 200 C.E., a philosophical law code, which was amplified by the TOSEFTA, a collection of complementary rules, ca. 300 C.E., then by the Jerusalem Talmud, a commentary to the Mishnah and the Tosefta, ca. 400 C.E., and finally by the Babylonian Talmud, ca. 600. The second of the two versions of the TALMUD forms the foundation for the Halakhic enterprise from its closure to our own day, with many commentaries, compilations of rulings (responsa), and codes of the law produced from 600 C.E. to the present day on the basis of the documents of late antiquity.

The Halakhah embodies the extension of God's design for world order, laid out in Scripture, into the inner-facing relationships of [1] God and Israel, [2] Israel's inner-order in its own terms, and [3] the Israelite's household viewed on its own in time and space and social circumstance. In its initial formulation in the Mishnah-Tosefta-Talmud, the Halakhah covered these topics:

1 Between God and Israel: The interior dimensions of Israel's relationships with God—[1] the division of Agriculture, [5] the division of Holy Things. The division of Agriculture defines what Israel in the Land of Israel owes God as his share of the produce of the Holy Land, encompassing also Israel's conformity to God's regulation on how that produce is to be garnered; the anomalous tractate, Berakhot, concerns exactly the same set of relationships. The division of Holy Things corresponds by specifying the way in which the gifts of the Land—meat, grain, oil, wine—are to be offered to Heaven, inclusive of the priesthood, as well as the manner in which the Temple and its staff are supported and the offerings paid for. Two tractates, moreover, describe the Temple and its rite, and one of them sets forth special problems in connection with the same. The sole anomalous tractate, Ḥullin, which takes up the correct slaughter of animals for secular purposes, belongs, because its rules pertain, also, to the conduct of the cult, not only to the household.

2 Within Israel's Social Order: The social order that is realized by Israelites' relationships with one another—

[4] the division of Damages: That division spells out the civil law that maintains justice and equity in the social order, the institutions of government and the sanctions they legitimately impose.

3 Inside the Israelite Household: The inner life of the household, encompassing the individual Israelite, with God—[3] the division of Women, [2] the division of Appointed Times, and [6] the division of Purities, as well as some singleton tractates such as Ḥullin. The division of Women deals with the way in which relationships of man and woman are governed by the rules of sanctification enforced by Heaven, which takes an interest in how family relationships are formed, maintained, and dissolved, and the effects, upon the family, of invoking Heaven's name in oaths. The division of Appointed Times addresses the effect upon the conduct of ordinary life of the advent of holy time, with special reference to the Sabbath and the pilgrim festivals (Passover, Tabernacles), the pilgrimage, and the intermediate days of festivals, the New Year and Day of Atonement, Fast Days, and Purim. While parts of some of these tractates, and nearly the whole of a few of them, concern conduct in the Temple, the main point of the tractates is to explore the impact upon the household and village of the Appointed times. The same interstitial position—between household and village, on the one side, and Temple and cult, on the other—serves the division of Purities. The laws of the tractates concern mainly the household, since the cleanness rules spelled out in those tractates concern purity at home. But, it goes without saying, the same uncleanness that prevents eating at home food that is to be preserved in conditions of cultic cleanness also prevents the Israelite from entering the restricted space of the Temple. But in the balance, the division concerns cleanness in that private domain that is occupied by the Israelite household.

Halakhah LeMoshe MiSinai (Hebrew: "A law revealed by God to Moses at Mount Sinai") Part of the Torah, often: transmitted orally and not in writing, until transcribed in a Rabbinic document.

Ḥaliṣah The rite of removing the shoe, described at Deuteronomy 25:9–10, by which the relationship between a childless widow and her surviving brother-in-law is severed; the widow publicly removes the shoe of her surviving brother-in-law who has refused to marry her, his deceased childless brother's widow.

Ḥallah [1] Bread for consumption on the Sabbath; [2] dough offering removed from bread-dough and handed over to the priest; [3] Mishnah tractate on dough offering, defining bread from which dough offering is required (chap. 1), kinds of grain that yield bread, kinds of dough; the process of separating dough offering (chaps. 2–3); the liability to the offering of mixtures of dough that is liable to dough offering and dough that is exempt (chaps. 3–4); liability to dough offering for bread prepared from grain grown outside of the land of Israel (chap. 4). In modern parlance, the braided Sabbath bread.

Ḥallal Male born to a priest but unfit for the priesthood; the offspring of a priest and a woman whom he is prohibited by the Torah from marrying, e.g., a divorcee; such an offspring is a profaned priest, that is, the offspring of a priest who does not possess the sanctity of the priesthood.

Hallel   Psalms 113–118, collectively designated as Hallel-Psalms, psalms of praise, recited on festival occasion, such as PASSOVER, SHABU'OT, and Tabernacles (see SUKKOT), and for the commemoration of the advent of the lunar month (*Rosh Hodesh*).

Hameṣ   Leaven or grain that is leavened, which is forbidden for use on PASSOVER.

Hamesh Megillot   (Hebrew: "Five Scrolls") The biblical books of Esther, Lamentations, Song of Songs, Qohelet (Ecclesiastes), and Ruth, read in the synagogue on PURIM, the Ninth of Ab (see AB, NINTH OF), PASSOVER, Tabernacles (see SUKKOT), and SHABU'OT, respectively.

Hannah (Hana)   Mother of the prophet Samuel, the prophet who founded the Israelite monarchy by anointing King Saul (see SAUL, KING) then replacing him with King David (see DAVID, KING) (1 Samuel 1–2). Hannah was barren and prayed for a child, whom she pledged to God's service. Her prayer was answered, and she dedicated her son, Samuel, as a servant of God. Her prayer forms the model of prayer in Judaism.

Hanukkah   (Hebrew: "dedication") An eight-day festival commemorating the victory of Judah Maccabbee and his followers over the Syrians, who, in 168 B.C.E., had outlawed the practice of Judaism, insisting instead that Jews assimilate into Hellenistic culture and pagan religious practices. In 164 B.C.E., Judah recaptured Jerusalem, purified the Jerusalem Temple, and relit the eternal light, which miraculously remained lit for eight days fueled by a single-day's supply of holy oil. Accordingly, Jews observe this festival, known also as the "Feast of Lights," by kindling an eight-branched   candelabra   (*Menorah*   or *Hannukiah*), adding an additional candle

each night until, on the final night of the festival, all eight branches as well as a ninth, which holds a candle used to light the others, are lit. This festive holiday also is marked by the giving of gifts, eating of fried foods (reminiscent of the oil), and playing of games, especially with a top (*Dreidel* or *Sevivon*) marked with the Hebrew acronym (nun, gimmel, hey, shin) for the slogan, "A great miracle happened there."

A minor holiday in early Rabbinic and medieval times, Hanukkah has become extremely popular in the contemporary period. This is explained by the appropriateness in modern thinking of Hanukkah's message, which focuses upon religious   freedom,   by   the   parallel between the Macabbean victory over the much more powerful Syrian army and the plight of modern-day Israel in its conflict with its Arab neighbors, and by the extent to which this joyous festival provides an opportunity for family activity and celebration. Especially in the Christian world, Jewish   celebration   of   Hanukkah   is spurred as well by the fact that Hanukkah falls in the same season as Christmas and

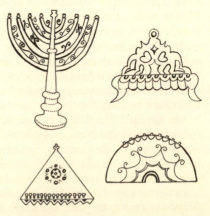

Hanukkah   Different styles of menorahs lit on hanukkah.

so provides Jews with a superficially parallel seasonal holiday.

Ḥanukkat HaBayit (Hebrew: Dedication of the House) A ceremony in which a MEZUZAH is affixed to the door-post of a home. Other than the benediction recited for the mezuzah ("Blessed are you, Lord our God … who has commanded us to affix the mezuzah"), the ceremony has no fixed structure or content, but generally includes readings or songs appropriate to the theme of God's bringing blessing and success upon those who dwell in the home being dedicated.

Hasidism A movement in Judaism that began in mid-eighteenth century Ukraine and Poland and continues to this day as a bastion of true belief and Torah-piety; a mystical movement drawing upon the resources of the QABBALAH, Hasidism began with emphases quite different from those of Rabbinic Judaism, which focused, e.g., upon the centrality of Torah learning. Hasidism instead focused on holy men as media of divine grace. These men, some of them endowed with profound learning in the Torah, were all exemplars of purity and piety. Taking shape around such charismatic personalities, Hasidic groups favored direct encounter with God over meeting God through study of Torah. Still, one Hasidic circle, today known as HABAD, and centered around the Hasidic dynasty deriving from the town of Lubovitch, ultimately found a central place in its piety for Torah study as well.

The mystic circles in Ukraine and Poland in the eighteenth century where Hasidism developed were distinguished from other Jews, for example, by special prayers, distinctive ways of observing certain religious duties, and the like. The first of a growing movement of ecstatics, Israel b. Eliezer *Baal Shem Tov*, known as "the Besht," worked as a popular healer. From the 1730s onward, he undertook travels and attracted to himself circles of followers in Podolia (Ukraine), Poland, and Lithuania, and elsewhere. When he died in 1760, he left disciples who organized the movement in southeastern Poland and Lithuania. Dov Ber inaugurated the institution of the Hasidic court and dispatched disciples beyond Podolia to establish courts of their own. Most of the major Hasidic circles originate in his disciples. Leadership of the movement passed to a succession of holy men, about whom stories were told and preserved. In the third generation, from the third quarter of the eighteenth century into the first of the nineteenth, the movement spread and took hold. Diverse leaders, called *zaddiqim* (see ṢADDIQ), holy men and charismatic figures, developed their own standing and doctrine.

Despite the controversies that swirled about the movement, many of Hasidism's basic ideas were not new. Hasidism drew heavily on available mystical books and doctrines, which from medieval times onward had won a place within the faith as part of the Torah. But Hasidism additionally lay great stress on joy and avoiding melancholy. It further maintained that the right attitude must accompany the doing of religious deeds: the deed could only be elevated when carried out in a spirit of devotion. The doctrine of Hasidism moreover held that in all of creation there are "holy sparks," waiting to be redeemed and reunified with God, which would occur when people used their appetites to serve God. Accordingly, before carrying out any religious deed, followers of Hasidism recite the formula, "For the sake of the unification of the Holy One, blessed be he, and his *shekhinah* [presence in the world]."

On this account, Hasids were criticized. But the fundamental pattern of life, the received world-view contained in the holy canon of Judaism—these defined the issues. Hasidism therefore constitutes a Judaism within Judaism—distinctive, yet in its major traits so closely related to Rabbinic Judaism as to be indistinguishable except in trivial details. But one of these mattered a great deal, and that is the doctrine of Ṣaddiqism: the ṣaddiq, or holy man, had the power to raise the prayers of the followers and to work miracles. The ṣaddiq was the means through which grace reached the world, the one who controlled the universe through his prayers. The ṣaddiq would bring humanity nearer to God and God closer to humanity. The Hasidim were well aware that this doctrine of the ṣaddiq —the pure and elevated soul that could reach to that realm of heaven in which only mercy reigns—represented an innovation. So too did the massive opposition to Hasidism.

By the end of the eighteenth century, powerful opponents, led by the most influential figures of Eastern European Judaism, characterized Hasidism as heretical. Its stress on ecstasy, visions, miracles of the leaders, its way of life of enthusiasm—these were seen as delusions, and the veneration of the ṣaddiq was interpreted as worship of a human being. The stress on prayer to the denigration of study of the Torah likewise called into question the legitimacy of the movement. In the war against Hasidism, the movement found itself anathematized, its books burned, its leaders vilified, even as individual ḥasids were forced out of their homes and Jewish communities and even imprisoned after complaints to the secular authorities.

Under such circumstances, the last thing anyone would anticipate would have been for Hasidism to find a place for itself within what would at some point be deemed Orthodoxy. But it did. By the 1830s, the original force of the movement had run its course, and the movement, beginning as a persecuted sect, now defined the way of life of the Jews in the Ukraine, Galicia, and central Poland, with offshoots in White Russia and Lithuania on the one side, and Hungary, on the other. The waves of emigration from the 1880s onward carried the movement to the West, and, in the aftermath of World War II, to the U.S.A. and the land of Israel as well. Today, the movement forms a powerful component of ORTHODOX JUDAISM, suggesting the capacity of Rabbinic Judaism to find strength by naturalizing initially alien modes of thought and piety. Rabbinic Judaism possessed the inner resources to make its own what began as a movement of criticism and radical reform of that same Judaism. (See BUBER, MARTIN.)

Haskalah   Jewish Enlightenment, eighteenth-century movement of rationalists. See EMANCIPATION.

Ḥavurah   In contemporary Judaism, a collective of individuals who gather for serious and intense prayer, study, and communal interaction. A creation of the 1960s and a central aspect of New Age Judaism, Ḥavurot often centered on a building in which some, or all, of the participants also lived. More recently the Ḥavurah has become a part of synagogue life itself, often comprising small groups of like-minded individuals within larger synagogue communities who gather for study, worship, or social activities. A hallmark of the Ḥavurah is the idea that individual Jews must control their own interaction with Jewish practices and sources. This is a conscious rejection of the modern American synagogue, viewed as a place in which most Jewish tasks are controlled and carried out by a few professionals: rabbis, cantors, and teachers.

Notably, as the idea of the Ḥavurah has entered the modern synagogue, it also transformed that institution, bringing to it ideals of lay participation, democratic governance, serious adult study programs, and participatory social action projects. In such settings, the rabbi becomes a teacher and co-participant rather than an administrator or surrogate practitioner of Judaism.

Ḥazakah   Presumption of right of possession or ownership through extended utilization of property; presumption of a fact; taking possession, e.g., through long-term use, thus: squatter's rights.

Hebrew Language   (Hebrew: *Ivrit*) The primary language of the Jewish people in the State of Israel and of Judaism throughout the world; used for Scripture, prayer, and study. It is attested to 1100 B.C.E. and evolved in three phases: biblical Hebrew (1100–1000 B.C.E., represented by poems in the Pentateuch and Exodus 15, Numbers 21:14–15, Judges 5); standard biblical Hebrew, 1000–550 B.C.E., covering most of the Pentateuch, the biblical books of Joshua, Judges, Samuel, Kings, most of the latter prophets, Psalms, and Proverbs; and late biblical Hebrew, embodied in the biblical books of Ezra, Nehemiah, Chronicles, Esther, Daniel. The Hebrew of the Dead Sea Scrolls continues late biblical Hebrew, for 200 B.C.E. to 70 C. E. In the next phase, the language is attested by the MISHNAH, ca. 200 C.E. It continued its development in medieval and modern times and remained a language of poetry and literature until it was revived for secular as well as sacred purposes in the resettlement of the Land of Israel, beginning in the late nineteenth century. In 1948, Hebrew was adopted as the official language of the State of Israel.

Hebrew Union College—Jewish Institute of Religion   Center for training Reform rabbis, teachers, cantors, communal administrators; campuses in Los Angeles, Cincinnati, New York City, and Jerusalem. Founded in Cincinnati in 1875.

Ḥeder   (Hebrew: "room") A one room school; elementary school for early education. In modern parlance, the Jewish equivalent of Sunday school.

Heqdesh   (Hebrew: "sanctified") Within the system of the Temple cult and sacrifices, a term designating that which has been sanctified for the Temple, either for the upkeep of the building or for use on the altar; designated for use only for the sanctuary and its purposes.

Heqqesh   In the midrashic literature, a principle of Scriptural exegesis that holds that if an analogy can be established between one classification and another, then the rule governing the one applies to the other.

Heschel, Abraham Joshua (1907–1972)   The leading theologian of Judaism in the twentieth century. Born in Poland, Heschel was educated in Warsaw, then in Vilna, Lithuania, and finally in Berlin, where he studied philosophy of religion. He taught in Germany until 1939, when he was expelled and returned to Warsaw. Through the efforts of Dr. Julian Morgenstern, president of Hebrew Union College (HUC), the Reform Rabbinical seminary in Cincinnati, he was brought to the U.S.A. in 1940. He taught at HUC for five years, and in 1945 moved to the Jewish Theological Seminary of America, in New York City, where he was professor until his death. In the 1950s, he did his systematic work, producing a philosophy of religion, *Man Is Not Alone* (1951) and *God in Search of Man* (1955). He wrote influential essays in religious philosophy, collected as

Man's Quest for God: Studies in Prayer and Symbolism (1954). His *The Insecurity of Freedom: Essays on Human Existence* (1966) addressed a broad audience of religious thinkers. In the late 1950s and through the 1960s he took an active role in the civil rights movement, marching with Martin Luther King in Selma, Alabama. He became known as the most prominent voice of Judaism in American public life. He also exercised considerable influence in the deliberations of the Second Vatican Council on the relationships of Christianity and Judaism. He is the single most influential theologian in American Judaism because of the broad perspective and profound knowledge exhibited in his writings.

Ḥeshvan   Counting from Nissan, the eighth month of the Jewish year, October-November.

Ḥiddush   (Hebrew: "innovation") In the study of Rabbinic literature, new point, insight, given as a comment on a classical text. Often ingenious; sometimes hair-splitting. See PILPUL.

Hillel   First-century Pharisaic leader; head of a school of Rabbinic studies and recognized by later Judaism as a founder of Rabbinic Judaism. Born in Babylonia, he is said to have gone to the land of Israel to study biblical exposition and is credited with developing a system of hermeneutics. One of his best-known teachings is, "Do not do unto others what you would not have them do unto you. That is the entire Torah. All the rest is commentary. Now go, study!"

Ḥillul HaShem   Hebrew term for the profanation of God's name or blasphemy. Alongside murder and adultery, blasphemy is one of the three actions one must not perform even on pain of death. In contemporary parlance, the term *ḥillul hashem* is used more generally to refer to doing something that brings Jews or Judaism into disrepute, particularly among non-Jews.

Ḥillul Shabbat   Profanation of the SABBATH through the violation of any of the restrictions that sanctify the Sabbath day.

Hirsch, Samson Raphael (1808–1888)   The first great intellect of ORTHODOX JUDAISM, sometimes called "neo-Orthodox." Hirsch's position laid stress on the possibility of living in the secular world and sustaining a fully Orthodox life. What made Hirsch significant was that he took that view not only on utilitarian grounds, as Samet says, "but also through the acceptance of its scale of values, aiming at creating a symbiosis between traditional Orthodoxy and modern German-European culture; both in theory and in practice this meant abandonment of Torah study for its own sake and adopting instead an increased concentration on practical halakhah." Hirsch himself studied at the University of Bonn, specializing in classical languages, history, and philosophy. So he did not think one had to spend all his time studying Torah, and in going to a university he implicitly affirmed that he could not define, within Torah study, all modes of learning. Gentile professors knew things worth knowing. But continuators of the Judaism of the dual Torah thought exactly the opposite, i.e. whatever is worth knowing is in the Torah.

Hirsch published a number of works to appeal to the younger generation. His ideal for them was the formation of a personality that would be both enlightened and observant, that is to say, educated in Western knowledge and observant of the Judaic way of life. This ideal took shape through an educational program that encompassed Hebrew language and holy literature, and also German, mathematics, sciences, and the like. In this way, he proposed to respond to the Reform view that Judaism in its received form constituted a barrier between Jews and German society. The Reform movement saw the received way of life as an obstacle to the sort of integration they thought wholesome and good. Hirsch concurred in the ideal and differed on detail. Distinctive Jewish clothing, in Hirsch's view, enjoyed a low priority. Quite to the contrary, he himself wore a ministerial gown at public worship, which did not win the approbation of the traditionalists, and when he preached, he encompassed not only the law of the Torah but other biblical matters, equally an innovation. Hirsch argued that Judaism and secular education could form a union. This would require the recognition of externals, which could be set aside, and the emphasis on the principles, which would not change. So Hirsch espoused what, in the ideas of those fully within the mentality of self-evidence, constituted selective piety, and, while the details differed, therefore fell within the classification of reform.

In his selections, Hirsch included changes in the conduct of the liturgy, involving a choir, congregational singing, sermons in the vernacular—a generation earlier sure marks of Reform. He required prayers to be said only in Hebrew and Jewish subjects to be taught in that language. He opposed all changes in the Prayer Book. At the same time, he sustained organizational relationships with the reformers and tried to avoid schism. By mid-career, however, toward the middle of the century, Hirsch could not tolerate the reformers' abrogation of the dietary laws and those affecting marital relationships, and he made his break, accusing the reformers of disrupting Israel's unity. In the following decades, he encouraged Orthodox Jews to leave the congregations dominated by Reform, even though, in the locale, such was the only synagogue. Separationist synagogues formed in the larger community. See ORTHODOX JUDAISM.

Historical School   School of thought in German traditional Judaism that laid heavy emphasis on historical research in determining what may or may not be subject to revision in the law of Judaism. See CONSERVATIVE JUDAISM.

Ḥol   (Hebrew: "secular") Not sanctified; contrasts with QODESH ("sanctified").

Ḥol HaMo'ed   Intermediate days of the festivals of Passover and Tabernacles. Servile labor is not to be performed between the first and the final festival days of the two eight-day festivals. See PASSOVER, SUKKOT.

Holocaust and Redemption, Judaism of   "The Holocaust" refers to the Germans' exterminationist anti-Semitism, the murder of nearly six million Jewish children, women, and men in Europe in 1933–1945. The "Redemption" is the creation of the State of Israel. This Judaic system—an ethnic ideology, not a religious formulation built out of the Torah—flourishes in the diaspora and, since the Six Day War of June 1967, has formed the principal force in the public life of Jews overall. In this Judaic system, "Israel" encompasses the ethnic group, the Jews of the diaspora, and the political entity, the State of Israel, accorded systemic priority. The ethnic-Jewish world view stresses the unique character of the murder of European Jewry and the providential and redemptive meaning of the creation of the State of Israel. This equation leads to active work in raising money and political support for the State of Israel. The urgent question is, why should

Jews be Jewish? And, within this view, the answer is: to continue the ethnic group that the Holocaust nearly wiped out, especially through the State of Israel, Jewry's answer to the Holocaust.

Different from Zionism, which held that "Israel" means only the state of Israel, and that Jews can legitimately live a full Jewish life only in the Jewish State, this system gives Jews living in America and elsewhere in the DIASPORA a reason and an explanation for being Jewish. This Judaism lays particular stress on the matched experiences of mid-twentieth century Jewry, the mass murder in death factories of six million of the Jews of Europe, and the creation of the State of Israel three years after the end of the massacre. The system as a whole presents an encompassing story, linking one event to the other as an instructive pattern and moves Jews to follow a particular set of actions as it tells them why they should be Jewish. This system tells ethnic Jews who they are, why they should be Jewish, what they should do because of that identification, and, it goes without saying, who the Jewish group is and how that group should relate to the rest of the world and to history.

At what point did the Judaism of Holocaust and Redemption take a position of paramount importance among the Jews of America and become the self-evident Judaism of the bulk of the organized Jewish community throughout the diaspora? Three factors are paramount: the Six Day War of 1967, the re-ethnicization of American life, and the transformation of the mass murder of European Jews into an event of narrative and world-destroying proportions. Why date the birth of the Judaism of Holocaust and Redemption to the 1967 War? People take as routine the importance of the State of Israel in American-Jewish consciousness. But in the 1940s and 1950s, American Jewry had yet to translate its deep sympathy for the Jewish state into political activity, on the one side, and the shaping element for local cultural activity and sentiment on the other. So, too, the memory of the destruction of European Jewry did not right away become "the Holocaust," as a formative event in contemporary Jewish consciousness. In fact, the re-ethnicization of the Jews could not have taken the form that it did—a powerful identification with the State of Israel as the answer to the question of "the Holocaust"—without a single, catalytic event.

That event was the 1967 War between the State of Israel and its Arab neighbors. When, on June 5, after a long period of threat, the dreaded war of "all against one" began, American Jews feared the worst. Six days later, they confronted an unimagined outcome, with territory held by Israel stretching from the Jordan River, to the Suez Canal, and the outskirts of Damascus. The trauma of the weeks preceding the war, when the Arabs promised to drive the Jews into the sea and no other power intervened or promised help, renewed for the post-Holocaust generation the nightmare of their parents. Once more, the streets and newspapers became the school for being Jewish. On that account, Judaism-in-formation took up a program of urgent questions. In the trying weeks before June 5, 1967, American Jewry relived the experience of the age of Hitler's Germany and the murder of the European Jews in death factories, when the daily newspaper taught lessons of Jewish history. Everybody knew that were he or she in Europe, death would be the sentence on account of the crime of Jewish birth. And the world was then indifferent. No avenues of escape were opened to the Jews who wanted to flee, and many roads to life were deliberately blocked by anti-Semitic and indifferent foreign service officials. The circumstance in 1967 was parallel. The Arab states threatened to destroy the State of Israel and murder its citizens. The Israelis turned to the world. The world again ignored Jewish suffering, and a new "Holocaust" loomed. But now the outcome was quite different. The entire history of the century at hand came under a new light. The Judaism of Holocaust and Redemption accounted for the events and came to function as the dominant system for ethnic Jews of the U.S.A and Western Europe.

Holy of Holies   (Hebrew: *devir*) The innermost holy place in the Temple of Jerusalem. Only the high priest could enter the area, and only on the Day of Atonement. There he burned incense and sprinkled sacrificial animal blood to atone for his own sins and those of the priesthood. The Holy of Holies was located at the west end of the Temple. In Solomon's Temple, it was the shrine for the ark of the covenant, which held the Torah, or teaching, of God to Moses. A small cedar altar overlaid with gold stood at the entrance.

Horayot   Mishnah tractate on the problem of collective sin, that is, erroneous decisions made by the instruments of government, as distinct from those made by individuals; collective expiation of guilt is effected through public institutions of government and instruction; focused upon Leviticus 4. The tractate defines the offering presented because of an erroneous decision by a court, chap. 1; the offering presented by a high priest who has unwittingly done what is contrary to the commandments of the Torah, the ruler, chap. 2; the individual, the anointed priest, and the community (chaps. 2–3) and offerings required for inadvertent sin from each class.

Hosea, Book of   First of the twelve minor prophets, active in the time of the king of Northern Israel, Jeroboam II (ca. 786–746 B.C.E.), who was active until around the fall of the northern kingdom of Israel in 721 B.C.E. Hosea's dominant theme is the Lord's compassion for ISRAEL, even though Israel had "gone awhoring" after Canaanite fertility rites. Israel would be punished, but the Lord would receive Israel back like a husband who accepts an unfaithful wife.

Hoshanah Rabbah   The seventh day of the festival of SUKKOT, in the liturgy of which the Hebrew word "Hoshanah" ("Save now!") frequently appears. On Hoshanah Rabbah there are seven processions around the synagogue, in which palm branches are carried in place of the LULAB, used in other processions during Sukkot.

Ḥullin   Mishnah tractate devoted to the slaughter of secular, or non-cultic, animals for everyday consumption; the preparation and use of meat for the table of the ordinary Israelite. The tractate begins with the rules of slaughter of animals; then come other dietary-rules, such as the law against slaughtering the dam and its young on the same day (Leviticus 22:28); the requirement to cover up the blood of a slaughtered beast; the taboo against the sciatic nerve (Genesis. 32:32); and cooking meat with milk (Exodus 23:19, 34:26, Deuteronomy 12:21); unclean food; gifts that are given to the priest: first, parts of an animal that has been slaughtered (Deuteronomy 18:4); second, the first fleece (Deuteronomy 18:4). The Babylonian Talmud contains a major commentary to this tractate.

Ḥumash   Another name for the Pentateuch or Five Books of Moses: Genesis, Exodus, Leviticus, Numbers, and Deuteronomy. The biblical narration is from the perspective of the loss and recovery of the

Land of Israel between 586 and 450 B.C.E., events of a distant past. Drawing upon materials from earlier times and reworking them in the light of the destruction of the Temple in 586 and the return of Israel to the Land of Israel in 530, the Pentateuch came to closure at ca. 450 B.C.E. In the Pentateuch, therefore, we deal with a composite of materials, each with its own viewpoint and traits. It was only after the destruction of the First Temple of Jerusalem in 586 B.C.E. that the Torah, that is, the Five Books of Moses, came into being, a pastiche of received stories, some old, some new, all revised for the purposes of the final authorship. It was in the aftermath of the destruction of that temple and the later restoration of the exile to the Land that that authorship wrote the origins of Israel, the Jewish people. In light of Israel's ultimate destiny, which the authorship took to be the loss and restoration of the Land, the origins of the people in its land took on their cogent meaning. Israel then began with its acquisition of the Land, through Abraham, and attained its identity as a people through the promise of the Land, in the covenant of Sinai, and the entry into the Land, under Joshua. Israel's history then formed the story of how, because of its conduct on the Land, Israel lost its land, first in the north, then in the south—despite the prophets' persistent warnings. From the exile in Babylonia, the authorship of the Torah recast Israel's history into the story of the conditional existence of the people. Everything depended on executing a contract: do this, get that, do not do this, do not get that—and nothing formed a given, beyond all stipulation. The task of that authorship demanded the interpretation of the condition of the present, and their message in response to the uncertainty of Israel's life beyond exile and restoration underlined that uncertainty of that life.

Ḥuppah   Marriage canopy, more generally, the marriage-rite of Judaism, invoking the great themes of the restoration of ISRAEL to the Land, and of Adam and Eve to Eden, the matching moment that forms a principal part of the master-narrative of Judaism. Present under the marriage canopy are Adam and Eve in Eden, and present, too, is the memory and hope of the Israelites beyond the destruction of Jerusalem in 586, destined once more to rejoice. At the Ḥuppah, the marriage canopy, which stands for the entire rite of uniting the bride and groom, the singular couple become Israelites restored to the Land, and Adam and Eve in Eden. The rite unfolds in stages, beginning before the couple reaches the marriage canopy, and ending long afterward. Seen in sequence, the rite follows this pattern: [1] KETUBAH is witnessed; [2] bride's veil is put in place by the groom; [3] under the Ḥuppah (1) betrothal, *erusin*; [4] under the Huppah, completion or (2) *nissuin*.

First, the KETUBAH, or marriage contract, is validated by the signatures of the witnesses. It guarantees support for the

Ḥuppah   A ḥuppah (wedding canopy) and the bridal couple.

wife in the event of divorce or death of the husband. Judaism lives in stories, but it also provides for the ordinary world. The bride is not only Eve, she is also a woman who bears responsibility to her husband, and the groom, Adam, is reciprocally responsible. So the Ḥuppah represents not only an occasion in Israel's story but a legal transaction by which the rights and obligations of each party have to reach the expression and guarantee of a contract.

Second, the groom places the veil over the bride's face, prior to the entry under the marriage canopy, and makes the following statement to her:

> May you, our sister, be fruitful and prosper. May God make you as Sarah, Rebecca, Rachel, and Leah. May the Lord bless you and keep you. May the Lord show you favor and be gracious to you. May the Lord show you kindness and grant you peace.

The blessing of the groom for the bride invokes the matriarchs of Israel.

Third, comes ERUSIN, betrothal. The union of a couple takes place in two stages, one, *erusin,* in which the woman is sanctified, or designated as holy, to a particular man, and the second, *nissuin,* in which the actual union is consecrated through the Seven Blessings. In ancient times, these stages took place with an interval of as much as a full year between them, the rite of designation (betrothal) separated from the consummation by twelve months. But in our own day, the wedding rite encompasses both. The first of the two is performed under the marriage canopy by the drinking of a cup of wine with this blessing:

> Blessed are you, our God, king of the universe, who creates the fruit of the vine.
>
> Blessed are you, Lord our God, king of the universe, who has sanctified us by His commandments and

commanded us concerning proper sexual relations, forbidding to us betrothed women but permitting to us married women through the rites of the Ḥuppah and sanctification. Blessed are you, Lord, who sanctifies His people Israel through the marriage canopy and the rite of sanctification.

Then there is a gift of a ring to the bride, with this formula:

> Behold you are sanctified to me by this ring in accordance with the tradition of Moses and Israel.

That concludes the betrothal. Then, fourth, come the Seven Blessings that mark the stage of *nissuin,* the fully realized union. The blessings are recited over a cup of wine, and these complete the rite under the Ḥuppah. They embody the chapters of the Israelite narrative that animate the occasion: Adam and Eve, Israel in Zion. The joy of the moment gives a foretaste of the rejoicing of restoration, redemption, return. Now the two roles become one in that same joy, first Adam and Eve, groom and bride, Eden then, the marriage canopy now:

> Grant perfect joy to these loving companions, as You did to the first man and woman in the Garden of Eden. Praised are You, O Lord, who grants the joy of bride and groom.

That same joy comes in the metaphors of Zion, the bride, and Israel, the groom. The joy is not in two but in three concentric moments, then, now, tomorrow, thus: Eden then, marriage party now, and Zion in the coming age:

> Praised are You, O Lord our God, King of the universe, who created joy and gladness, bride and groom, mirth, song, delight and rejoicing, love and harmony, peace and companionship. O Lord our God, may there ever be

heard in the cities of Judah and in the streets of Jerusalem voices of joy and gladness, voices of bride and groom, the jubilant voices of those joined in marriage under the bridal canopy, the voices of young people feasting and signing.

Praised are You, O Lord, who causes the groom to rejoice with his bride.

The joy of this new creation prefigures the joy of the Messiah's coming, hope for which is very present in this hour. And when he comes, the joy then will echo the joy of bridge and groom before us. Zion the bridge, Israel the groom, united now as they will be reunited by the compassionate God—these stand under the marriage canopy.

Impurity Jewish concepts of impurity (Hebrew: *tum'ah*) and purity (*tohorah*) carry forward Pentateuchal commandments that the people of Israel must avoid certain sources of contamination, the principal one of which is the corpse (Numbers 19). Uncleanliness affects the conduct of three activities: eating, procreation, and attendance at the Temple. When the priests ate their priestly rations, they were to do so in a condition of cultic cleanliness. Furthermore, all Israelites are to abstain from unclean foods and from sexual relations during a woman's menstrual period or when affected by the uncleanliness of the sexual organs to which Leviticus 15 makes allusion. All Israelites also must become clean to participate in the Temple cult, which would affect many at the time of the pilgrimage festivals, PASSOVER, SHABU'OT (Pentecost), and Tabernacles (see SUKKOT). In addition, among the forms of Judaism that flourished in Second Temple times, some groups, such as the PHARISEES, the ESSENES, and those represented by law codes found in the DEAD SEA SCROLLS, kept the rules of cultic purity in eating food at home, not in the Temple, a practice that did not characterize the bulk of the communities of Judaism. After the Jerusalem Temple was destroyed in 70 C.E., when attaining cleanliness to participate in the cult no longer pertained, rules of uncleanliness governing food and sexual relations continued to apply, as they do in Judaism to the present day. But in matters of public worship it was the Temple, not the synagogue, to which considerations of cleanliness applied, and no one would refrain from attending synagogue worship by reason of having become unclean (*tameh*), for instance, by having attended a funeral.

At the heart of the system of impurity and purity is the idea that semen or vaginal blood that cannot carry out the purpose for which it was intended, which is participation in the process of procreating life, is a source of uncleanliness. Such non-productive semen, such vaginal flow outside of the normal cycle of procreation—violate their innate purpose. They do so of themselves, not by man's or woman's intervention. Of such violations of the natural law and the purposive definition of the media of procreation, the Israelite has to take heed. Man or woman cannot generate by an act of deliberation an unclean body fluid, whether genital semen or genital blood, which is deemed unclean only if it flows naturally; nor can they form by an act of will a source of uncleanliness represented by the corpse or the dead creeping thing.

After the destruction of the Jerusalem Temple, the goal of the system of purity and impurity is for life to be created and maintained as if it were lived in the holy Temple, protected from the sources of contamination that would pollute the Temple. Perhaps, embodying the perfection of the natural world, the Temple—as if here and now—stands for Eden then and there. For the paramount aspiration of Judaism is to restore humanity to Eden, ISRAEL to the Land of Israel. For if, as is blatant, uncleanliness denies access to the Temple and its surrogates and counterparts in the households of Israel, then cleanliness must open the way to sanctification. Uncleanliness attended to, cleanliness attained, all media of restoration of cleanliness, Israel's natural condition, set the household of Israel en route to sanctification, localized in the Temple down below, matched by Heaven up above, realized by the household here and now.

Isaac   Second son of ABRAHAM, after ISHMAEL, but Abraham's only child by SARAH (Genesis 21). He was bound on an altar at God's command by Abraham, who was prepared to obey God and offer him as a sacrifice (Genesis 22) (see AQEDAH). At the last moment, God provided a ram in place of Isaac. The readiness of Abraham to sacrifice his son, and of Isaac to be sacrificed, is held in Judaism to be a source of great merit for Abraham's and Isaac's descendants, the people of Israel. The sounding of the ram's horn on the New Year (ROSH HASHANAH) is meant to call to mind the merit of Abraham and Isaac at the time that their descendants are subject to divine justice and need God's forgiveness. Through his wife Rebecca, Isaac was father of JACOB and Esau. He is the vehicle for passing the divine blessing from Abraham onward, rather than Ishmael. Rebecca and Jacob tricked Isaac into giving Jacob the blessing of the firstborn (Genesis 27:1–40), though Esau was born to Isaac first via Hagar, Rebecca's handmaid.

Isaiah   [1] Prophet whose words are recorded in the biblical book of Isaiah, chapters 1–39; active in Jerusalem between 750 and 700 B.C.E. He advised King Hezekiah, then king of Judea, to trust in God and to stand firm against the Assyrian invasion of 701 B.C.E. and not to surrender. The Assyrians had already conquered the Northern Kingdom of Israel and had taken the ten northern tribes into exile in Assyria, the northern part of present day Iraq. Hezekiah stood firm and the Assyrians broke off the siege. [2] The prophet whose words are recorded in the biblical book of Isaiah, chapters 40–55. He was active in the time of

the Second Temple, ca. 500 B.C.E., and prophesied that Israel's sin had been atoned for by the destruction of the Temple in 586 B.C.E. and God had reconciled with the people of Israel. [3] The prophet of a somewhat later period whose words are recorded in the biblical book of Isaiah, chapters 56–66.

Ishmael   [1] Son of Abraham and Hagar. [2] Rabbinic sage of ca. 100 C.E.

Israel   [1] In the Bible, a name given to the patriarch JACOB after he wrestled with a divine messenger (Genesis 32:28). This name, often found in the phrase "people of Israel" or "children of Israel," came to designate all of the descendants of Jacob, who, whether from birth or as a result of personal choice, recognize God and accept God's rule set forth in the Torah. The term "Israel" thus covers all who accept the Torah as the sole and complete revelation of God's will and who affirm belief in one God alone. [2] In some biblical references in the books of Samuel, Kings, and Chronicles, the territory promised by God to the people of Israel is referred to as the Land of Israel. This usage becomes common throughout later Rabbinic and post-Rabbinic Jewish writings. [3] In contemporary usage, the term Israel refers to the modern State of Israel, the Jewish State, and Land of Israel refers to the State of Israel plus other areas that, in ancient times, comprised the total territory of the people of Israel.

Israelite   A member of one of the tribes of ancient Israel, whose history, culture, and religion are described in the Hebrew Bible. The term "Israelite" distinguishes the religious practices of the children of ABRAHAM and SARAH from the religion of Judaism that emerged out of the biblical faith and that has been followed since the late biblical period by the people commonly referred to as Jews. In the eighteenth and early nineteenth centuries, some westernized Jews adopted the term "Israelite" to refer to themselves as adherents of the monotheistic faith of the Hebrew Scriptures but not as practitioners of Judaism, defined—negatively in their view—by its attention to a code of obligatory law and ritual.

Iyyar　Second month of the Jewish year, April-May.

J

Jacob Also called Israel, son of Isaac and Rebecca, father of the people of Israel's twelve tribal progenitors. All Israel then is called "the house of Jacob." Jacob got the name Israel when, returning to the Land from Mesopotamia, he wrestled with a mysterious angel (Genesis 32:24–30), who changed his name from Jacob to Israel, meaning, "May God strive." In Genesis 49, he bestows blessings on his sons. In Rabbinic literature of the first six centuries C.E., Jacob's life is deemed to symbolize later events in the history of Jacob's children, Israel; he represents the nation as a whole, and his antagonists, Esau—his brother— and Laban—his father-in-law, are identified with Rome.

Jehovah Transliteration of the divine name, based on a misunderstanding of the Hebrew letters YHWH. Jews do not pronounce this name of God (the tetragrammaton) but instead use the word *Adonai,* usually translated as "Lord." To indicate this replacement, in Hebrew texts, the vowels of the word *Adonai* appear under the Hebrew consonants YHWH. Some translators have mistakenly read this combination as JeHoVaH.

Jeremiah Prophet in Jerusalem, ca. 620 to 580 B.C.E., before the destruction of Jerusalem by the Babylonians in 586. He warned that God would not protect Jerusalem if Israel violated the covenant that God made with them in the Torah (Jeremiah 7 and 26). He advised Israel to submit to Babylonia and accept the punishment brought by God through the Babylonians. After the conquest of Jerusalem, he was forced to go into exile to Egypt, where he died. He is credited with the authorship of the book of Lamentations, which mourns for the destruction of the Temple and of Jerusalem.

Jerusalem City conquered by King David and made the political and religious capital of the Israelite nation. In the religion Judaism, it is the place God chose for the building of the Temple that the people of Israel were to construct for divine worship and sacrifice, as spelled out in the biblical book of Deuteronomy.

Jew, Jewish An ethnic identity bearing religious consequence. In the classical tradition, followed today by Orthodox and Conservative Judaism, a Jew is a person who is born of a Jewish mother or who has converted to Orthodox Judaism; in Reform and Reconstructionist Judaism, a Jew is a person born of a Jewish mother or of a Jewish father or who has converted to Judaism. Status bestowed by birth or gained by conversion represents the melding of the ethnic and genealogical with the religious and theological. In dealing with the Jews, there is no way radically to distinguish the ethnic from the religious. In general, though, the words "Jew" and "Jewish" stress the ethnic character of the Jews as a group.

Jewish Revolt The First War against Rome, fought in the Land of Israel, both in Galilee and then in Judea, 67–73 C.E. The war began with a Temple riot and the revolt was led by the Zealots thereafter. It reached its climax in August, 70 C.E., when on the ninth day of the Hebrew month of Ab, the Temple was captured and burned by the Romans. Resistance continued for some time. The Second

War against Rome was fought in the land of Israel under the leadership of the Simeon bar Kokhba (see MESSIAH), 132–135 C.E., probably in the expectation that after the three generations had passed, Israel would regain Jerusalem, as had happened in the aftermath of the loss of Jerusalem in 586 B.C.E. and its restoration three generations later. The war was fiercely fought against Rome which was then at the height of its power. When it was over, the Jews were forbidden to enter Jerusalem. The Temple was plowed over and a pagan temple dedicated to Jupiter was constructed in its place.

Jewish Theological Seminary of America   The Conservative movement's center for training rabbis, teachers, cantors, community administrators, and scholars of Judaism; founded in New York City in 1888 by Sabato Morais. A campus now exists in Jerusalem as well.

Jezebel   The wife of Ahab, king of northern Israel, ca. 843 B.C.E. She violated the exclusive worship of the Lord and defied the prophets of the Lord, Elijah, and Elisha. She was the daughter of the priest-king of Phoenicia, ruler of Tyre and Sidon, and persuaded Ahab to introduce the worship of the god Ba'al Melkart. She had most of the prophets of the Lord killed. In 1 Kings 21:5–16, the story is told of how she seized the vineyard of Naboth of Jezreel, who had refused to give it up. She had him charged with blaspheming God and the king, and so he was stoned to death. Elijah confronted Ahab in the vineyard and predicted his and his wife's downfall. The prediction came true.

Job   The principal character in the biblical book of Job, which addresses the problem of human suffering: how can a just God explain the human condition, the prosperity of the wicked, and the suffering of the righteous? The book is in two parts, a prose prologue and epilogue, Job 1:1–2:13, 42:7–17, and a poetic discussion, Job 3:1–42:6. The story told in the prologue and epilogue concerns a pious and prosperous man who loses his children, health, and wealth. Job is being tested before the Lord by the prosecutor, Satan. He will not curse God for the unfair treatment. At the end, he receives his health and wealth and a new set of sons and daughters. The poems involve two soliloquies, discourses of three friends trying to explain what has happened with Job's rebuttals ("Job's comforters"), a hymn, an oath of innocence, speeches of a younger friend, and God's intervention with questions spoken from the whirlwind, answered by Job.

Joseph   The biblical patriarch Jacob's eleventh son. The stories about Joseph, Genesis 37, 39–50, portray him as victim of a conspiracy of his jealous brothers, but destined for great things. His brothers sold him into slavery in Egypt and, after he was imprisoned on a false charge, he was rescued by his power to interpret dreams. He became a viceroy to Pharaoh, whom he served well. He foresaw a coming famine and in the seven lush years stored grain to sustain Egypt in the seven lean years that followed. His brothers came down to Egypt to buy grain during the famine, and he made himself known to them and reconciled with them. He brought them to the land of Goshen, where the people of Israel dwelt for a long time. During the period of the rule of the Pharaoh served by Joseph, they were treated well. But later on, a succeeding Pharaoh embittered their lives and enslaved them. The Israelites who left Egypt in the Exodus took Joseph's bones with them and reburied him in the Promised Land.

Josephus   A first-century C.E. general and historian of the Jews. His great works were *The Jewish War*, which he wrote shortly after the defeat of the Jews by the Romans and the fall of Jerusalem and destruction of the Temple in 70 C.E., and *The History of the Jews*, a recapitulation of the narratives of Scripture joined with an account of affairs to his own time. Josephus had been a general in the First War against Rome (67–73 C.E.) but surrendered and went over to the Roman side. After the war, he wrote to conciliate Roman opinion to the Jews and explained that the war was the work of zealots but did not represent the greater part of the people of Israel in the Land of Israel, all the more so the Jews living outside of the Land. In his autobiography, *The Life*, he justified his conduct during the war.

Joshua   [1] Biblical book about the Israelites' entry into and conquest of the land of Canaan under Joshua, the successor to Moses. Joshua was selected by Moses as his successor and leader of Israel from the wilderness into the Promised Land. Joshua conquered the Land and divided it among the tribes. He had been one of the twelve spies who were sent to scout out the Land from the wilderness, and only he and Caleb had brought back a good report. The book of Joshua records the story of his leadership in the conquest of the Land of Israel and division of the Land among the twelve Israelite tribes. [2] A Rabbinic sage of the later first century C.E., a disciple of Yohanan ben Zakkai and a leading authority in the Mishnah.

Jubilee   (Hebrew: *Yovel*) The fiftieth year, marked at the end of seven Sabbatical cycles. In the Jubilee year, the land lies fallow, slaves are released, debts are remitted, and all land purchased since the previous Jubilee is returned to its original owner (Leviticus 25:8–17). The Jubilee

ceased to be observed after the destruction of the Second Temple in 70 C.E.

Jubilees, Book of   A narrative work in fifty chapters in Hebrew written in ca. 1560 B.C.E. that retells the biblical stories from Genesis 1 through Exodus 20. The book is presented as a divine revelation to Moses from an angel on Mount Sinai. The retelling of the story is in accord with a chronology that employs time units of seven and forty-nine years (a jubilee). The angels revealed to Enoch the correct length of the solar year, 364 days exactly, evenly divisible into fifty-two weeks. The author shows that the ancient biblical heroes engaged in practices that in fact arose only long after their time. For example, ABRAHAM kept the Festivals of Unleavened Bread (PASSOVER) and of Tabernacles (SUKKOT).

Judah Halevi (1080–1141)   Jewish poet, philosopher, and physician, born in Spain. At the end of his life he set out for Jerusalem, reaching Egypt in 1140, where he died. One of the best known medieval Hebrew poets, he introduced forms of Arab poetry into Hebrew verse, writing frequently of his longing for Zion. Alongside his more than 800 extant poems, he is best known for his major philosophic work, *The Kuzari*, which takes the form of a dialogue between a rabbi and the pagan king of the Khazars—a kingdom that had, several centuries earlier, considered Islam and Christianity and then adopted Judaism—who seeks spiritual direction. In this work, Halevi asserts that Judaism is superior to Christianity and Islam, since the God of Israel is known through the received tradition and not through philosophy, with its syllogisms and mathematical reasoning. Halevi thus objected to the indifference of philosophy to the comparative merits of the competing traditions. In philosophy's approach, religion is recommended, but which religion does not matter much. For the majority religions, such an indifference may have been tolerable, but not for a minority destined any day to have to die for their particular profession of faith.

Martyrdom, such as Jews faced, will not be rendered tolerable by adherence to the "unmoved mover," the God anyone may reach through reason. Only for the God of Israel will a Jew give up his or her life. By its nature, philosophy thus is insufficient for the religious quest. It can hardly compete with the *history* of the Jewish people, a history recording extraordinary events starting with revelation. Philosophy has nothing to do with Sinai, with the Promised Land, with prophecy. On the contrary, the Jew, expounding religion to the king of the Khazars, begins not like the philosopher with a disquisition on divine attributes, nor like the Christian who starts with the works of creation and expounds the Trinity, nor like the Moslem who acknowledges the unity and eternity of God. Rather, he begins by recounting the miraculous history of the Exodus, revelation, forty years in the wilderness, the conquest of the Land of Israel, the appearance of prophets, and the certainty of reward for those who follow the divine law and punishment for disobedience.

In the continuation of the dialogue, the pitiful condition of Israel is turned into the primary testimony and vindication of Israel's faith. That Israel suffers is the best assurance of divine concern. The suffering constitutes the certainty of coming redemption. In the end, the Jew parts from the king in order to undertake a journey to the Land of Israel. There he seeks perfection with God. To this the king objects. He thought the Jew loved freedom, but the Jew finds himself in bondage by imposing duties obligatory in residing in the Land of Israel. The Jew replies that the freedom he

seeks is from the service of men and the courting of their favor. He seeks the service of one whose favor is obtained with the smallest effort: "His service is freedom, and humility before him is true honor." He, therefore, turns to Jerusalem to seek the holy life. Here we find no effort to identify Judaism with rational truth, but rather the claim that the life of the pious Jew stands above—indeed constitutes the best testimony to—truth.

The source of truth is biblical revelation. History, not philosophy, testifies to the truth and in the end constitutes its sole criterion. Philosophy claims reason can find the way to God. Halevi says only God can show the way to God, and he does so through revelation, and, therefore, through history. For the philosopher, God is the object of knowledge. For Halevi, God is the subject of knowledge. And Israel has a specifically religious faculty that mediates the relationship to God. Halevi seeks to explain the supernatural status of Israel. The religious faculty is its peculiar inheritance and makes it the core of humanity. But while the rest of humanity is subject to the laws of nature, Israel is subject to supernatural, divine providence, manifested in reward and punishment. The very condition of the Jews, in that God punishes them, verifies the particular and specific place of Israel in the divine plan.

Judah the Patriarch   Head of the Jewish community in the Land of Israel; in 200 C.E. promulgated the MISHNAH; combined learning and political power.

Judaism   A religion, meaning a mode of organizing the social order that encompasses [1] a worldview, or ethos (belief), [2] a way of life or ethics (practice), and [3] a community of practitioners who identify themselves by appeal to that worldview and through the practice of that way of life (community). Judaism is a religion that, for its world view, knows God through the Torah; [2] for its way of life carries out the religious obligations of building a holy community that the Torah sets forth; and [3] regards the community of the faithful as continuing that same "Israel" as the one to which the Scriptures are addressed, thus, a community that is covenanted with God through the Torah.

Within Judaism, no single creed rules everywhere, no minimal principles of the faith govern through time. The documents accepted as normative within Judaism contain contradictions, and different communities of Judaism hold divergent opinions. Like the other ancient and enduring religions, Judaism is hardly uniform, so that it is more appropriate to speak of "Judaisms" than of a single, uniform, harmonious Judaism. Over time, opinions change, and new writings are viewed as authoritative. But no teaching authority, such as the Pope and the Bishops for Roman Catholic Christianity, exercises institutional authority in Judaism to define the teachings of the faith. Nor does a consensus of the faithful tell us which teachings enjoy broad acceptance and represent the faith and which prove marginal or schismatic. So how are we to know what are the principal, normative teachings of Judaism?

The SIDDUR, or prayerbook, serves as the authoritative source of the teachings of Judaism because it defines what praying Israel means by God, Torah, Israel, Creation, Revelation, Redemption, and other principal components of theological Judaism. The Siddur (and associated liturgical texts), in its classical formulation followed by Orthodox and Conservative Judaisms, and, with revisions, by Reform and Reconstructionist Judaisms as well, functions as the model for nearly all communities of Judaism and by its nature serves as a compendium of the main teachings of the

faith. While there are thousands of editions and translations, the principal parts of the Siddur are uniform, or nearly uniform for most communities of Judaism today and all of them for long centuries before our own time.

The order of prayer, weekdays and holy days, always entails three units: the recitation of the SHEMA, which is a proclamation of God's unity and dominion; the Amidah, which presents prayers of supplication, said standing in near-silence, then repeated; and the ALENU, the statement of the praying community of its obligation to praise God alone (see SHEMONEH ESREH). These three components of public worship iterate the community's faith about the central issues of Judaism: its view of God, of the Israel comprised by the worshipping community, and of the human situation of humanity addressing God.

The teachings of Judaism involve three principal components—a story of creation, one of revelation, and one of redemption—that can be articulated in a single sentence: God created the world, revealed the Torah, and will redeem the people of Israel—to whom God revealed the Torah—at the end of time through the sending of the Messiah. This set of mythic statements expresses the covenant between God and Israel: the keeping of the religious requirements of the Torah as an expression of loyalty to the covenant between God and Israel will lead to redemption.

Why should these principal teachings of Judaism have made sense and proved plausible for the community of Israel over a long period of time, even until our own day? The reason is that the critical issues of the Jews' historical life—Why do we matter? Why should we go forward? How long will this situation last?—are dealt with in the liturgy and its doctrines in a profound and transcendent way. The Jews have had to suffer for their faith and accept the condition of a despised minority, a pariah people, everywhere they have lived. Even in Europe and North America today, many people look down on the Jews and think ill of them, and in the Muslim world Jews are despised. The faithful Jews, for their part, have always had the choice of accepting the dominant religion of their place of residence—Christianity in the West, Islam in the Middle East—and so of leaving their condition as a pariah people. And some did. But most did not, just as the Jews of the modern period chose and continue to choose to be Jews, no matter what. Why should they do this? Why do they do this? And what does it mean?

In the classical story of Judaism, the meaning is found in the correspondence of heaven and earth. The world was created for the sake of the Torah; the Torah was revealed for the sake of Israel; and Israel, keeping the covenant through the Torah, will be redeemed in the end of time. To the world, the holy community may seem to be pariahs, but Judaism knows they are God's children—princes and princesses. The life of Torah is sweet and serene. The rhythms of creation and Sabbath, revelation and Torah-study, and redemption and festivals (Passover, Tabernacles, Pentecost) join the lives of individual men and women to the patterns of the transcendent and the holy. From the perspective of Judaism lived by the Jewish people, the suffering has been the proof and vindication of the faith of Torah. The very regularity of creation—the waves on the ocean, the majesty and permanence of the mountains and the valleys—stands as witness to the truth of the faith of Torah, which is what Judaism is.

K

Kaplan, Mordecai See RECONSTRUC-
TIONIST JUDAISM

Karaism A form of Judaism that
rejects the doctrine of the dual Torah, that
is, the Rabbinic doctrine that at Sinai God
revealed the Torah to be transmitted
through two media, written and oral.
Focusing on that central belief, Karaism
denied that God revealed to Moses at
Sinai more than the Written Torah and
explicitly condemned belief in an oral
one. Karaism rested on four principles: (1)
the literal meaning of the biblical text; (2)
the consensus of the community; (3) the
conclusions derived from Scripture by the
method of logical analogy; (4) knowledge
based on human reason and intelligence.
It took shape in the eighth century, beginning after the rise of Islam, and advocated
the return to Scripture as against tradition,
inclusive of Rabbinic tradition. The sect
originated in Babylonia in the period following the creation of the Babylonian
Talmud, on the one side, and the rise of
Islam, on the other. The movement itself
claimed to originate in biblical times and
to derive its doctrine from the true priest,
Ṣadok. The founder of the movement,
Anan b. David, imposed DIETARY LAWS
that were stricter than those of the Rabbis,
and in other ways legislated a version of
the law of a more strict character than the
talmudic authorities admitted. The basic
principle predominated that Scriptures
were to be studied freely, independently,
and individually. No uniformity of view
could then emerge. Given the stress of
Rabbinic Judaism on the authority of the
Talmud and related canonical documents,
one could not expect a more precise
statement of the opposite view. See
KARAITES.

Karaites A sect in Judaism, founded
by Anan b. David in ca. 700 that affirmed
Scripture alone, unmediated by tradition.
The Karaites explicitly rejected the conception of God's revealing to Moses at
Sinai an oral Torah in addition to the written Torah and maintained that only the
written Torah—the Pentateuch—was
valid for Judaism. Influential in Middle
Eastern Jewish communities as opponents of Rabbinic Judaism, the Judaism
that held God revealed an Oral Torah,
now written down in the Talmud of
Babylonia and other documents, the
Karaites were declared schismatic and
marriage between them and Rabbanite
Jews ultimately was banned by the latter.
What marked Karaites was the rejection
of such customs as observance of HANUK-
KAH, use of certain ritual objects, rigid
application of scriptural laws on the Sabbath, ritual cleanness, and consanguine-
ous marriage. They prohibited use of light
and fire on the Sabbath and travel beyond
2,000 yards of the home. They required
washing hands and feet and removing
shoes before entering the synagogue or
reading from the Torah. The liturgy of the
Karaite synagogue differed from that of
the rabbinate one as well. The Karaite
system of Judaism therefore accepted the
authority and law only of the Pentateuch
and applied that law in as literal a way as
possible. During the Shoah, the Rabbis
whom the Germans consulted ruled that
the Karaites were not Jews, and the Germans did not murder the Karaites in their
territories.

Karet (Hebrew: "extirpation") In classical Judaism, premature death at the hands of heaven; dying before one's time, which is defined as prior to age 60.

Karo, Joseph Born in Spain in 1488, lived in Turkey, then in Safed, in the Land of Israel, from 1536 until his death in 1575; author of the code of Jewish law called *Shulḥan Arukh*, he was both a master of law and a mystic. His code of law remains authoritative to this day, and the record of his mystical experiences, in *Maggid Mesharim*, is still read. He first wrote a commentary, called *Bet Yoseph*, on the then-authoritative code of law, the *Arba'ah Turim*, and then abbreviated the law in his own code, which served Jews of Sephardic origin. Jews of Ashkenazic origin adopted it when their customs were included. Consequently, Karo became the single most important authority in the practice of Judaism from his time to the present.

Kashrut See DIETARY LAWS.

Kavvanah (Hebrew: "intent, intention, intentionality") In Judaism, the attitude that motivates a given action, the intention of the person who performs the action: what he hopes to accomplish—effect or prevent. This intentionality governs the action's classification, e.g., as to its effect or lack of effect, acceptability or lack of acceptability, under the law of Judaism.

Kavvanah refers to the freedom to form and implement one's own will. People match God in possessing freedom of will. The sole player in the cosmic drama with the power to upset God's plans is the human. In humanity, God has not *met* but *made* his match. But free will reaches concrete expression only in the deeds people do by reason of the plans or intentions they shape on their own. The high value accorded by God to a person's voluntary act of accepting God's dominion, the enthusiastic response made by God to a person's supererogatory deeds of uncoerced love and uncompelled generosity, the heavy emphasis upon the virtues of self-abnegation and self-restraint—these emblematic traits of the coherent theology attest to the uncertainty of humanity's response that, from the beginning, God has built into creation. For the one power that lies beyond the rules of reason, that defies predicting, is each person's power to make up his or her own mind.

Intentionality is critical in doing one's religious duties; one must not utilize the Torah and the commandments for an inappropriate purpose. Even when it comes to doing religious deeds, intentionality dictates the value of what is done; while one may well perform one's obligation to Heaven through correct action, without matching intentionality, still, to study the Torah to achieve honor negates the action. Purity of heart, desire to serve God and not to aggrandize oneself—these govern the effect of the act. The correct intentionality is to carry out the requirements of the Torah for their own sake, not for the sake of a reward. This is expressed, first of all, in terms of Torah-study itself, and, further, in the setting of carrying out the commandments. One must study the Torah for an appropriate motive, which is not to gain prestige and honor but to love God.

Intentionality forms the systemic dynamics of the entire structure of sanctification and morality that Judaism constructs. It is the principal variable, because it is the one thing that God has created that is possessed of its own autonomy. That is why, also, it is intentionality that explains sin, and it is sin that accounts for the imperfect condition of the world and of Israel therein.

Kayoṣé Bo BeMaqqom Aḥer   In the midrashic literature, a principle of Scriptural exegesis that holds that a difficulty in understanding a given verse may be solved by appeal to the comparison with another verse that exhibits points of similarity.

Kelal Uperat   (Hebrew: "the governing principle, the particularization thereof") In the midrashic literature, a principle of reading Scripture that holds that a general principle given in one verse followed by a particularization of the same governing principle in another verse is limited to the items particularized in the corresponding verse; or a particular rule may be generalized in the same manner.

Kelal Yisrael   (Hebrew: "Universal Israel") In Judaism, all Jews all together are held to be responsible for one another and for the sins of each. The generality of Israel as a moral entity is called *Kelal Yisrael*, that is, the whole of the community of Israel, or, alternatively, *Knesset Yisrael*, the Community of Israel. The modern theologian, Solomon Schechter, translated the concept into "Catholic Israel," which he interpreted to mean that, alongside tradition, the legitimate content of Jewish thought and practice is determined by what the Jewish people as a whole believe and do. In the classic Rabbinic exegesis of Scripture, particularly in Song of Songs Rabbah, the Community of Israel is personified as the beloved of God, who speaks to Israel through the love-song, and KNESSET YISRAEL speaks to God as well.

Kelim   Mishnah tractate devoted to sources of uncleanness, in particular, the susceptibility to uncleanness of various pots and pans, made of diverse materials: earthenware utensils (chaps. 2–10); metal utensils (chaps. 11–14); other materials (wood, leather; chaps. 15–18); suscep-tibility of utensils to diverse types of uncleanness and the end of susceptibility; connection (chaps. 19–24); the components of an object (chap. 25); leather objects, woven materials, fabrics, glass utensils (chaps. 26–30).

Keritot   Mishnah tractate on sins for the commission of which one is punishable by extirpation, if one deliberately does the deed, or a sin offering, if one does so inadvertently, or a suspensive guilt offering, in the case of doubt. Thus: occasions on which one is obligated to present a sin offering (chaps. 1–2), a single sin offering and multiple sins (chaps. 2–3); and a suspensive guilt offering (chaps. 4–6).

Ketubah   Marriage contract specifying obligations of husband to wife. See KETUBOT.

Ketubim   (Hebrew: "Writings," "Hagiographa") The last third of the tripartite division of the Hebrew Scriptures (TORAH, NEBI'IM, Ketubim), referring to the biblical books of Psalms, Proverbs, Ecclesiastes, Job, Chronicles, Ruth, Song of Songs, Lamentations, Esther, Daniel, Ezra, Nehemiah.

Ketubot   Mishnah tractate on marriage settlements, dealing with the formation of a marriage, with attention to the material rights of the parties to the marital union: the wife (chaps. 1–2); the maiden and her marriage contract, conflicting claims in that regard (chaps. 1–2); the materials rights of the husband and the father (chaps. 3–5); the fine paid to the father (Deuteronomy 21:22) for rape or seduction (chap. 3); the father's rights (chap. 4), and the husband's rights (chap. 5); then the reciprocal responsibilities and rights of the husband and wife for the duration of the marriage (chaps. 5–9); the wife's   duties   to   the   husband,   the husband's to the wife; the dowry; the marital rights and duties of the wife (chap. 7); property rights of the wife (chap. 8); finally, the cessation of the marriage and collecting the marriage settlement covered by the contract (chaps. 9–13); imposing an oath; multiple claims on an estate and the wife's claim; support of the widow; rights to and collection of a marriage contract, special cases; then case-books.

Kilayim   Mishnah tractate on the prohibition against hybridization: plants (chaps. 1–7), animals (chap. 8); mixed fibers, wool and linen (chap. 9). Special attention focuses on growing different kinds of plants together; plants that are or are not regarded as diverse kinds with one another; grafting; sowing different kinds of crops in the same space or adjacent spaces; vines and other crops.

Kings, Books of   The two books of Kings complete the story of Israel begun in the biblical books of Deuteronomy, Joshua, Judges, and Samuel. The entire sequence was worked out after the destruction of the First Temple in 586 B.C.E., during Babylonian Exile in ca. 550 B.C.E. The main theme is that Israel has suffered calamity by reason of not keeping the law of the Torah. 1 Kings begins with the end of the story of David (chaps. 1–2). The reign of Solomon is covered in 1 Kings 3–11, then the reigns of the kings of Judah and Israel from the beginning of the divided kingdom, in ca. 930 B.C.E., to the fall of Northern Israel in 721 B.C.E., in 1 Kings 12–17; and then the story of the kings of the southern kingdom of Judah, to 586 B.C.E. (2 Kings 18–25). The various kings are judged by whether or not they accepted the sole legitimacy of Jerusalem's Temple and of the worship of the Lord; Hezekiah and Josiah are approved in the south, none of their northern counterparts is accepted. The fall of Israel, then

Judah, is explained by apostasy. But the people will return to the glory of David's rule over a united Israelite people.

Kippah   Skull cap, worn by males as a mark of piety and humility. Nowadays, sometimes worn by females as well. There is no explicit biblical injunction to cover the head, but the custom, enacted as a Rabbinic injunction, is ancient and pervasive.

Kippurim   Tosefta tractate devoted to the Day of Atonement and its rites. Amplifies Mishnah tractate YOMA, on the same topic.

Kislev   Counting from Nisan, the ninth month of the Jewish calendar, in November-December, in which HANUKKAH falls.

Knesset Yisrael   (Hebrew: "Assembly of Israel") The Jewish people as a whole, also referred to as KELAL YISRAEL.

Kohen   (Hebrew: "Aaronide priest") Individual authorized by reason of birth to carry out Temple sacrifices and other rites. Aaron, brother of Moses, was consecrated as the first Israelite priest, and from him all Israelite priests trace their origin via the male line. Scripture holds that the priests are the tribe of Levi, one of the Israelite tribes. The LEVITES had no land assigned to them in the Land of Israel; they were counted separately in the census; they were supported by a tithe of the crop of the Land. The Levites were chosen for God's service by reason of their loyalty, when others strayed. This is the picture of Leviticus 8–10. Priests were sanctified and had to keep purity laws and were restricted in whom they might marry; they could not contract corpse uncleanness except for near of kin. They also taught instruction to the people, administered the Temple, and maintained its facilities. In contemporary synagogues, the Kohen has the honor of being called first to the Torah. The Kohen also bestows the priestly blessing on specified liturgical occasions, daily in the state of Israel, on festivals in the diaspora. See BIRKAT KOHANIM.

Kol Nidrei   (Aramaic: "all vows") A declaration that all vows made rashly during the year and not carried out are null and void; recited at the beginning of synagogue worship on the eve of YOM KIPPUR. In light of the importance of the statement made in the Kol Nidrei declaration, that entire evening's worship commonly is referred to as Kol Nidrei.

Kolel   An institution of higher talmudic study, generally attended by married men who are supported by a stipend.

Kosher   A variant of the Hebrew word "kasher," meaning "fit" or "proper;" term applied to anything suitable for use according to Jewish law, especially with reference to food and the DIETARY LAWS.

Kuzari, Book of   See JUDAH HALEVI.

L

Ladino   Judeo-Spanish, also known as Spaniole or Judezmo; Spanish written in Hebrew characters, preserving the medieval language of the Sephardim.

Lag BeOmer   (Hebrew: "33d [day] of the Omer") The thirty-third day of the seven-week period of Counting of the Omer (see OMER), the first sheaf of barley harvested on the second day of PASSOVER and presented in the Jerusalem Temple at SHABU'OT (Leviticus 23:15). While the origins of Lag BeOmer, a semi-holiday, are obscure, tradition holds that it marks the cessation of a plague that killed students of Rabbi AQIBA; it is, accordingly, a day of celebration for scholars. The mourning practices traditionally kept during the rest of the Counting of the Omer do not apply on this day. It is also a day of pilgrimage to the grave of R. Simeon b. Yohai, author of the ZOHAR and to the grave of R. Meir Baal HaNess in Morocco.

Lamed Vav   Thirty-six men of humble vocation not recognized, but by whose merit the world exists; they bring salvation in crisis.

Lamentations   Biblical book of alphabetical acrostic poems mourning the destruction of the Temple of Jerusalem by the Babylonians in 586 B.C.E.; recited on Tisha BeAb (see AB, NINTH OF); attributed to JEREMIAH.

Lamentations Rabbati   Rabbinic presentation of the book of Lamentations, completed ca. 500–600 C.E. Lamentations concerns the destruction of the Temple in 586 B.C.E. The theme of Lamentations Rabbati is Israel's relationship with God, and its message is that the covenant still and always governs that relationship. Therefore, everything that happens to Israel makes sense and has meaning; Israel is not helpless before its fate but controls its own destiny. Israel and God have mutually agreed to bind themselves to a common Torah; the rules of the relationship are such that an infraction triggers a penalty; but obedience to the Torah likewise brings reward, which is redemption. Thus, ISRAEL suffers because of sin, but God will respond to Israel's atonement, on the one side, and loyalty to the covenant, on the other. And when Israel has attained the merit that accrues through the Torah, God will redeem Israel.

Leprosy   See ṢARA'AT.

Levaiah   (Hebrew: "accompanying") The accompanying of the deceased to the grave, thus funeral. The burial rite at the graveside is laconic. The prayers are exceedingly brief. One prayer that is commonly recited is as follows:

> The dust returns to the earth, as it was, but the spirit returns to God, who gave it. May the soul of the deceased be bound up in the bond of life eternal. Send comfort, O Lord, to those who mourn. Grant strength to those whose burden is sorrow.

It is also common to intone the prayer, *El Male' Rahamim*, "O God full of Compassion," after which the body is placed in the grave. Three pieces of broken pottery have been laid on eyes and mouth as signs of their vanity. A handful of dirt from the Land of Israel is laid under the head.

The family of the deceased recites the

QADDISH. The family as well as the assembled now shovel dirt into the grave, fulfilling the obligation to bury the dead. Then two lines are formed, leading away from the grave, and the mourners who pass through these lines are given the blessing: "May the Omnipresent comfort you among the others who mourn for Zion and Jerusalem." The appeal to Zion and Jerusalem refers to the Temple of old, which people mourn until the coming restoration, thus a messianic and eschatological reference, the only one made at the funeral. The mourners remain at home for a mourning period of seven days (SHIVA) and continue to recite the memorial Qaddish for eleven months.

Levi The biblical patriarch Jacob's third son by his wife Leah. Moses and Aaron, the brother of Moses and the first high priest, were descendants of Levi. Through Aaron, the Israelite priesthood was assigned to the tribe of Levi.

Levir See YABAM.

Levites Caste of Temple acolytes and assistants; singers of Psalms during Temple rites; descendents of Levi, the third son of Jacob by his wife Leah, but distinguished from the priests (*Kohanim*), who derive as well from the line of Aaron, the brother of Moses.

Leviticus The third book of the Pentateuch; describes the Levitical rites of the tabernacle in the wilderness. The sacrificial laws form the first part (chaps. 1–7); consecration of the priesthood and their office (chaps. 8–10); the laws of ritual purity (chaps. 11–15); the ritual for Yom Kippur, the day of atonement (chap. 16); laws governing the holiness of the people (chaps. 17–26); and a supplement on vows (chap. 27).

Leviticus Rabbah A Rabbinic treatment of the biblical book of Leviticus that, like Genesis Rabbah, asserts that the laws of history may be known out of Scripture's narratives and that these laws, so far as Israel is concerned, focus upon the holy life of the community. If ISRAEL obeys the laws of society aimed at Israel's sanctification, then the foreordained history, resting on the merit of the ancestors, will unfold as Israel hopes. So there is no secret to the meaning of the events of the day, and Israel, for its part, can affect its destiny and effect salvation. The authorship of Leviticus Rabbah has thus joined the two great motifs, sanctification and salvation, by reading a biblical book, Leviticus, that is devoted to the former in the light of the requirements of the latter. In this way, they made their fundamental point, which is that salvation at the end of history depends upon sanctification in the here and now.

To prove these points, the authors of Leviticus Rabbah make lists of facts that bear the same traits and show the working of rules of history. These lists through the power of repetition make a single point or prove a social law of history. The catalogues of exemplary heroes and historical events serve a further purpose. They provide a model of how contemporary events are to be absorbed into the biblical paradigm. Since biblical events exemplify recurrent happenings, sin and redemption, forgiveness and atonement, they lose their one-time character. At the same time and in the same way, current events find a place within the ancient, but eternally present, paradigmatic scheme. So no new historical events, other than exemplary episodes in lives of heroes, demand narration because, through what is said about the past, what was happening in the times of the framers of Leviticus Rabbah would also come under consideration.

Nearly all of the chapters of Leviticus

Rabbah deal with the national, social condition of Israel: (1) Israel's setting in the history of the nations, (2) the sanctified character of the inner life of Israel itself, (3) the future, salvation of Israel. So the biblical book that deals with the tabernacle in the wilderness, which sages understood to form the model for the Temple later on built in Jerusalem, now is shown to address the holy people. That is no paradox, rather a logical next step in the exploration of sanctification. Leviticus really discusses not the consecration of the cult but the sanctification of the nation—its conformity to God's will laid forth in the Torah, and God's rules. Leviticus Rabbah executes the paradox of shifting categories, applying to the nation and its history the category that in the book subject to commentary pertained to the holy place and its eternal condition. The nation now is like the cult then, the ordinary Israelite now like the priest then. The holy way of life lived now, through acts to which merit accrues, corresponds to the holy rites then. The process of metamorphosis is full, rich, complete.

Lulab Palm branch into which is inserted springs of willow and myrtle and which is carried together with a citron (ETROG) during synagogue worship on the festival of SUKKOT (Tabernacles) to fulfill the requirement of Leviticus 23:40: "And you shall take on the first day the fruit of goodly trees, branches of palm trees, and boughs of leafy trees, and willows of the brook; and you shall rejoice before the Lord your God seven days." Scripture views these species as representing the bounty of the Land of Israel and so as

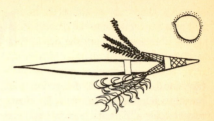

Lulab Lulab and etrog used during worship on Sukkot.

appropriately used in a celebration of the harvest season.

Luria, Isaac (1534–1572) Jewish mystic and ascetic, born in Safed in the Land of Israel, formed his own theoretical system of mystical doctrine, deriving from experiences of direct communication from "other worlds." His principal problem was how God, who is all in all, could create the world, there being no space outside of God for such a creation. His answer was that God first of all contracted or withdrew "from himself into himself," and in doing so made possible existence outside of the Divine. A second doctrine concerned the light of creation; the primordial light of creation spilled over, so the sparks of divine light fell into lower spheres of being. This is called "the breaking of the vessels." The task then is to restore these fallen sparks and souls to their proper place, and the healing of the cosmic order is called *tiqqun*, repair or restoration. Restoration is accomplished through human actions, which have spiritual significance in restoring the divine sparks to their proper place.

M

Ma'amad (Hebrew: "delegation") A priestly delegation. In Temple times, twenty-four different priestly watches were in charge of the Jerusalem Temple, and for each watch there was a *ma'amad* (delegation), made up of priests, Levites, and Israelites. When the time came for a particular watch to go up to Jerusalem, its priests and Levites went up with it.

Ma'ariv The evening worship service, known formally as Arvit, consisting of the SHEMA and its blessings, the SHEMONEH ESREH, and ALENU. Unlike in morning and afternoon prayers, even when the Ma'ariv service is recited in a congregational setting, the Shemoneh Esreh is not repeated, as it was originally considered optional in the evening.

Ma'aser (Hebrew: "tithe") A tenth of the herd and crop, set aside for the Lord, to be used for the Temple, priesthood, and other scheduled castes.

Ma'aser 'Ani (Hebrew: "poorman's tithe") A tenth of the crop to be distributed among the local poor in the third and sixth years of the Sabbatical cycle.

Ma'aser Sheni (Hebrew: "second tithe") A tithe separated in the first, second, fourth, and fifth years of the Sabbatical cycle and brought to Jerusalem for consumption there. This is the title of a Mishnah tractate on eating second tithe in Jerusalem and on prohibited uses of produce designated as second tithe (chaps. 1–2); transferring the status of second tithe to coins, to be brought in its stead to Jerusalem and used for the purchase of food to be eaten there (chaps. 2–4); and some special problems (chap. 5).

Ma'aserot (Hebrew: "tithes") Mishnah tractate on the conditions under which produce becomes subject to the law of tithing (chap. 1); procedures by which harvested produce is rendered liable to the removal of tithes (chaps. 1–4), including processing and storage of untithed produce, bringing produce into the courtyard or home, preparation of produce for use in the meal; cases of doubt and unmet conditions and incomplete procedures, e.g., edibility, harvest, processing, and the like (chaps. 4–5). The tractate is commented on in the Jerusalem Talmud but not in the Babylonian Talmud.

Mabul (Hebrew: "flood") A massive inundation of the whole earth brought about by God when he saw how corrupt the earth was (Genesis 6:12). God instructed NOAH, the only righteous man in his generation, to build an ark of gopher wood and to take up residence in it, "For I am about to bring the Floodwaters upon the earth to destroy all flesh; everything on earth shall perish" (Genesis 6:17). But God established a covenant with Noah and his family: "for you alone have I found righteous before me in this generation" (Genesis 7:1). The flood came from the fountains of the great deep and from the floodgates of the sky and lasted for forty days and forty nights (Genesis 7:11–12). Noah's sons, Shem, Ham, and Japheth, were the progenitors of all humanity thereafter.

Magen David (Hebrew: "Shield of David") Six-pointed star composed of two interwoven triangles; a widely used decorative and magical symbol from ancient times and on; used as a distinctively Jewish symbol only from the seventeenth century or later. Its contemporary centrality as a symbol of Judaism is due to its adoption, in the nineteenth century, by the Zionist movement, which led to its placement on the flag of the state of Israel. Under the National Socialists (Nazis), every Jew in Germany, later on in all German-occupied Europe, had to display a yellow star as a sign of being Jewish.

Magic Bowls   A pottery bowl on which was written a magical formula, used to drive away evil spirits or to invoke the help of a deity in preserving and protecting individuals or a family. During the Talmudic period, in roughly 300–600 C.E., such bowls were in common use in Babylonia by Christians, Mazdeans, Mandeans, and Jews. Bowls used in Jewish homes often were prepared by Jews not involved with or representative of the Rabbinical academies. At the same time, certain Rabbinic figures were deemed potent in driving away particular demons and so appear with frequency on these bowls.

The formulas used on magic bowls and the deities invoked are common across religious traditions. The bowls apparently were prepared by professionals, for instance, by Jews for both Jewish and non-Jewish use. A practitioner would be hired to produce a bowl not because of his denomination but because of his reputation for success. Accordingly, for the most part, identification of a bowl's origin depends upon the script in which the incantation was prepared: Aramaic letters are Jewish; Syriac script indicates a Christian source; and Mandean lettering suggests a Mandean origin.

The majority of known magic bowls were found during excavations in Nippur in 1888–1889. They were found upside down in the ruins of houses, with one or more bowls found in almost every house as well as in cemeteries (where they apparently served to lay ghosts at rest). The bowls were used by individuals and families seeking protection for houses and property, e.g., cattle, often with a particular concern for domestic sexual life and unborn babies. Lilis and Liliths, thought to prey upon women and children and to produce offspring with human beings, are common targets of the bowls.

The chief element of the bowls is an incantation composed of repeating phrases, words, or syllables believed to have the power to bind favorable powers or demons to some designated action. Angels, in Jewish bowls, and deities, on pagan ones, frequently are adduced, and there appears to have been an attempt to use as many names as possible. The spell's main power, however, derived from terminology declaring that the demon has been rendered unable to exercise its control, for instance, that it is "bound, sealed, countersealed, exorcised, hobbled, and silenced." The separation of a Lilith from her victim often is expressed in terms of a writ of divorce (see GET). Jewish texts frequently refer to the angels Michael, Gabriel, and Raphael. The name YHWH also occurs, often broken down into individual, repeated, letters or syllables.

Mah Nishtannah   Often translated, "Why is this night different from all other nights?," the opening words of four questions asked by child at the PASSOVER *seder*. More accurately to be rendered "How different is this night from all other nights!" The response to this statement lists four specific ways in which the *seder* meal is distinctive.

Maḥzor   Prayer book for the New Year and Day of Atonement, containing the unique liturgy for those days;

distinguished from the *siddur*, which contains the liturgy for weekdays, Sabbaths, and the festivals of PASSOVER, SUKKOT, and SHABU'OT.

Maimonides (1135–1204)

Known as Rambam (an acronym for **R**abbi **M**oses **b**en **M**aimon), he was a distinguished student of the Talmud and Jewish law, a community authority, a great physician, and a leading philosophical thinker of his day. His achievement was to synthesize a neo-Platonic Aristotelianism with biblical revelation. His *Guide to the Perplexed,* published in 1190, was intended to reconcile the believer to the philosopher and the philosopher to faith. For him, philosophy was not alien to religion but identical with it, for truth was, in the end, the sole issue. Faith is a form of knowledge; philosophy is the road to faith. His proof for the existence of God was Aristotelian. He argued from creation to Creator, but accepted the eternity of the world. In Maimonides' view, God is so distinctive as to be insusceptible of definition through traits normally attributed to humans ("good," "kind," "powerful," etc.). God accordingly is purged of all sensuous elements, so that all one can say is that God is God—nothing more—for God can only be *known* as the highest cause of being.

What then of revelation? Did God not say anything about himself? And if he did, what need for reasonings such as these? For Maimonides, prophecy, like philosophy, depends upon the Active Intellect. Prophecy is a gift bestowed by God upon humanity. The Torah and commandments are clearly important but are not ultimately beyond question or reasonable inquiry. They, however, survive the inquiry unimpaired. The Torah fosters a sound mind and body. The greatest good, however, is not simply to study Torah but to know God, that is, to worship and love God.

Piety and knowledge of Torah serve merely to prepare people for this highest achievement. Study of Torah thus loses its usual character within Rabbinic Judaism as an end in itself and is rendered into a means to a philosophical goal. This constituted a most striking transformation of the old values.

Maimonides provided a philosophical definition of Judaism, a list of articles of faith he thought obligatory on every faithful Jew. These are: (1) existence of God; (2) His unity; (3) His incorporeality; (4) His eternity; (5) the obligation to worship Him alone; (6) prophecy; (7) Moses as the greatest of the prophets; (8) the divine origin of Torah; (9) the eternal validity of Torah; (10) God's knowledge of man's deeds; (12) His promise to send a messiah; and (13) His promise to resurrect the dead. The words of the philosopher were thus transformed into a message of faith, at once sufficiently complex to sustain critical inquiry according to the canons of the day and simple enough to bear the weight of the faith of ordinary folk. Maimonides' "God without attributes" is still guide, refuge, stronghold. It is a strange and paradoxical fate for the philosopher's teachings. (See YIGDAL.)

Makhshirin Mishnah tractate devoted to elucidation of conditions set by Leviticus 11:34, 37 for susceptibility to uncleanness of produce; produce is susceptible to uncleanness when harvested and then deliberately watered. Makhshirin treats the issue of intentionality in watering the produce (chap. 1); water that is capable of imparting susceptibility mixed with water that is not (chap 2); absorption of water (chap. 3); water that serves one purpose, its status as to a secondary purpose (chaps. 3–5); liquids not used intentionally do not impart susceptibility (chap. 5); liquids that can impart susceptibility to uncleanness (chap. 6).

Makkot   (Hebrew: "blows") Mishnah tractate devoted to those punishable by flogging for perjury (chap. 1); the penalty of exile and those who are subject to it (chap. 2); and others penalized by flogging and how the penalty of flogging is administered (chap. 3). Both Talmuds devote important and lengthy expositions to this tractate.

Malachi, Book of   The last of the Twelve Minor prophetic books of the Hebrew Scriptures, written sometime after 450 B.C.E. The book consists of six sections, each taking the form of a question and an answer. The prophet defends God's justice, questioned because of the unfulfilled expectations of an end of time. Malachi emphasizes the requirement of correct worship, condemns divorce, and announces that the day of judgment will come soon. Those faithful to the worship of the Lord and moral responsibilities will be glad, the unfaithful will be cursed.

Mal'akh HaMavet   Angel of death; referred to in the TALMUD as the divine agent that brings death at the proper time.

Malkhuyyot   Verses of Scripture devoted to God's sovereignty, found as a section of the New Year Additional Service (*Musaf*).

Mamzer   Offspring of a union of people who are genealogically ineligible for marriage to each other and whose union is penalized by extirpation, particularly an incestuous one (e.g., catalogued at Leviticus 18). A Mamzer may only marry another person in that same status, and this stigma is permanent, passing on to future generations. Contrary to common contemporary usage, the term Mamzer does not apply to the offspring of unmarried parents, since the child of parents who are genealogically free to marry is never illegitimate in Jewish law. Mamzer therefore cannot be translated as "bastard."

Manoah   The father of Samson, depicted in Judges 13 as a pious and God-fearing man. He questioned an angel who appeared to his then-barren wife, announcing the coming birth of a son, regarding how the son was to be raised and how he might honor the individual who brought tidings of the child's impending birth.

Ma'oz Tsur   "Fortress, Rock [of My Salvation];" title and initial words of a HANUKKAH hymn song in the Ashkenazic rite after the kindling of the Hanukkah candles; normally rendered in English as "Rock of Ages." The song is of German origin, probably from the thirteenth century.

Maror   Bitter herbs, consumed at the Passover *seder* in remembrance of the bitter life of the Israelite slaves in Egypt.

Mashal   Parable, formed by a narrative that compares one situation to another. Common in Rabbinic literature of late antiquity.

Mashgiah   (Hebrew: "inspector") Supervisor of rituals, particularly ritual slaughter and the preparation of foods according to the restrictions of kashrut (see DIETARY LAWS); must be expert in laws, pious, and God-fearing. An ignorant person, motivated by financial gain, cannot supervise religious rites.

Maskil   *Illuminé*, i.e., enlightened person, follower of the *Haskalah* (Enlightenment), secularizing movement in East and Central European Jewry from the eighteenth century onward.

Massekhet   (Hebrew: "tractate") A

topical subdivision of the Mishnah, Tosefta, Talmud, or other Rabbinic documents.

Matzah   Unleavened bread, used during the eight-day festival of PASSOVER in place of leavened bread. Referred to in the HAG-GADAH as "the bread of affliction." Eaten as a matter of religious duty on the first day of Passover.

Mazal Tov   (Hebrew, literally: "a good star") The Hebrew word for guiding star is *mazal* (planet), so that the blessing *mazal tov* means, "under a propitious star," i.e., "good luck." This is a commonplace greeting and blessing at festive occasions, e.g., a wedding, Bar Mitzvah, or circumcision. See ASTROLOGY.

Medinat Yisrael   Hebrew: "The State of Israel," referring to the modern Jewish state.

Megillah   (Hebrew: "scroll") Usually, the scroll of Esther, read at Purim. This is also the name of a Mishnah tractate on the reading of the scroll of Esther on Purim; the tractate covers the rules of reading the Megillah (chaps. 1–2); the laws of syna-gogue property and liturgy, lections of Scripture in the synagogue (chaps. 3–4).

Meḥitzah   A partition in a synagogue separating male from female worshippers, found today primarily in Orthodox congre-gations. Separation of the sexes was abol-ished by the nineteenth-century Reform movement, which developed a policy of family pews. It has been abandoned as well in Conservative congregations, which fea-ture mixed seating.

Me'ilah   Mishnah tractate devoted to sacrilege (Leviticus 5:15–16); sacrilege of sacrifices in particular (chaps. 1–3); when the laws of sacrilege apply; stages in the status of an offering, cultic property not

subject to sacrilege; sacrilege of Temple property in general (chaps. 4–5).

Mekhilta Attributed to R. Ishmael
A legal midrash covering Exodus 12:1–23:19, 31:12–13, and 35:1–3; the docu-ment is variously dated, but ca. 250 is presently favored by many scholars (though rejected with reason by others). It presents composites of three kinds of materials: 1) *ad hoc* and episodic exegeses of some passages of Exodus; 2) a group of argumentative essays that set forth theological principles; 3) topical articles, some of them sustained, about important subjects of the Judaism of the dual Torah. The compilation's main points similarly fall into three classifica-tions: 1) generalizations about the charac-ter of Scripture, 2) rules for correct conduct, and 3) theological teachings, with special reference to the relationship between ISRAEL and God and the impli-cations of that relationship for the fate of Israel among the nations. The first two are not significant in volume and intellectual dimensions; the third is enormous and important.

At the heart of the theology expressed in Mekhilta Attributed to R. Ishmael is the idea that by performing religious duties Israel was redeemed, and prepara-tion of the rite of PASSOVER well in advance was the religious duty to which redemption of Israel would serve as reward. What God says he will do, he does. Wherever Scripture indicates that God has said something, we can find in some other passage precisely what he had said. This means that by carefully reading Scripture, we are able to identify the rules that govern history and salvation. The vindication of Moses' demands turns the demands into prophecies. This is under-lined by the careful delineation of the degradation and humiliation of Pharaoh.

And then comes the striking contrast between the reverence in which Israelites hold the rule of God and the humiliation of the Egyptian ruler. People get what is coming to them. Divine punishment is inexorable, so too divine reward. When God exacts punishment of the nations, His name is made great in the world. Merit is what saved Israel at the sea. The issue to be pursued is, what sort of merit, e.g., deriving from what actions or persons? The acts of healing of the Holy One, blessed be He, are not like the acts of healing of mortals. The redemption at sea prefigures the redemption at the end of time. Faith in God is what saves Israel.

God punishes the arrogant person by exacting a penalty precisely from that about which such a person takes pride. With that in which the nations of the world take pride before Him He exacts punishment from them. Numerous cases on a long line of instances, based upon historical facts provided by Scripture, serve to demonstrate that proposition. Israel is unique among the nations. Mortals have the power to praise and glorify God. God takes many forms. The Lord is master of all media of war. The Lord needs none of those media. The Lord is a man of war, but the Lord is in no way comparable to a man of war, making war in a supernatural way, specifically by retaining, even while making war, the attributes of mercy and humanity. God is just, and God's justice insures that the worthy are rewarded and the unworthy are penalized. God responds to human actions and attitudes. Those who oppose Israel are as though they opposed God. God is unique and God's salvation at the sea will be repeated at the end of time.

Israel gained great merit because it alone was willing to accept the TEN COMMANDMENTS. The Israelites deserve praise for accepting the Torah. The "other gods" are not really gods at all. They are called

"other" for various reasons. Suffering is precious and will not be rejected. One must not act in regard to God the way the outsiders treat their gods. They honor their gods in good times, not in bad, but Israel, exemplified by JOB, honors God in bad times as much as in good. These fundamental principles of faith hardly exhaust the theological and normative statements in Mekhilta Attributed to R. Ishmael. They represent only those convictions that are spelled out in massive detail and argued with great force, the points of emphasis within a vast fabric of faith.

Melavveh Malkah (Hebrew: "accompanying the Queen") A Sabbath meal and festivities held at end of the day to prolong the outgoing Sabbath.

Menaḥot [1] Meal offerings; [2] Mishnah tractate on meal offerings in the Temple; improper intention and invalidating meal offerings (chaps. 1–4); proper preparation of meal offerings (chaps. 5–9); special meal offerings (chaps. 10–11); vows in connection with meal offerings (chaps. 12–13).

Menorah (Hebrew: "candelabrum") In general usage, the nine-branched candelabrum used at HANUKKAH (Hebrew: *hanukkiah*). The term originally pertained specifically to the seven-branched candelabrum used in the ancient Tabernacle (see Exodus 25) and then the Jerusalem Temple (see 1 Kings 7:49); this seven branched candelabrum is the most frequently found Jewish symbol in antiquity; it has been adopted as well as the official symbol of the modern State of Israel.

Meshumad (Hebrew: "apostate") A Jew who commits apostasy, giving up the faith of Judaism for some other faith. In Judaism in biblical times, this was

identified with going over to Greek culture
or treasonable action on behalf of the
Roman government. In later periods, it was
identified with giving up the Torah and
accepting Christianity. According to classical Jewish law, a Jewish apostate
remains a Jew, though he or she is a sinner;
reversion to Judaism accordingly requires
no rite of return. A person born a Jew or
converted to Judaism never loses that identification, whatever he or she does. (See
GER.)

Messiah   (Hebrew: "annointed one") A
leader commissioned through an act of
anointing, e.g., the anointed priest, the
anointed leader in battle, or, in particular,
the anointed one to come as eschatological
king to rule at the end of days. In Rabbinic
Judaism, the idea of a divinely sanctioned
leader who will resurrect the dead at the
end of days first becomes prominent in the
Jerusalem Talmud, ca. 400 C.E. A contrast
is drawn between the failed messiah Simeon bar Kokhba, a Jewish general of the
second century war against Rome, who
exemplifies arrogance against God, and
the true Messiah, who will be humble, a
master of the Torah, and a model of self-
sacrifice. Bar Kokhba lost the war because
of arrogance and, in particular, because he
ignored the authority of sages. The Talmud
presents, by contrast, a fully exposed doctrine of *the* Messiah, the one who will save
Israel: who he is, how we will know him,
what we must do to bring him: the Messiah
will be a sage, the Messiah will come when
Israel has attained the condition of sanctification marked by profound humility and
complete acceptance of God's will.

The climax of the matter comes in an
explicit statement that the practice of conduct required by the Torah will bring about
the coming of the Messiah. Taanit 1:1 of
the Jerusalem Talmud contains the most
striking expression of this viewpoint:

J   "The oracle concerning Dumah. One
is calling to me from Seir, 'Watchman, what of the night? Watchman,
what of the night?' (Isaiah 21:11)."

K   The Israelites said to Isaiah, "O our
Rabbi, Isaiah, what will come for us
out of this night?"

L   He said to them, "Wait for me, until I
can present the question."

M   Once he had asked the question [of
God], he came back to them.

N   They said to him, "Watchman, what of
the night? What did the Guardian of
the ages tell you?"

O   He said to them, "The watchman says:
'Morning comes; and also the night. If
you will inquire, inquire; come back
again' (Isaiah 21:12)."

P   They said to him, "Also the night?"

Q   He said to them, "It is not what you are
thinking. But there will be morning
for the righteous, and night for the
wicked, morning for Israel, and night
for idolaters."

R   They said to him, "When?"

S   He said to them, "Whenever you want.
He too wants [it to be]—if you want it,
He wants it."

T   They said to him, "What is standing in
the way?"

U   He said to them, "Repentance: 'Come
back again' (Isaiah 21:12)."

V   R. Aha in the name of R. Tanhum b. R.
Hiyya, "If Israel repents for one day,
forthwith the son of David [i.e. the
Messiah] will come.

W   "What is the Scriptural basis? 'O that
today you would hearken to his
voice!' (Psalm 95:7)."

X   Said R. Levi, "If Israel would keep a
single Sabbath in the proper way,
forthwith the son of David will come."

Y   What is the Scriptural basis for this
view? "Moses said, Eat it today, for
today is a Sabbath to the Lord; today

you will not find it in the field" (Exod. 16:25).

Z And it says, "For thus said the Lord God, the Holy One of Israel, 'In returning and rest you shall be saved; in quietness and in trust shall be your strength.' And you would not (Isaiah 30:15)."

The Messiah will come any day that Israel makes it possible. If all Israel will keep a single Sabbath in the proper way, the Messiah will come. If all Israel will repent for one day, the Messiah will come. "Whenever you want …," the Messiah will come. In this way, the Talmud shows that the system of religious observance, including study of Torah, has salutary power, that the purpose of the law is to attain Israel's salvation: "If you want it, God wants it too." The one thing Israel commands is its own heart; the power it yet exercises is the power to repent. These suffice. The entire history of humanity will respond to Israel's will, to what happens in Israel's heart and soul. And, with Temple in ruins, repentance can take place only within the heart and mind.

Mezuzah (Hebrew: "doorpost") A parchment containing the first two paragraphs of the *Shema* (Deuteronomy 6:4–9, 11:13–21), the proclamation of God's unity and dominion over ISRAEL that is recited twice a day by observant Jews. The parchment is rolled tightly and placed in a case, then attached to the doorpost of a house (and, often, on the doorposts of individual rooms of a house as well) in which a Jew dwells. This carries out literally the obligation expressed at Deuteronomy 6:9, that one write God's commandments on the doorposts of one's house.

Middot [1] Mishnah tractate that describes the layout of the Temple: watch posts and gates (chap. 1); Temple Mount (chap. 2); altar and porch (chap. 3),

Mezuzah A mezuzah on a doorpost surrounded by different styles of mezuzah.

sanctuary and courtyard (chaps. 4–5). [2] See VIRTUE.

Midrash (Hebrew: "exegesis") A term routinely used to convey three distinct, if related, meanings. In common use, the word Midrash may refer to:

1 a distinctive *process* or *method* of interpretation,
2 a compilation of the results of that process, that is, a book that collects a set of exegeses,
3 a single unit of exegesis that uses that method, e.g., the interpretation or set of interpretations of a single biblical verse.

While the specific referent of the term Midrash depends upon the context in which it appears, in all of its meanings, Midrash signifies a distinctively Rabbinic mode of reflecting upon Scripture. In Judaism, Scripture is subjected to the close reading represented in the Midrash for two purposes, to explore and systematize norms of action (the law; HALAKHAH) set forth in Scripture, yielding the sub-category Midrash Halakhah, and to identify norms of attitude or belief, virtue and proper motivation. Encased in narrative form, these teachings of an ethical and moral character are called

AGGADAH, or lore, which yields the sub-category Midrash Aggadah.

Exegesis of Scripture was never unique to Rabbinic Judaism and its writings. On the contrary, the interpretation of the Hebrew Scriptures was a convention of all systems of Judaism from before the closure of Scripture itself; no one, including the sages who stand behind Rabbinic literature, began anywhere but in the encounter with the Written Torah. Everyone read Scripture as the foundation of their distinctive Judaic system.

Collecting and organizing documents of exegeses of Scripture in a systematic way developed in a quite distinct circumstance, however, one that is particular to Rabbinic Judaism. For Rabbinic literature, the circumstance was defined by the requirement of MISHNAH exegesis. The Mishnah's character itself defined a principal task of Scripture-exegesis. Standing by itself, providing few proof texts to Scripture to back up its rules, the Mishnah bore no explanation of why the Jews should obey its rules. Brought into relationship to Scriptures, by contrast, the Mishnah gained access to the source of authority by definition operative in the Jewish people. Accordingly, the work of relating the Mishnah's rules to those of Scripture got under way alongside the formation of the Mishnah's rules themselves. It follows that explanations of the sense of the document, including its authority and sources, would draw attention to the written part of the Torah.

We may classify the Midrash compilations in three successive groups: exegetical, propositional, and exegetical-propositional (theological).

[1] Exegetical Discourse of Halakhah of the Pentateuch: One important dimension, therefore, of the earliest documents of Scripture exegesis, the Midrash compilations that deal with LEVITICUS, NUM-BERS, and DEUTERONOMY, measures the distance between the Mishnah and Scripture and aims to close it. The question is persistently addressed in analyzing Scripture: precisely how does a rule of the Mishnah relate to, or rest upon, a rule of Scripture? That question demanded an answer, so that the status of the Mishnah's rules, and, right alongside, of the Mishnah itself, could find a clear definition. Collecting and arranging exegeses of Scripture as these related to passages of the Mishnah first reached literary form in SIFRA, to Leviticus, and in two books, both called SIFRE, one to Numbers, the other Deuteronomy. All three compositions accomplished much else. For, even at that early stage, exegeses of passages of Scripture in their own context and not only for the sake of Mishnah exegesis attracted attention. But a principal motif in all three books concerned the issue of Mishnah–Scripture relationships.

A second, still more fruitful path in formulating Midrash clarifications of Scripture also emerged from the labor of Mishnah exegesis. As the work of Mishnah exegesis got under way, in the third century, exegetes of the Mishnah and others alongside undertook a parallel labor. They read the Scriptures in the way in which they were reading the Mishnah itself. That is to say, they began to work through verses of Scripture in exactly the same way—word for word, phrase for phrase, line for line—in which, to begin with, the exegetes of the Mishnah pursued the interpretation and explanation of the Mishnah. Precisely the types of exegesis that dictated the way in which sages read the Mishnah now guided their reading of Scripture as well. And, as people began to collect and organize comments in accord with the order of sentences and paragraphs of the Mishnah, they found the stimulation to collect and organize comments on clauses and verses of Scripture. This kind of verse-by-verse exegetical work got under way in the Sifra and the two Sifres, but reached fulfillment in GENESIS RABBAH which presents a line-for-line reading of the Book of Genesis. Characteristic of the narrowly-exegetical phase of Midrash-compilation is the absence of a single, governing proposition, running through the details. It is not possible, for example, to state the main point, expressed through countless cases, in the Sifra or Sifre to Deuteronomy.

[2] From Exegesis to Proposition: A further group of Midrash compilations altogether transcends the limits of formal exegesis. Beyond these two modes of exegesis—search for the sources of the Mishnah in Scripture, line-by-line reading of Scripture as of the Mishnah—lies yet a third, an approach we may call "writing with Scripture," meaning, using verses of Scripture in a context established by a propositional program independent of Scripture itself. To understand it, we have to know how the earliest of the two versions of the Talmud read the Mishnah. The Jerusalem Talmud's authors not only explained phrases or sentences of the Mishnah in the manner of Mishnah and Scripture exegetes. They also investigated the principles and large-scale conceptual problems of the document and of the law, given only in cases in the Mishnah itself. That is to say, they dealt with a given topic, a subject and its rule, the cases that yield the rule, but with an encompassing problem, a principle, and its implications for a number of topics and rules.

This far more discursive and philosophical mode of thought produced for Mishnah exegesis sustained essays on principles cutting across specific rules. Predictably, this same intellectual work extended from the Mishnah to Scripture. Exegesis of Scripture beyond that focused on words, phrases, and sentences produced discursive essays on great principles or problems of theology and morality. Discursive exegesis is represented, to begin with, in LEVITICUS RABBAH, a document that reached closure, people generally suppose, sometime after Genesis Rabbah, thus ca. 450, marking the shift from verse-by-verse to syllogistic reading of verses of Scripture. It was continued in PESIQTA DERAB KAHANA, organized around themes pertinent to various holy days through the liturgical year, and PESIQTA RABBATI, a derivative and imitative work.

[3] Saying One Thing through Many Things: Writing with Scripture reached its climax in the theological Midrash compilations formed at the end of the development of Rabbinic literature. A fusion of the two approaches to Midrash exegesis, the verse-by-verse amplification of successive chapters of Scripture and the syllogistic presentation of propositions, arguments, and proofs deriving from the facts of Scripture, was accomplished in the third body of Midrash compilations: RUTH RABBAH, ESTHER RABBAH Part I, LAMENTATIONS RABBATI, and SONG OF SONGS RABBAH. Here we find the verse-by-verse reading of scriptural books. But at the same time, a highly propositional program governs the exegesis, each of the compilations meaning to prove a single, fundamental theological point through the accumulation of detailed comments.

The Babylonian TALMUD: Halakhah and Aggadah, Mishnah and Midrash in a Single Definitive Document: The Babylonian Talmud accomplished the fusion of Mishnah and Scripture exegesis in a single compilation. The authors of units of discourse collected in the Babylonian Talmud drew together the two, hitherto distinct, modes of organizing thought, either around the Mishnah or around Scripture. They treated both Torahs, oral and written, as equally available in the work of organizing large-scale exercises of sustained inquiry. So we find in the Babylonian Talmud a systematic treatment of some tractates of the Mishnah. And within the same aggregates of discourse, we also find (in somewhat smaller proportion to be sure, roughly 60 percent to roughly 40 percent in a sample made of three tractates) a second principle of organizing and redaction. That principle dictates that ideas be laid out in line with verses of Scripture, themselves dealt with in cogent sequence, one by one, just as the Mishnah's sentences and paragraphs come under analysis, in cogent order and one by one.

Midrash Rabbah   Compilation of Midrash collections devoted to the books of GENESIS, EXODUS, LEVITICUS, NUMBERS, DEUTERONOMY, and the Five Scrolls: ESTHER, ECCLESIASTES, LAMENTATIONS, RUTH, and SONG OF SONGS. Some of the documents derive from late antiquity, others are medieval in origin.

Midrash Tanhuma   A Midrash compilation in which a rabbi, Tanhuma, is often cited; a collection of such Midrash exegeses, covering the whole of the Pentateuch, was printed under the title Midrash Tanhuma by Salomon Buber in 1885. The earliest of the included text derives from the period after 800 C.E.

Minhag   (Hebrew: "custom") A traditional practice or way of doing things, not understood to be strictly required by Jewish law. A *minhag* thus is distinguished from a *mitzvah*, or religious obligation. The term is frequently used to describe variations in liturgical or other everyday customs that developed over time among Jews living in diverse geographical or cultural settings.

Minḥah   Afternoon prayers, consisting of Psalm 145 (ASHREI), the AMIDA, and ALENU; corresponds to the daily whole offering presented at dusk in the Jerusalem Temple.

Minyan   Number needed for quorum for worship; ten. Counted for a minyan: women and men, in Reform, Conservative, Reconstructionist Judaism; men only, in Orthodox Judaism.

Miqvah   Ritual bath for immersion to wash away impurity. The miqvah is a pool carved into rock or otherwise built into the ground and containing a minimum of 40 seahs of water (an uncertain amount, representing as little as 250 or as many as 1000 quarts). So as to represent the flowing water that Scripture states is to be used for immersion, the water of the miqvah may never have been contained in a vessel. Rainwater, melted snow or ice, or other flowing water is used for this purpose. See PURIFICATION, RITES OF.

Miqvaot   Mishnah tractate on immersion pools (see MIQVAH), centered on the kind of collection of water that serves to remove uncleanness (chaps. 1–5); doubts in connection with immersion and immersion pools (chap. 2); the union of pools to form the requisite volume of water (chaps. 5–6); mixtures of water and wine, mud, water in various localities (chaps. 7–8); the use of the immersion pool, the problem of interposition between the flesh and the water (chaps. 8–10).

Miracles   Extraordinary events that have no possible human or natural cause are recognized in the Hebrew Bible and in later forms of Judaism as deriving from the direct intervention of God in the human sphere. In the Rabbinic literature, such occurrences are referred to by the term *nes*, signifying a "wondrous event" and roughly comparable to the English term "miracle." In the Hebrew Bible, events that violate the natural order more commonly are designated as "signs" (*'otot*), a term that points to the distinctive role miracles play in ancient Israelite theology. In the Hebrew Bible, God performs miracles for the explicit purpose of demonstrating His power and informing people of His desires and plans. In light of this purpose, events such as the Ten Plagues that God brought against the Egyptians are more than simply "miracles." Rather, such remarkable happenings have a specific theological function, as signs of the absolute power of God and proof that Moses speaks for God when he states what is expected of the Egyptians.

The function of miracles in the Bible is clear from the distinction Scripture makes between a miracle and a mere magic trick. Magic can be performed by magicians of all peoples (Exodus 7:22) and is not a source of knowledge about God or God's will. Miracles, by contrast, are unparalleled manifestations of God's will that function as saving acts on behalf of God's people. Miracles are at once signs of what God desires and proof of God's ability to accomplish His will.

In the biblical view, people thus come to know God and God's demands primarily because God personally and directly reveals these things. Rather than from theological or philosophical speculation, knowledge of God and of what God demands results from the wondrous deeds through which God reveals Himself in the world. As in the case of the Exodus from Egypt, such signs occur in particular in the context of God's saving acts, which express God's sovereignty and bring salvation to God's people. But such miracles pertain as well to individuals, as in the marvelous works of God described in the Psalms (see., e.g., Psalm 9:1–2). In all, miracles constitute the foundation for the Israelites' acceptance of God's sovereignty, as Isaiah 25:1–2 makes explicit:

> O Lord, Thou art my God; I will exalt Thee, I will praise Thy name; for Thou hast done wonderful things, plans formed of old, faithful and sure. For Thou hast made the city a heap, the fortified city a ruin; the palace of aliens is a city no more, it will never be rebuilt.

From the destruction of a fortified city to the placement of a rainbow in the heaven (Genesis 9:13), God's extraordinary acts instruct people of God's will and assure them of God's saving powers.

In later Jewish history, the biblical view gives way to a perspective that largely rejects the idea that miracles should be expected or that they even are an appropriate way for God's will to be made known. As a result of the historical events of the first centuries C.E., which saw the destruction of the Jerusalem Temple, the failed Bar Kokhba revolt (see MESSIAH), and the loss of Israelite sovereignty to Rome, first under pagans and then Christians, both the political and theological contexts in which Jews previously had interpreted the events of history—viewing them as the result of the miraculous intervention of God into the human sphere—were dramatically altered. If God could work miracles, why did he now not miraculously return the nation to its former glory?

In the new setting, rather than either denying the power of God to perform miracles, on the one hand, or promising that miracles will again occur, on the other, the sages who shaped Rabbinic Judaism rethought the biblical perspective on what can and should be expected of God. The destruction of the Temple and the failed revolt under Bar Kokhba had made clear to these rabbis that the Jewish people were not well served by ambitious political leaders who insisted that God would immediately and miraculously fulfill the biblical promise of Jewish sovereignty over the Land of Israel. In the Rabbinic view, rather, Jews were better off forgetting the notion of God's wondrous actions in history and accepting, instead, Roman political domination. Under this domination, rather than depending upon miracles, the people developed modes of piety independent of priestly and nationalistic aspirations, unconcerned with what was happening on the stage of history.

The result of this thinking was that, under Rabbinic leadership, Jews continued to pray for the rebuilding of the Temple, the re-establishment of animal sacrifice, and renewed Israelite sovereignty, all to be achieved through God's personal and miraculous intervention in history. But these things now were seen not as matters for this day but as signifiers of the advent of the messianic age. They would be events of the end of time, not aspects of this world, expected to come about today or tomorrow. The Rabbinic ideology thus refocused the people's concerns from the events of political history, which are far beyond the control of the individual, to events within the life and control of each person and family. What came to matter were the every-day details of life, the recurring actions that define who we are and that demarcate what is truly important.

Thus, even as Talmudic rabbis acknowledged that miracles occur and are evidence of God's action in the world, they proposed that miracles are neither an appropriate foundation for faith nor the expected method through which God would in their own day protect individuals or the Israelite people as a whole. Indeed, the rabbis went so far as to portray miracles as attempts by God inappropriately to

coerce the people to accept God's rule. Insofar as a coerced "faith" is not a legitimate faith at all, the rabbis even declared God's redeeming of the people from Egypt an inappropriate foundation for the Israelites' accepting of the covenant (Babylonian Talmud Shabbat 88a):

A   "And they [that is, the people of Israel, after the Exodus, camped at Sinai] stood below the mount" (Exodus 19:17):

B   Actually underneath the mountain.

C   Said R. Abdimi bar Hama bar Hasa, "This teaches that the Holy One, blessed be He, held the mountain over Israel like a cask and said to them, 'If you accept the Torah, well and good, and if not, then there is where your grave will be.'"

D   Said R. Aha bar Jacob, "On this basis there is ground for a powerful protest against the Torah [since it was imposed by force]."

E   Said Raba, "Nonetheless, the generation of the time of Ahasuerus accepted it, as it is written, 'The Jews ordained and took it upon themselves'* (Esther 9:27)—they confirmed what the others [at the time of Sinai] had already accepted."

God's actions against the Egyptians did more than to help the Israelites to recognize God's power and sovereignty. Rather, God's miracles created a circumstance of compulsion, in which the people of Israel had no choice but to accept the Torah. Having witnessed God's overwhelming power and willingness to drown an entire army, the people stood in

---

*The verse continues: "and their descendants and all who joined them, that without fail they would keep these two days according to what was written and at the time appointed every year."

the wilderness with nowhere to go, no means of defending themselves, and insufficient provisions. The rabbis imagine this circumstance as comparable to standing "beneath" Sinai, for the people's refusal to accept God's covenant would certainly have meant their being left to die in the wilderness. The rabbis see as a more appropriate foundation for faith the events described in the biblical book of Esther, in which the name of God never appears but in which the people saw their own victory as predicated upon the divine will, a kind of miracle that had nothing to do with God's intervention into the natural order.

Jews thus came increasingly to insist that each individual has the power and obligation to use his or her own intellect and everyday actions to come to know God and to work to create a better world, a world of holiness and sanctification, as God wishes it to be. In its confrontation with the real world in which people live, the biblical image of God's power to act through miracles yielded to the belief that people themselves have and must use their power to transform the world. It is here, rather than in God's intervention in the human realm, that the rabbis saw the real miracle of God's power.

Mishnah   A philosophical law code, completed ca. 200 C.E., covering topics of both a theoretical and practical character. It was produced under the sponsorship of JUDAH THE PATRIARCH (*nasi*), the ethnic ruler of the Jews of the land of Israel. It comprises sixty-two topical subdivisions (tractates), divided by topics among six divisions, as follows:

1 Zera'im (Agriculture): Berakhot (Blessings); Peah (the corner of the field); Demai (doubtfully tithed produce); Kilayim (mixed seeds); Shebi'it (the seventh year); Terumot (heave offering or priestly rations); Ma'aserot (tithes); Ma'aser Sheni (second tithe); Hallah (dough offering); Orlah (produce of trees in the first three years after planting, which is prohibited); and Bikkurim (first fruits).

2 Mo'ed (Appointed Times): Shabbat (the Sabbath); Erubin (the fictive fusion meal or boundary); Pesahim (Passover); Sheqalim (the Temple tax); Yoma (the Day of Atonement); Sukkah (the festival of Tabernacles); Besah (the preparation of food on the festivals and Sabbath); Rosh Hashanah (the New Year); Ta'anit (fast days); Megillah (Purim); Mo'ed Qatan (the intermediate days of the festivals of Passover and Tabernacles); Hagigah (the festal offering).

3 Nashim (Women): Yebamot (the levirate widow); Ketubot (the marriage contract); Nedarim (vows); Nazir (the special vow of the Nazirite); Sotah (the wife accused of adultery); Gittin (writs of divorce); Qiddushin (betrothal).

4 Neziqin (Damages or civil law): Baba Qamma, Baba Mesia, Baba Batra (civil law, covering damages and torts, correct conduct of business, labor, and real estate transactions); Sanhedrin (institutions of government; criminal penalties); Makkot (flogging); Shabuot (oaths); Eduyyot (a collection arranged on other than topical lines); Hora'ot (rules governing improper conduct of civil authorities);

5 Qodashim (Holy Things): Zebahim (every day animal offerings); Menahot (meal offerings); Hullin (animals slaughtered for secular purposes); Bekhorot (firstlings); Arakhin (vows of valuation); Temurah (vows of exchange of a beast for an already consecrated beast); Keritot (penalty of extirpation or premature death);

Me'ilah (sacrilege); Tamid (the daily whole offering); Middot (the layout of the Temple building); Qinnim (how to deal with bird offerings designated for a given purpose and then mixed up);

6   Purity (Tohorot): Kelim (susceptibility of utensils to uncleanness); Ohalot (transmission of corpse-uncleanness in the tent of a corpse); Negaim (the uncleanness described in Leviticus 13–14); Paraḥ (the preparation of purification-water); Tohorot (problems of doubt in connection with matters of cleanness); Miqvaot (immersion-pools); Niddah (menstrual uncleanliness); Makhshirin (rendering susceptible to uncleanness produce that is dry and so not susceptible); Zabim (the uncleanness covered at Leviticus 15); Tebul-Yom (the uncleanness of one who has immersed on that self-same day and awaits sunset for completion of the purification rites); Yadayim (the uncleanness of hands); Uqsin (the uncleanness transmitted through what is connected to unclean produce).

In volume, the sixth division covers approximately a quarter of the entire document. Topics of interest to the priesthood and the Temple, such as priestly fees, conduct of the cult on holy days, conduct of the cult on ordinary days and management and upkeep of the Temple, and the rules of cultic cleanness, also predominate in the first, second, fifth, and sixth divisions. Rules governing the social order form the bulk of the third and fourth. Of these tractates, only Eduyyot is organized along other than topical lines, for it collects sayings on diverse subjects attributed to particular authorities. The Mishnah as printed today always includes ABOT (sayings of the sages), but that document reached closure about a generation later than the Mishnah. While it serves as an apologetic, insisting that the Mishnah has the status of revelation, it does not conform to the formal, rhetorical, or logical traits characteristic of the Mishnah overall.

Focus of the Mishnah: The stress of the Mishnah throughout on the priestly caste and the Temple cult points to its principal concern, which centers upon sanctification, understood as the correct arrangement of all things, each in its proper category, each called by its rightful name. The Mishnah thus takes as its model of holiness the condition of the world at the time of creation, as portrayed in Genesis Chapter 1, and the image of the Temple cult, as set forth in Leviticus. In line with this view of holiness, the thousands of rules and cases that comprise the Mishnah express in concrete language abstract principles of hierarchical classification, that is, of the proper order of all things. These principles define the document's method and mark it as a work of philosophical character. Not only this, but a variety of specific, recurrent concerns, for example, the relationship of being to becoming, actual to potential, the principles of economics, the politics, correspond point-by-point to comparable ones in Graeco-Roman philosophy, particularly the Aristotelian tradition. This stress on proper order and right rule and the formulation of a philosophy, politics, and economics, within the principles of natural history set forth by Aristotle, explain why the Mishnah makes a statement to be classified as philosophy, concerning the order of the natural world in its correspondence with the supernatural one.

The Mishnah's Philosophy. Method and Propositions: The system of philosophy expressed through concrete and detailed law presented by the Mishnah consists of a coherent logic and topic, a cogent worldview, and a comprehensive way of living. It is a worldview that speaks of transcendent things, a way of life in response to the supernatural meaning of what is done, a heightened and deepened perception of the sanctification of ISRAEL in deed and in deliberation. Sanctification thus means two things, first, distinguishing Israel in all its dimensions from the world in all its ways; second, establishing the stability, order, regularity, predictability, and reliability of Israel in the world of nature and supernature in particular at moments and in contexts of danger. Danger means instability, disorder, irregularity, uncertainty, and betrayal. Each topic of the system as a whole takes up a critical and indispensable moment or context of social being. Through what is said in regard to each of the Mishnah's principal topics, what the system expressed through normative rules as a whole wishes to declare is fully expressed. Yet if the parts severally and jointly give the message of the whole, the whole cannot exist without all of the parts, so well joined and carefully crafted are they all.

The Mishnah's system therefore focused upon the holiness of the life of Israel, the people, a holiness that had formerly centered on the Temple. The logically consequent question was, what is the meaning of sanctity, and how shall Israel attain, or give evidence of, sanctification? The answer derived from the original creation, the end of the Temple directing attention to the beginning of the natural world that the Temple had embodied. For the meaning of sanctity, the framers therefore turned to that first act of sanctification, the one in creation. It came about when, all things in array, in place, each with its proper names, God blessed and sanctified the seventh day on the eve of the first Sabbath. Creation was made ready for the blessing and the sanctification when all things were very good, that is to say, in

their rightful order, called by their rightful name. An orderly nature was a sanctified and blessed nature, so dictated Scripture in the name of the Supernatural. So, to receive the blessing and to be made holy, all things in nature and society were to be set in right array. Given the condition of Israel, the people, in its Land, in the aftermath of the catastrophic war against Rome led by Bar Kokhba (see MESSIAH) in 132–135 C.E., putting things in order was no easy task. But that is why, after all, the question pressed, the answer proving inexorable and obvious. The condition of society corresponded to the critical question that obsessed the system-builders.

Mishneh Torah (Hebrew: "Repetition of the Torah") In the late twelfth century, the first complete systematic compilation of biblical and Rabbinic law, produced by the great Jewish philosopher and legal scholar Moses Maimonides (see MAIMONIDES) (1135–1204). Maimonides organized the commandments of Judaism in fourteen categories, leading his admirers to refer to the work as Yad haḤazakah, that is, "The Mighty Fourteen" (in Hebrew, a wordplay on the expression "the mighty hand;" see, e.g., Deuteronomy 4:34, "Yad" meaning hand and consisting of the two letters of the alphabet that represent the number fourteen). Maimonides' innovations in the Mishneh Torah were 1) his writing in Hebrew instead of Talmudic Aramaic, 2) his use of his own classificatory system instead of the six-part division found in the prior talmudic literature, 3) his willingness to decide the law on the basis of texts other than the Babylonian Talmud, heretofore considered solely authoritative, and 4) his decision to give his view of the law without presenting citations to the original sources or indicating dissenting opinions. Especially as a result of this final innovation, the Mishneh Torah was, upon its appearance, bitterly attacked. Even so, the work was soon accepted as authoritative, and it served as the foundation for all later Jewish legal codes. Despite this success, Maimonides' express purpose in writing the Mishneh Torah, to facilitate study of Jewish law without reference to the original talmudic sources, was not accomplished. Rather, the Mishneh Torah itself became a prime subject of analysis and interpretation, with Maimonides' approach to and understanding of the talmudic texts with which he worked being carefully and completely analyzed much as those texts themselves had previously been studied.

Mishpat   (Hebrew: "justice," "jurisprudence.") By "justice," Judaism understands transactions that are fair, equitable, proportionate, commensurate. That God is just and metes out justice answers Abraham's question at Sodom, "Will not the judge of all the earth do justice?" (Genesis 18:25). In place of fate or impersonal destiny, chance, or simply irrational, inexplicable chaos, God's plan and purpose everywhere come to realization in a rational way. By rational, Judaism understands, commensurate to the moral character of a deed is the reward or the punishment thereof. God above all does justice and binds himself to do justice.

Talmudic Judaism learns that God's will is realized in the moral order of justice from Scripture, where God makes himself manifest. World order is best embodied when sin is punished, merit rewarded. That body of evidence that Scripture supplied recorded human action and divine reaction, on the one side, and meritorious deed and divine response and reward, on the other. It consisted of consequential cases, drawn from both private and public life, to underscore

sages' insistence upon the match between the personal and the public, all things subject to the same simple rule. That demonstration of not only the principle but the precision of measure for measure, deriving from Scripture's own record of God's actions, takes pride of place in the examination of the rationality of the sages' universe. The principle that all existence obeys rules, and that these rules embody principles of justice through specific punishment for particular sin, precise reward of singular acts of virtue, defined the starting point of all rational thought and the entire character of sages' theological structure and system.

Here is sages' account of God's justice, which is always commensurate, both for reward and punishment, in consequence of which the present permits us to peer into the future with certainty of what is going to happen. We note the sages' identification of the precision of justice, the exact match of action and reaction, each step in the sin, each step in the response, and, above all, the immediacy of God's presence in the entire transaction (Mishnah Sotah 1:7):

A   By that same measure by which a man metes out [to others], do they mete out to him:

B   [The woman accused of unfaithfulness, Numbers 5] primped herself for sin, the Omnipresent made her repulsive.

C   She exposed herself for sin, the Omnipresent exposed her.

D   With the thigh she began to sin, and afterward with the belly, therefore the thigh suffers the curse first, and afterward the belly.

E   But the rest of the body does not escape [punishment].

According to Scripture, a woman accused of adultery drinks a potion of "bitter water," which produces one impact for the guilty, another for the innocent. Scripture describes it in this language: "If no man has lain with you … be free from this water of bitterness that brings the curse. But if you have gone astray … then the Lord make you an execration … when the Lord makes your thigh fall away and your body swell; may this water … pass into your bowels and make your body swell and your thigh fall away" (Numbers 5:20–22). The sages' point is that, through the ritual of the bitter waters, perfect justice is achieved, for the punishment for the guilty woman's sin matches, measure for measure, the character of the sin itself.

If sages had to state the logic that imposes order and proportion upon all relationships—the social counterpart to the laws of gravity—they would point to justice: what accords with justice is logical, and what does not is irrational. Ample evidence derives from Scripture's enormous corpus of facts to sustain in sages' view that the moral order, based on justice, governs the affairs of men and nations.

Mitzvah A commandment, precept, or religious duty; the opposite of a sin (*averah*). In the plural (*mitzvot*), the term is used to encompass biblical and Rabbinic law as a whole and, hence, to refer to the complete system of Jewish religious, ethical, and social practices. In contemporary parlance, Jews additionally use the term mitzvah to refer simply to a good deed, whether or not the deed is required by religious law. This usage is presaged in the Talmud, where the term also on occasion is applied to meritorious acts that are not religious obligations.

The Talmud states that there are a total of 613 (Heb.: *Taryag*) *mitzvot*. Two hundred and forty-eight of these, said to correspond to the number of organs in the human body, are positive responsibilities, while three hundred and sixty-five, equaling the number of days in the year, are prohibitions (Babylonian Talmud, Makkot 23b). While medieval and modern thinkers have catalogued the commandments in conformity with these numbers, no agreed upon system has emerged.

Judaism demarcates commandments expressly stated in Scripture from those that have their source in Rabbinic interpretation. Jews further distinguish important commandments from less significant ones (although Judaism in general demands that all *mitzvot* be equally observed). Within these divisions, prohibitions, which ban a certain action, generally are deemed the weightiest of the commandments. This is because transgressing a prohibition results from a physical action on the part of the individual, so that the individual can clearly be said to have sinned. This is unlike the failure to perform a positive responsibility, which may not comprise a sin at all. One positive precept, for instance, states that Jews living in the diaspora should make a pilgrimage to the Land of Israel. A Jew who fails to do so does not enjoy the spiritual benefit of having fulfilled that particular mitzvah. But this failure is in no way a sin.

The obligation to observe the commandments commences at the age of majority, calculated in pre-modern times as thirteen for boys and twelve for girls (see BAR MITZVAH). (In contemporary practice, the age of thirteen generally is used for both.) Prior to reaching the age of majority, children are instructed in the observance of Jewish law, but their failure to do so is not considered a transgression.

While classical Judaism obligates men to follow all the commandments, it exempts women from positive precepts that must be performed at a fixed time, for example, statutory prayer, which must be recited at set times in the morning, afternoon, and night. The exemption of women from such obligations was on the theory that household responsibilities might preclude their fulfilling them at the required time. In Reform, Reconstructionist, and, largely, in Conservative Judaism, this distinction between men and women has been abolished.

Mitzvat 'Aseh (Hebrew: "A commandment requiring an action") A religious duty involving an act of commission, by contrast to a Mitzvat Lo Ta'aseh, a religious duty involving an act of omission or restraint. Thus, the commandment requiring the consumption of unleavened bread on the eve of Passover is a Mitzvat 'Aseh, while the prohibition against consuming leaven during that same festival is a Mitzvat Lo Ta'aseh. The first delineates what one must do, the second what one may not do.

Mitzvat Lo Ta'aseh A religious duty involving an act of omission, restraint. See MITZVAT 'ASEH.

Mitnaged (Hebrew: "opponent;" pl.: *Mitnaggedim*) In the eighteenth century, the designation given rationalists and talmudists who vehemently opposed emergent HASIDISM. Later, the term came simply to refer to non-Hasidic Lithuanian Judaism, with its focus upon talmudic study, retention of the Polish liturgical rite, and its rejection of charismatic leaders such as were found in the Hasidic world.

Mizbeah (Hebrew: "altar") Place near which animal offerings were slaughtered, and on which their blood was tossed; fires were maintained for burning up certain parts of the sacrificial beast and other offerings, e.g., grain and wine; the outer altar of the Jerusalem Temple stood in the open, with a fire maintained on it, and offerings of various kinds, after the daily whole offering at dawn and until the same at dusk, were presented. Only priests could approach the altar and minister there. The power of the altar is to sanctify that which is placed upon it. According to the Mishnah, this applies only so long as what is set upon the altar is suitable for an offering, e.g., sheep or turtledoves but not lions or chickens, which, if put up on the altar, are simply removed therefrom.

Modern Orthodoxy See ORTHODOX JUDAISM.

Mo'ed Hebrew term for a festival or appointed time; name of the second division of the Mishnah and Talmud, devoted to the observance of appointed times both in the home and in the Jerusalem Temple.

Mo'ed Qatan Mishnah tractate devoted to the intermediate days of a festival, with special interest in labor that may or may not be performed between the first and final festival days of Tabernacles and Passover (chaps. 1–2); commerce on the intermediate days of a festival (chaps. 2–3); burial of the dead and mourning on the intermediate days of the festival (chap. 3).

Mohel Ritual circumciser, who performs the rite of BERIT MILAH, which marks the entry of a newborn male into the Jewish covenant with God; not to be confused with a surgeon or obstetrician who performs a circumcision as a medical procedure.

Monotheism The doctrine that there is only one God, who is creator of heaven and earth, who revealed the Torah to Israel, and who, at the end of time, will redeem those that accept his dominion. Judaism is a religion of ethical monotheism, meaning, the one and only God is not only all powerful but also just and merciful. The will of this one, unique God, made manifest through the Torah, governs. Further, God's will, for both private life and public activity, is rational. In place of fate or impersonal destiny, chance, or simply irrational, inexplicable chaos, God's plan and purpose everywhere come to realization. So Judaism identifies God's will as the active and causative force in the lives of individuals and nations. Monotheism is not a matter of arithmetic—one God against many gods. Rather, the Lord, who made Himself known in the Torah, is the one and only God of all the world.

How do monotheism and polytheism differ? A religion of numerous gods finds many solutions to one problem, a religion of only one God presents one solution to many problems. Life is seldom fair. Rules rarely work. To explain the reason why, polytheisms adduce multiple causes of chaos, a god per anomaly. Diverse gods do various things, so that ordinarily outcomes conflict. Monotheism, by nature, explains many things in a single way. One God rules. Life is meant to be fair, and just rules are supposed to describe what is ordinary, all in the name of that one and only God. So, in monotheism, a simple logic governs to limit ways of making sense of things. But that logic contains its own dialectics. If one true God has done everything, then, since He is God all-powerful and omniscient, all things are credited to, and blamed on, Him. In that case He can be either good or bad, just or unjust—but not both. Responding to the generative dialectics of monotheism, Judaism systematically reveals the justice of the one and only God of all creation. God is not only God but also good.

The four principles of Judaism's monotheist theology of a merciful, just God are these:

1   God formed creation in accord with a plan, which the Torah reveals. World order can be shown by the facts of nature and society set forth in that plan to conform to a pattern of reason based upon justice. Those who possess the Torah—ISRAEL—know God and those who do not—the gentiles—reject him in favor of idols. What happens to each of the two sectors of humanity, respectively, responds to their relationship with God. Israel in the present age is subordinate to the nations, because God has designated the gentiles as the medium for penalizing Israel's rebellion, meaning through Israel's subordination and exile to provoke Israel to repent. Private life, as much as the public order, conforms to the principle that God rules justly in a creation of perfection and stasis.

2   The perfection of creation, realized in the rule of exact justice, is signified by the timelessness of the world of human affairs, their conformity to a few enduring paradigms that transcend change (theology of history). No present, past, or future marks time, but only the recapitulation of those patterns. Perfection is further embodied in the unchanging relationships of the social commonwealth (theology of political economy), which assure that scarce resources, once allocated, remain in stasis. A further indication of perfection lies in the complementarity of the components of creation, on the one side, and, finally, the correspondence between God and man, in God's image (theological anthropology), on the other.

3   Israel's condition, public and personal, marks flaws in creation. What disrupts perfection is the sole power capable of standing on its own against

God's power, and that is human will. What humans control and God cannot coerce is the human capacity to form intention and therefore choose either arrogantly to defy, or humbly to love, God. Because humans defy God, the sin that results from their rebellion flaws creation and disrupts world order (theological theodicy). The paradigm of the rebellion of Adam in Eden prevails, the act of arrogant rebellion leading to exile from Eden thus accounting for the condition of humanity. But, as in the original transaction of alienation and consequent exile, God retains the power to encourage repentance through punishing human arrogance. In mercy, moreover, God exercises the power to respond to repentance with forgiveness, that is, a change of attitude evoking a counterpart change. Since, commanding its own will, humanity also has the power to initiate the process of reconciliation with God, through repentance, an act of humility, humans may restore the perfection of that order that through arrogance they have marred.

4   God will ultimately restore that perfection that embodied His plan for creation. In the work of restoration death that comes about by reason of sin will die, the dead will be raised and judged for their deeds in this life, and most of them, having been justified, will go on to eternal life in the world to come. The paradigm of man restored to Eden is realized in Israel's return to the Land of Israel. In that world or age to come, however, that sector of humanity that through the Torah knows God will encompass all of humanity. Idolators will perish, and humanity that comprises Israel at the end will know the one, true God and spend eternity in his light.

Moses   [1] Prophet of Israel, who led the Israelite slaves out of Egyptian bondage and through the wilderness, to the plains of Moab, at a distance from the Land of Israel on the other side of the Jordan. He was not permitted to enter the Promised Land, that is, the land that God promised to give the Israelites though he was allowed to see it from a distance on the summit of Mount Nebo, where he is buried. He was born to an Israelite slave family. Pharaoh, the king of Egypt, had decreed that the Israelites were to murder all their sons. But Moses' mother hid him in the rushes of the Nile, where Pharaoh's daughter found him and raised him as her own son. He was raised as an Egyptian prince. When he was forty, he killed an Egyptian whom he saw oppressing an Israelite, and fled from Egypt to Midian. He married the daughter of the priest Jethro, and, as a shepherd for his father-in-law, encountered a wonder in the wilderness: a bush that burned but was not consumed. God appeared to Moses at the bush and revealed His name to him and commanded him to go back to Egypt and instruct Pharaoh to free the Israelite slaves. This he did, and, after performing various miracles involving plagues upon Egypt for withholding the right to leave, Moses succeeded in leading the people out of Egypt and into the wilderness of Sinai. There, at Mount Sinai, Moses went up and received God's Teaching. [2] *Moshe Rabbenu*: "Moses our rabbi," or: "our master:" Talmudic representation of Moses as sage and rabbi, studying Torah as God's first disciple, teaching Torah to Joshua, his disciple, and onward through time.

Mumar   See MESHUMAD.

Musaf   (Hebrew: "Additional [service]") A service of worship that corresponds to the additional offerings that, while the Jerusalem Temple stood, were presented in the Temple on the Sabbath, festivals, and holy days. The additional service liturgy recounts the Temple offerings on those occasions.

Musar   (Hebrew, literally: "chastise-ment;" "instruction in right behavior," "morality") A movement in modern Judaism emphasizing study and practice of ethical conduct, founded by Israel Salanter (1810–1883).

Mysticism   See QABBALAH.

N

Nabi   See NEBI'IM.

Nashim   (Hebrew: "Women") The third division of the Mishnah, on women and family law, comprising tractates Yebamot (Levirate marriage); Ketubot (marriage-contracts); Nedarim (vows), Nazir (the Nazirite vow), Sotah (the wife accused of adultery), Qiddushin (betrothals); Gittin (writs of divorce). Attention focuses upon the point of disorder marked by the transfer of a woman from the status provided by one man to that provided by another, e.g., from father to husband or, after divorce or the husband's death, from that husband's house back to that of the father. See WOMEN.

Nasi   (Hebrew: "patriarch") In the first centuries C.E., the ethnarch of the Jews, as an ethnic group; principal authority, prince. Title accorded to Judah, Patriarch of the Jews of the Land of Israel, in the late second century, who sponsored the Mishnah and made it the normative law. Recognized as the governor of the Jewish community of the Land of Israel by the Roman government until the early fifth century.

Nathan   Prophet in the time of King David, in ca. 1000 B.C.E. (2 Samuel 11–12). Nathan confronted David after David arranged for the death of his general, Uriah, so that he could marry Uriah's wife, who had become his concubine. Nathan declared, "Have you murdered—and then inherited!" His condemnation of the king's conduct represents the first time that a king was called to account by a prophet speaking in God's name.

Nathan of Gaza   Prophet of Shabbetai

Zvi (see SABBATEANISM), who announced that Shabbetai was the Messiah.

Nazir   Mishnah tractate on the NAZIRITE, with special attention to the vow that he or she takes (chaps. 1–4); the offerings presented by a Nazirite at the end of the period of abstinence (chaps. 4–5); restrictions on the Nazirite: grape and wine, hair-cutting, corpse-uncleanness (chaps. 6–9).

Nazirite   One who, in line with Numbers 6, vows to abstain from wine, haircuts, and contracting corpse-uncleanliness.

Nebelah   (Hebrew: "carrion") Road-kill; beasts that have died of natural causes or through means other than proper, ritual slaughter, which, under the restrictions of kashrut (see DIETARY LAWS), are forbidden for consumption.

Nebi'im   (Hebrew: "Prophets;" singular: *Nabi*') [1] A man or woman whom God has selected as a messenger to deliver his statement; [2] In the Hebrew Scriptures, the prophetic books, comprising Joshua, Judges, Samuel, Kings, Isaiah, Jeremiah, Ezekiel, and the twelve minor prophets: Hosea, Joel, Amos, Obadiah, Jonah, Micah, Nahum, Habakkuk, Zephaniah, Haggai, Zechariah, and Malachi.

Nebo, Mount   Mountain in the plains of Moab from which, before his death, MOSES, forbidden to enter the Promised Land, was able to see the Land.

Nedarim   (Hebrew: "Vows;" singular: *Neder*) [1] Vows in the nature of the statement, "This food is Qorban," meaning, it is to be regarded by me as in the status of an offering and hence prohibited to me; [2] Mishnah tractate on vows; the language of vows, euphemisms, language of limited or nil effect (chaps. 1–3); binding effects of vows (chaps. 4–8); absolution of vows (chaps. 8–11), e.g., by a father for the daughter and the husband for a wife (chaps. 10–11); vows not subject to abrogation (chap. 11).

Neder See NEDARIM.

Nega'im (Hebrew: "dermatological irregularities") [1] Appearance of certain peculiar formations on the skin, signifying uncleanness, e.g., by reason of having gossiped, referred to at Leviticus 13–14; [2] Mishnah tractate on the uncleanness signified by the skin ailment described at Leviticus 13–14, covering marks of the skinailment in general and the bright spot (chaps. 1–8); the boil and the burning (chap. 9); scaly skin (chap. 10); the bald spot on forehead and temple (chap. 10); garments and houses affected by the same marks (chaps. 11–13); the process of purification of a person affected by the skin ailment (chap. 14).

Ne'ilah (Hebrew: "Locking [of the gates]" "closure") Closing service at end of YOM KIPPUR, at nightfall when fast ends.

Nephilim Giants begotten by the sons of God and the daughters of men, as recounted in Genesis 6:4.

Neshekh (Hebrew: "usury") Any fee paid for waiting for the return of money that one has lent; this covers fees in kind, such as free rent, or even fees in personal services. These are absolutely forbidden in transactions between Israelites but permitted between Israelites and gentiles. Israelites may pay interest to gentiles or collect it from them; in interactions with other Israelites, this is strictly forbidden.

Netilat Yadayim Hand-washing prior to meals, not for hygienic purposes but to attain cultic cleanness, corresponding to the priests' state of cleanness before carrying out the rites at the Temple altar. The rite of Netilat Yadayim, in which water is poured from a vessel onto each hand, is carried out before eating any meal that includes bread.

New Age Judaism A term referring to new modes of Jewish practice and belief that emerged in the late twentieth century as a result of Judaism's encounter with the American counter-culture and in reaction to the feeling of many young adults that American Judaism had become stultified and, to be meaningful, needed to be reformulated. The hallmarks of New Age Judaism are a new spirituality, including a mixing of traditional Jewish mysticism (QABBALAH) and the meditative practices of eastern religions, egalitarianism and inclusiveness, and, at base, a belief that, to be meaningful, the religious experience must be personal and participatory.

A central aspect of New Age Judaism is the Ḥavurah, which emerged in the 1960s as a place for serious and intense prayer and study, often centered in a building in which some, or all, participants also lived. A hallmark of the Ḥavurah is the idea that individual Jews can control their own interaction with Jewish practices and sources. This is a conscious rejection of the modern American synagogue, viewed as a place in which most Jewish tasks are controlled and carried out by a few professionals: rabbis, cantors, and teachers. Notably, by the end of the twentieth century, the Ḥavurah had transformed and became a part of synagogue life itself, often comprising small groups of like-minded individuals within the setting of larger synagogue communities. In other settings, the Havurah constituted a model for synagogues that focused on the idea of lay participation, democratic governance, serious adult study programs, and social action projects. In such settings, the rabbi is seen as a teacher rather than an administrator or surrogate practitioner of Judaism.

Alongside the Havurah, New Age Judaism is marked by an increased focus on the education of adults as well as children in the practices, history, and theology of Judaism; decentralized, non-corporate charities, in which individual donors have a direct say in how their money is used; and new styles of Jewish music, using the guitar and combining contemporary pop and folk idioms with Hasidic and Eastern European traditions. This is different from the earlier Reform preference for organ and choir and the Conservative movement's favoring of traditional cantorial music.

Within its ritual practices, New Age Judaism focuses on the personal and on ritual as a path to healing in moments of vulnerability. Thus, ceremonies have been developed for mourning for infertility, abortion, or miscarriage, recovery after rape; rituals similarly have been created to respond to divorce, getting a new job, losing a job, and retirement. While traditional life cycle rituals primarily marked the individual's bonding to Torah and community, these newer ones witness many phases of the individual's life, seeking to bring Judaism's wisdom to bear on all personal times of passage.

Neziqin   Fourth division of the Mishnah, devoted to civil law and damages, the court system and the administration of justice, comprised of tractates Baba Qamma (torts), Baba Mesia (transactions), Baba Batra (partnerships), Sanhedrin (courts of law), Makkot (penalties), Abodah Zarah (dealings with gentiles), Shebu'ot (guilt offerings, oaths), Horay'ot (erroneous decisions of court), Abot, and Eduyyot.

Niddah   (Hebrew: "Menstruating woman") [1] A menstruant, whose status regarding what she may and may not do is defined at Leviticus 15; [2] Mishnah tractate devoted to the uncleanliness of the menstruating woman set forth in Leviticus 15; definition of unclean excretions (chaps. 2–5); rules applicable at various ages (chaps. 5–6); doubts in connection with unclean excretions (chaps. 6–9); dissent of the House of Shammai on the same topics (chaps. 9–10).

Niggun   Melody; traditional tune for prayer.

Nisan   First month of the Jewish year. The first full moon of Nisan after the vernal equinox marks the celebration of PASSOVER.

Nissim   See MIRACLES.

Nissuin   Consummation of a marriage. See HUPPAH.

Noah   The only person from Adam, for the ten generations thereafter, whom God found righteous. On that account, God chose Noah to survive the flood that would wipe out all of humankind on account of its wicked ways (Genesis 6–9). Noah became the founder of a new humankind, and, according to Genesis 10, all the nations of the world go back to his three sons, Shem, Ham, and Japheth (see MABUL).

Northern Kingdom of Israel   The ten northern tribes of Israel, who broke away after Solomon's rule and abandoned Jerusalem and the Temple in favor of an independent state of their own. The northern kingdom of Israel lasted until the Assyrian conquest of 701 B.C.E.

Numbers, Book of Fourth of the Five Books of Moses. The Israelites wandering in the wilderness are portrayed from when they left Sinai to before they entered the Promised Land. The people are depicted as rebellious and ungrateful, and God is represented as sustaining them nonetheless. The work opens with a census of Israel, chaps. 1–4, then the law of the wife accused of adultery, chap. 5; the Nazirite, someone who vows not to drink wine or get a haircut, renunciation taken as marks of sanctification, chapter 6; setting up the Tabernacle in the wilderness and dedicating it, chaps. 7–10; complaints of the people against Moses and God, chaps. 11–14; the offerings of the altar to the Lord, chaps.15, 28; the rebellion of Koraḥ, who opposed Moses, chap.16; the priesthood of Aaron, chaps. 17–18; purity and removing corpse uncleanliness, chapter 19; Moses brings water out of a rock, chap. 20; Israel's wars with the Canaanites and Siḥon and Og, chap. 21; the prophet produced by the nations, Balaam comes to curse Israel in behalf of Moab but stays to bless, chaps. 22–24; the Israelites get involved with Moabite women, chaps. 25; a census, chap. 26; and some miscellaneous items.

O

Ohalot   Mishnah tractate devoted to the uncleanness that is spread by a tent located over the body of a corpse, in line with Numbers 19; centered on diverse modes of imparting uncleanness and sources of uncleanness in general (chaps. 2–3); tents as a medium for spreading corpse-uncleanliness (chaps. 3–16); sources of uncleanliness analogous to human remains (chap. 16). This tractate is complemented by the Tosefta tractate Ahilot, but not commented upon in either version of the Talmud.

Olah   An offering that is wholly burned up on the altar fires in the Temple in Jerusalem, yielding no share of the sacrifice for either the officiating priest or the person in behalf of whom the offering is presented.

Olam HaBa'   (Hebrew: "The world to come") The period beginning at the end of history, with the advent of the Messiah to raise the dead for judgment, the last judgment, and the entry of nearly all the people of Israel to eternal life. Marking the final condition of world order, this period signifies the realization of correct and perfect relationships between God and humanity at large, God and Israel in particular. With those who reject God having been disposed of for eternity in the grave, the age to come finds its definition as the time of total reconciliation between God and Adam. It is the age when humanity embodied in Israel loves God and accepts God's dominion and completes the work of repentance and atonement for acts of rebellion that marred this world in its day.

Resurrection concerns the individual Israelite, with some further implications for the whole of Israel. Then the world to come that follows encompasses all Israel. Resurrection embodies salvation for the private person, the world to come, redemption for the entire holy people, now at the end encompassing all of humankind within Israel. The age, or world, to come (the Hebrew term *olam* may sustain either the locative, "world," or the temporal-ordinal, "age") completes, and necessarily forms the final chapter, of the theology of the Torah. The age that is coming will find Adam's successor in Eden's replacement, that is, resurrected, judged, and justified Israel—comprising nearly all Israelites who ever lived—now eternally rooted in the Land of Israel.

When the sages of classical Judaism speak of the world to come, their language signifies a final change in relationship between God and humanity, a model of how God and humanity relate that marks the utter restoration of the world order as originally contemplated. That is the way humanity and God conduct the cosmic transaction that God had intended from the beginning and for eternity—time having no place in God's ordering of creation. Israel's master-narrative yields this account: Adam loses Eden, Israel, the new Adam, loses the Land, then Israel repents, the dead are raised, Israel is restored to the Land, and eternal life follows. So here the story comes full circle that commences with God's creation of a perfect world defined by a just order.

The world to come concludes the eschatological series that comprises [1] past, [2] present, [3] Israel's collective repentance, [4] the age (days) of the Messiah, [5] days of the war of Gog and Magog, [6] the resurrection of the dead, [7] the judgment, and onward to the last things at [8] the world to come. A single sentence captures the story: *When Israel returns to God, God will restore their fortune in the model of Adam and Eve in Eden.* Importantly, this sentence is explicitly built on the verb-root "return," which in the causative yields the term "restore," and which also lies behind the Hebrew word *teshubah,* "repentance." It thereby defines the condition—the people of Israel's return or repentance—that will lead to the advent of the age to come, which encompasses the action of God's returning matters to their original condition.

Inheriting the Garden of Eden bears precisely the meaning of inheriting the world to come; there is no difference, and the two, Eden and world to come, are, in classical Judaism, interchangeable when sages speak of what happens after death, on the one side, or after resurrection and judgment, on the other. For Israel, entering the world to come after resurrection and judgment marks a home-coming. At the moment of entry into the world to come, humanity returns to its original condition, in God's image, after God's likeness, as the complement and conclusion of creation. Here is the ultimate point of correspondence in classical Judaism's system of perfecting the world under God's rule.

Olam HaZeh This world, antonym of the world to come, *Olam HaBa'.*

Old Age According to Talmudic Judaism, the period of life commencing at 60, ripe old age at 70; a mark of wisdom. Death before age 60 is counted as extirpation, a form of penalty for a sin. Once a person reaches age 60, he or she knows that that penalty has not been incurred for any reason. Age is the requirement of wisdom and understanding, but the value of age depends on knowledge of the Torah. "When sages grow old, their minds

become serene, when the ignorant grow old, their minds become agitated."

Old Testament See SCRIPTURE.

Omer The first sheaf of barley cut in the harvest, offered on the second day of PASSOVER, sixteenth of Nisan at which point the new crops of grain are permitted for use; forty-nine days are counted, on each of which the omer was offered in the Temple, until Pentecost; with the exception of the thirty-third day, this was observed as a period of mourning. See LAG BEOMER.

Oneg Shabbat (Hebrew: "Sabbath delight") Celebration of the Sabbath, often held on Friday night, involving singing and dancing and celebration of the holy day (see MELAVVEH MALKAH).

Oral Torah See TORAH SHEBE'AL PEH.

Orlah [1] Produce of a tree in the fourth year after it is planted; [2] Mishnah tractate on the status of fruit during the first three years after the planting of a fruit tree, during which time, in accord with Leviticus 19:23, the fruit may not be used. In the fourth year, the produce is in the status of Second Tithe, to be brought to Jerusalem and eaten there (see MA'ASER SHENI). The tractate defines a fruit tree as a tree principally intended for food production (chap. 1) and considers issues involving the planting of fruit trees, e.g., does replanting an old tree create a new growth, subject again to the restrictions of Orlah? Mixtures between prohibited and permitted produce are sorted out (chap. 2); the prohibitions against the use of fruit in the first three years of the tree's growth extend to using it for dye or weaving, for fire or coals, or in mixtures (chap. 3). Orlah also means "foreskin."

Orthodox Judaism Movements in modern Judaism that affirm the divine revelation and eternal authority of the Torah, oral and written. It regards the laws of the Torah as God's imperatives and insists on complete obedience to those laws, as interpreted by the great Rabbinic sages. The Torah records things that really happened, words that God articulated to the named prophets, the conditions that God has set forth to make Israel a suitable abode for his presence on earth.

While Orthodoxy is diverse and divided, it may be divided into two main divisions, integrationist and self-segregationist. The former favors the integration of the Jews into the national life of the countries of their birth and regards ZIONISM as integral to Judaism. The latter advocates the social and cultural segregation of holy Israel from other people in the countries where they live, including the state of Israel, and within the self-segregationist camp are communities of Orthodox Judaism that do not regard Zionism as integral to Judaism or that even reject Zionism and the state of Israel altogether. Indicators such as clothing, language, above all, education differentiate integrationist from segregationist Judaisms. Integrationist, or "modern-Orthodox" Jews keep and study the law of the Torah but include in the curriculum subjects outside of the sciences of the Torah. Self-segregationist Orthodox Jews study only the sacred sciences, represented by the literature of the Torah.

Integrationist-Orthodox Judaism originated among Jews who rejected Reform and made a self-conscious decision to remain within the way of life and worldview that they had known and cherished all their lives. They framed the issues in terms of change and history. The Reformers held that Judaism could change and that Judaism was a product of history. The Orthodox opponents denied that Judaism could change and insisted that Judaism, derived from God's will at Sinai, was eternal and supernatural, not historical and man-made. Integrationist-Orthodox Judaism dealt with the same urgent questions as did REFORM JUDAISM, questions raised by political emancipation, but it gave different answers to them. As a result, Integrationist-Orthodoxy formulated a mode of Jewish life that, like Reform, encouraged participation in and enjoyment of the benefits of the modern world. Jews may wear clothing that non-Jews wear, may live within a common economy with non-Jews, and may, in diverse ways, take up a life not readily distinguished from the lives lived by people in general. But even as it permitted this entry into the cultures of the countries in which Jews lived, Integrationist-Orthodoxy insisted, unlike the Reformers, that other equally important aspects of life—diet, the calendar of holy days, and sacred convocations, the content and language of prayer—remain in the category of the sacred and could not be dismissed or changed. See HIRSCH, SAMSON RAPHAEL.

Otot   See MIRACLES.

P

Palestine Secular name of the Land of Israel. Originally the Roman name for the Land of Israel, adopted after the defeat by the Romans of the JEWISH REVOLT of 132–135 C.E. led by Bar Kokhba.

Parah Mishnah tractate devoted to the preparation of purification-water described in Numbers 19, through the burning of a red heifer and the mixing of its ashes with running water. The red heifer is defined (chaps. 1–2); the rite is described in a narrative (chap. 3); the conduct of the rite is then set forth in laws (chap. 4); the purity of utensils used in the rite (chap. 5); mixing the ash and the water (chap. 6); drawing the water (chaps. 6–8); water used for the rite (chaps. 8–9); uncleanness and the purification rite (chap. 9–11); hyssop used for sprinkling the purification water (chaps. 11–12); the rules of sprinkling the water (chap. 12).

Pareve Within the system of dietary regulations, neutral, in the category of neither dairy products (milk, cheese) nor meat, and therefore permitted for preparation and consumption alongside either of those other categories of food. Besides fruits and vegetables, the category of Pareve includes fish and eggs.

Parokhet (Hebrew: "curtain") In the synagogue, the curtain that veils the ark in which the Torah scrolls are kept. In Scripture, the term refers to the curtain that enclosed the Holy of Holies in the wilderness tabernacle (Exodus 26:31–33).

Passover Festival celebrated from the first full moon after the vernal equinox, the full moon of Nisan, that commemorates the Exodus from Egypt, described in the first fourteen chapters of the biblical book of Exodus; with Tabernacles and Pentecost, one of Judaism's three pilgrimage festivals, on which, in biblical times, all Israelite males were obligated to appear at the Temple in Jerusalem (Deuteronomy 16:16). Particular emphasis is upon the unleavened bread eaten by the Israelites as a result of their hasty departure from Egypt (Exodus 12). Passover is celebrated for seven (in the diaspora, eight) days, the first and last day (in the diaspora, two days) of which are holy days and the middle days of which are in the status of HOL HAMO'ED. On the first night (in the diaspora, two nights), the events of the Exodus are relived through a ritual meal, called a SEDER, at which the text of the HAGGADAH is read. During the entire duration of the Passover, Jews are forbidden from consuming, or even possessing, leavened products. Theologically,

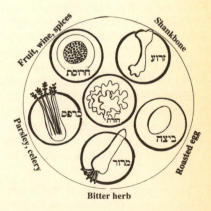

Passover The Seder Plate holding the symbolic foods referred to during the Passover Seder.

Passover signals the beginning of Israel as a free people called from the slavery of Egypt to bondage to the Torah. Passover carries Israel to Sinai freely to accept God's rule in the Torah. Referred to as "the season of our liberation," Passover is where the people Israel starts.

The home-ritual of the Passover Seder tells the story of the Exodus by explaining the symbols present on the table:

The Youngest Present: Why has this night been made different from all other nights? On all other nights we eat bread whether leavened or unleavened, on this night only unleavened; on all other nights we eat all kinds of herbs, on this night only bitter ones; on all other nights we do not dip herbs even once; on this night, twice; on all other nights we sit at the table either sitting or reclining, on this night we all recline.

To this comes the reply:

The Presiding Person: We were the slaves of Pharaoh in Egypt; and the Lord our God brought us forth from there with a mighty hand and an outstretched arm. And if the Holy One, blessed be He, had not brought our fathers forth from Egypt, then surely we, and our children, and our children's children, would be enslaved to Pharaoh in Egypt. And so, even if all of us were full of wisdom and understanding, well along in years and deeply versed in the tradition, we should still be bidden to repeat once more the story of the exodus from Egypt; and he who delights to dwell on the liberation is one to be praised.

The story of Israel then is spelled out, and in the course of the narrative, the people of Israel is defined:

Long ago our ancestors were idol-worshippers but now the Holy One has drawn us to His service. So we read in the Torah: And Joshua said to all the people, "Thus says the Lord, God of Israel: From time immemorial your fathers lived beyond the river Euphrates, even to Terah, father of Abraham and of Nahor, and they worshipped idols. And I took your father Abraham from beyond the river and guided his footsteps throughout the land of Canaan. I multiplied his offspring and gave him Isaac. To Isaac I gave Jacob and Esau. And I set apart Mount Seir as the inheritance of Esau, while Jacob and his sons went down to Egypt."

All of it is deeply relevant to successive generations of Jews who celebrate Passover, for it says who those assembled around the table really are, and for whom they really stand. They in the here and now stand for "our ancestors," Abraham, Isaac, and Jacob.

All those present: Blessed is He who keeps His promise to Israel…for the Holy One set a term to our bondage, fulfilling the word which He gave our father Abraham in the covenant made between the divided sacrifice: Know beyond a doubt that your offspring will be strangers in a land that is not theirs, four hundred years they shall serve and suffer. But in the end I shall pronounce judgment on the oppressor people and your offspring shall go forth with great wealth

So Israel defines itself: a family, a people, saved by God from bondage. Through the natural eye, we see ordinary folk, not much different from their neighbors in dress, language, or aspirations. The words they speak do not describe reality and are not meant to. When Jews say of themselves, "We were the slaves of Pharaoh in Egypt," they know they never felt the lash; but through the eye of faith that is just what they have done. It is their liberation, not merely that of long-dead forebears, that they now celebrate. One theme stands out: we, here and now, are really living then and there. So for example:

> We were slaves in of Pharaoh in Egypt and the Lord our God brought us forth from there with a mighty hand and an outstretched arm. And if the Holy One, blessed be He, had not brought our fathers forth from Egypt, then we and our descendents would still be slaves to Pharaoh in Egypt. And so, even if all of us were full of wisdom, understanding, sages and well informed in the Torah, we should still be obligated to repeat again the story of the exodus from Egypt; and whoever treats as an important matter the story of the Exodus from Egypt is praiseworthy.

The symbols on the table—the unleavened bread, the bitter herbs, the lamb bone, and the like—explicitly invoke the then and there in the here and now. First comes the unleavened bread:

> This is the bread of affliction, which our ancestors ate in the land of Egypt. Let all who are hungry come and eat with us, let all who are needy come and celebrate the Passover with us. This year here, next year in the land of Israel; this year slaves, next year free people.

Now the message is announced in so many words:

> This is the promise that has stood by our forefathers and stands by us. For neither once, nor twice, nor three times was our destruction planned; in every generation they rise against us, and in every generation God delivers us from their hands into freedom, out of anguish into joy, out of mourning into

festivity, out of darkness into light, out of bondage into redemption.

Passover tells the story of Israel through time, not one time only, but all time, and its message is, "God delivers us from their hands," and that is the point that the story of Passover registers:

> For ever after, in every generation, *every Israelite must think of himself [or herself] as having gone forth from Egypt* [italics added]. For we read in the Torah: "In that day thou shalt teach thy son, saying: All this is because of what God did for me when I went forth from Egypt." It was not only our forefathers that the Holy One, blessed be He, redeemed; us too, the living, He redeemed together with them, as we learn from the verse in the Torah: "And He brought us out from thence, so that He might bring us home, and give us the Land which He pledged to our forefathers."

The story relived at the Passover Seder turns Jews' lives into a metaphor, Jews into actors, the everyday meal into drama. What continues today to speak so ubiquitously, with such power, that pretty much everybody who wants in joins in is a message that penetrates to the heart of people who remember the murder, in the near-past, of up to six million Jews, and who know, in the near at hand of anti-Semitism, that they too are a minority and at risk.

Patriarch Ethnarch of the Jews, as an ethnic group; principal authority, prince. Title accorded to Judah, Patriarch of the Jews of the Land of Israel in the late second century, who sponsored the Mishnah and made it the normative law. Recognized as the governor of the Jewish community of the Land of Israel by the

Roman government, pagan, then Christian, until the early fifth century.

Peace offering   See SHELAMIM.

Peah   [1] The corner of the field, left for the poor; in accord with Leviticus 19:9, 23:22; [2] Mishnah tractate on the rules of gifts to the poor. The tractate discusses the corner of the field (chaps. 1–4); gleanings to be left for the poor (chaps. 4–5); the forgotten sheaf (chaps. 5–7); grape gleanings, the defective grape cluster, to be left for the poor (chap. 7); general rules governing gifts to the poor (Deuteronomy 14:28–29), covering when the poor may glean, claims of the poor to produce, and the minimum requirement of poor man's tithe (chap. 8).

Pe'ot   (Hebrew: "corners;" "earlocks") Leviticus 19:27 forbids removing hair at corners of head, interpreted as meaning not to cut earlocks.

Pentateuch   The Five Books of Moses, comprised of Genesis, Exodus, Leviticus, Numbers, and Deuteronomy. See TORAH, HUMASH.

Pesahim   Mishnah tractate devoted to Passover, with special attention to preparation for PASSOVER (chaps. 1–4), involving removing leaven and avoiding what ferments; the Passover offering on the night of the fourteenth of Nisan, including slaying the offering and eating it (chaps. 5–9); and the Passover SEDER (chap. 10).

Peshat   Literal meaning of Scripture; contrasting with *derash,* or homiletical interpretation.

Pesiqta deRab Kahana   A Midrash compilation organized around the synagogue liturgy, with the readings of Scripture for various holy days or special Sabbaths expounded. Like LEVITICUS RABBAH, Pesiqta deRab Kahana formulates propositions that are demonstrated over and over

again through the discussion of specific verses of Scripture. In each case, a single verse stands at the head, and all the other verses that are discussed are brought into relationship with that verse, so as to expound the message of the holy occasion on which that verse is read in synagogue worship.

Pesiqta deRab Kahana follows the synagogal lections from early spring through fall, in the Western calendar, from late February or early March through late September or early October, approximately half of the solar year, twenty-seven weeks, and somewhat more than half of the lunar year. On the very surface, the basic building block is the theme of a Sabbath distinguished by a particular lection or portion of Scripture that is read in the synagogue alongside the everyday cycle of Scripture-readings.

Pesiqta Rabbati   A medieval Midrash compilation that concerns the special occasions of the synagogue calendar. Imitating Pesiqta, the fifty-three compositions of Pesiqta Rabbati present distinct chapters that focus on liturgical occasions. Though derivative and imitative, the document does a creditable job of carrying forward the program of the Pesiqta deRab Kahana's authors and compilers.

Treating the special Sabbaths from Hanukkah in December through the Days of Awe and Tabernacles in the following September and October, the order of passages of Pesiqta Rabbati is the same as those of Pesiqta deRab Kahana. Some of the compositions are lifted from the prior Pesiqta, but most are original. The imitative character of the later Pesiqta—form and substance alike—is proven by a simple fact. The authorship of Pesiqta Rabbati has simply recapitulated the liturgical program of the authorship of the earlier Pesiqta. The main difference between the documents is in the greater cogency attained by Pesiqta deRab Kahana.

Pharaoh   In the Exodus story, the ruler of Egypt. According to the story told in the book of Exodus, the Pharaoh who favored the Israelites died, and a new Pharaoh arose. He feared that the Israelites were too many and strong and would escape from the land, so he enslaved them, and forced them to built for him the store cities of Pithom and Raamses (Exodus 1:5–11). When Moses came to Pharaoh and asked him to allow Israel to leave, Pharaoh persistently refused, resisting the sequence of miracles performed by Moses and the plagues brought on by him, until, finally, with the death of all the firstborn of Egypt, he acceded. But he pursued the fleeing Israelites, who crossed the Reed (Red) Sea on dry land; when Pharaoh and his legions followed, the Sea closed in on them and they drowned.

Pharisees   (Hebrew: *Perushim*; "separatists") A party in ancient Judaism teaching that "traditions" in addition to Scripture were revealed at Sinai. These traditions were preserved among prophets and sages down to the Pharisaic party; the Pharisees espoused the prophetic ideals and translated them to everyday life of Jewry through legislation. The Pharisees were distinguished from other groups in ancient Judaism by their belief in: (1) the immortality of the soul; (2) the existence of angels; (3) divine providence; (4) freedom of will; and (5) the resurrection of the dead.

A sect within Judaism before the destruction of the Jerusalem Temple in 70 C.E., the Pharisees stressed the importance of observing cultic rules of sanctification, including tithing. These involved Scripture's laws concerning the correct preparation of food, including the proper separation of tithes for the support of the priesthood and other scheduled castes. The

book of Leviticus had furthermore laid down rules governing uncleanness, its sources and affects. The result of contact with uncleanness was not hygienic but, mainly, cultic: one affected by uncleanness could not enter the Temple (e.g., Leviticus 12, 13–14, 15). Scripture's concern for cleanness or uncleanness thus derived from the desire to protect the cult and Temple from the dangers seen to lurk in the sources of uncleanness.

By contrast, the earliest purity rules found in the Mishnah, which many assume have Pharisaic origins, deal with domestic matters. The fundamental assumption throughout is that one eats in a state of cultic cleanness not only food deriving from the Temple altar, but meals eaten at home. The further and more important assumption is that ordinary people, and not only priests, keep those rules. Put together, the two premises point to a group that is made up of lay people pretending to be priests, who treat their homes as temples, their tables as altars.

The Pharisaic stress on the sanctification of the home and the paradigmatic power of the Temple for the home points to a extreme position within the priestly paradigm of the Pentateuch. What the priests wanted for the Temple, the Pharisees wanted for the community at large. And in that way the Pharisees carry to a radical extreme the fundamental premise of the priests' Torah of Moses. While we have slight access to positions taken in the first century by the Pharisees on other matters, what we do know allows us to characterize the Pharisaic system as a Judaism of sanctification. No wonder, then, that Pharisees, by all accounts, affirmed the eternity of the soul (as Josephus says) or the resurrection of the dead (as Luke's picture of Paul in Acts maintains). For the way of sanctification led past the uncleanness of the grave to the renewed purity of the living person, purification out of the most unclean of all sources of uncleanness, the realm of death itself. The pattern of sanctification of the everyday brought immediacy to the cosmic pattern of death and resurrection. For the nation earlier and always, and for the individual even now, in the priests' system of the Torah of Moses, as much as in the Pharisees' system, life flowed from the altar, nexus of heaven and earth. See SADDUCEES, ESSENES.

Philosophy Philosophy of Judaism entails the systematization of beliefs into an abstract structure of thought. As an important phase in the history of Judaism, philosophical thinking about Scripture and tradition began in response to the advent of Islamic philosophy. The rise of Islam from the seventh century C.E. brought important intellectual changes, because of the character of Islamic culture. Rabbinic Judaism accommodated that new mode of thought. Specifically, Muslim theologians, responding to Greek philosophy translated (not uncommonly by bilingual Jews) into Arabic, developed a mode of thought along philosophical lines, rigorous, abstract, and scientific, with special interest in a close reading of Aristotle, founder of the philosophical tradition of criticism. Rabbinic sages in the Islamic world then naturalized philosophy within the framework of Judaism. They thought philosophically about religious data; and they engaged with counterparts in Islam and Christianity and produced a common philosophy of religion as well.

The new thinking and the issues it generated represented a challenge to traditional doctrine and thought. While in ancient times, a school of Judaic philosophy in the Greek-speaking Jewish world, represented by Philo of Alexandria, read Scripture in the light of philosophical modes of thought, the sages of the Talmud did not follow that generalizing and speculative mode of thought. They read Scripture within a different framework altogether. But as the Judaic intellectuals of Islam faced the challenge of Muslim rationalism and philosophical rigor, they read Scripture and the Oral Torah in a new way. Their task was to reconcile and accommodate the principles of the one with the propositions of the other. In medieval Islam and Christendom, no Judaic intellectuals could rest easy in the admission that Scripture and science, in its philosophical form, came into conflict.

That is why alongside study of Torah a different sort of intellectual-religious life flourished in Judaism. It was the study of the tradition through the instruments of reason and the discipline of philosophy. The philosophical enterprise attracted small numbers of elitists and mainly served their specialized spiritual and intellectual needs. But they set the standard, and those who followed it included the thoughtful and the perplexed—those who took the statements of the tradition most seriously and, through questioning and reflection, intended to examine and then effect them. The Rabbinic philosophers of Judaism, moreover, were not persons who limited their activities to study and teaching. They frequently occupied high posts within the Jewish community and served in the high society of politics, culture, and science outside the community as well. Though not numerous, the philosophers exercised considerable influence, particularly over the mind in an age that believed reason and learning, not wealth and worldly power, were what really mattered.

Philosophy flourished in a world of deep religious conviction. The issues of philosophy were set, not by lack of belief, but by deep faith. Few, if any, denied providence, a personal God, and a holy book revealed by God through his chosen messenger. Everyone believed in reward and punishment, in a last judgment, and in a settling of accounts. The Jewish philosopher had to cope with problems imposed not only by the classical faith but also by the anomalous situation of the Jews themselves. That situation was perceived within the theology of the Torah that told the story of Israel as Adam's counterpart and opposite, covenanted with God. The question of justice loomed large: How was philosophy to account reasonably for the homelessness of God's people, who were well aware that they lived as a minority among powerful, prosperous majorities—Christian or Muslim?

The new context of intellectual competition contributed a new question: If the Torah were true, why did different revelations claiming to be based upon it flourish, while the people of Torah suffered? Why ought one to remain a Jew, when every day one was confronted by the success of the daughter religions? Conversion was always a possibility—an inviting one even under the best of circumstances—for a member of a despised minority. The search was complicated by the formidable appeal of Greek philosophy to medieval Christian and Islamic civilization. Its rationalism, its openness, its search for pure knowledge challenged all revelations. Philosophy called into question all assertions of truth verifiable not through reason but only through appeals to a source of truth not universally recognized. Reason thus stood, it seemed, against revelation. Mysterious divine plans came into conflict with allegations of the limitless capacity of human reason. Free inquiry might lead anywhere and so would not reliably lead to the synagogue, church, or mosque. And not merely traditional knowledge, but the specific propositions of faith and the assertions of a

holy book had to be measured against the results of reason. Faith *or* reason—this seemed to be the choice.

For the Jews, moreover, the very substance of faith—in a personal, highly anthropomorphic God who exhibited traits of character not always in conformity with humanity's highest ideals—posed a formidable obstacle. Classical conundrums of philosophy were further enriched by the obvious contradictions between belief in free will and belief in divine providence. Is God all-knowing? Then how can people be held responsible for what they do? Is God perfect? Then how can He change His mind or set aside His laws to forgive people? No theologian in such a cosmopolitan, rational age could begin with an assertion of a double truth or a private, relative one. The notion that something could be true for one party and not for another, or that faith and reason were equally valid and yet contradictory were ideas that had little appeal. And the holy book had to retain the upper hand. These, then, are the issues with which the philosophers of Judaism from medieval times to the present day have had to struggle.

Pidyon Shebuyim (Hebrew: "ransoming of captives") Term referring to the religious duty to ransom an Israelite captured by slave traders or kidnappers; according to talmudic law, the community as a whole is responsible for ransoming captives.

Pilpul (Hebrew: "pepper") The method of dialectical reasoning used in the study of talmudic law. See TALMUDIC DIALECTICS.

Pittsburgh Platform Creed of REFORM JUDAISM, issued in Pittsburgh in 1885 by the CENTRAL CONFERENCE OF AMERICAN RABBIS and emphasizing who is

ISRAEL, with that doctrine exposing the foundations of the way of life and world view that the Reform movement at that time conceived:

> We recognize in the Mosaic legislation a system of training the Jewish people for its mission during its national life in Palestine, and today we accept as binding only its moral laws and maintain only such ceremonies as elevate and sanctify our lives, but reject all such as are not adapted to the views and habits of modern civilization.... We hold that all such Mosaic and Rabbinical laws as regular diet, priestly purity, and dress originated in ages and under the influence of ideas entirely foreign to our present mental and spiritual state.... Their observance in our days is apt rather to obstruct than to further modern spiritual elevation.... We recognize in the modern era of universal culture of heart and intellect the approaching of the realization of Israel's great messianic hope for the establishment of the kingdom of truth, justice, and peace among all men. We consider ourselves no longer a nation but a religious community and therefore expect neither a return to Palestine nor a sacrificial worship under the sons of Aaron nor the restoration of any of the laws concerning the Jewish state....

The Pittsburgh Platform takes up each component of the system in turn. Israel once was a nation ("during its national life") but today is not a nation. It once had a set of laws that regulate diet, clothing, and the like. These no longer apply, because Israel now is not what it was then. Israel forms an integral part of Western civilization. The reason to persist as a distinctive group was that the group has its work to do, namely, to realize the messianic hope for the establishment of a kingdom of truth, justice, and peace. For that purpose Israel no longer constitutes a nation. It now forms a religious community.

Individual Jews now live as citizens in other nations. Difference is acceptable at the level of religion, not nationality, a position that accords fully with the definition of citizenship of the Western democracies. The worldview then emphasizes an as-yet unrealized but coming perfect age. The way of life admits to no important traits that distinguish Jews from others, since morality, in the nature of things, forms a universal category, applicable in the same way to everyone. The theory of Israel then forms the heart of matters, and what we learn is that Israel constitutes a "we," that is, that the Jews continue to form a group that, by its own indicators, holds together and constitutes a cogent social entity.

All this, in a simple statement of a handful of rabbis, forms a full and encompassing Judaism, one that, to its communicants, presented truth of a self-evident order. But it was also a truth declared, not discovered, and the self-evidence of the truth of the statements competed with the self-awareness characteristic of those who made them. For they could recognize the problem that demanded attention: the reframing of a theory of Israel for that Israel that they themselves constituted: that "we" that required explanation. No more urgent question faced the rabbis, because, after all, they lived in a century of opening horizons, in which people could envision perfection. World War I would change all that, also for Israel. By 1937, the Reform rabbis, meeting in Columbus, Ohio, would reframe the system, expressing a world view quite different from that of the half-century before.

Piyyut   Synagogue poetry, deriving from the first centuries and through the beginning of modernity.

Pogroms   Race riots against the Jews, involving looting, destruction of property, violence against persons, rape, and murder; common in nineteenth-century Czarist Russia and twentieth-century Germany; a foretaste of the Holocaust. See SHOAH.

Post-exilic   Term that refers to the period in Jewish history following the exile of ancient Israel in 586 B.C.E. by the Babylonians to Babylonia, that is, the area around Baghdad in present day Iraq. The Babylonian exile came to an end after three generations when, in 538 B.C.E., the Persians, under the king and world-ruler Cyrus, restored to Jerusalem the Israelites who had been taken to Babylonia. Later on, in ca. 450, the Persians sent a Jewish viceroy, Nehemiah, who, together with Ezra the Scribe, completed the project of restoring Jerusalem and rebuilding the Temple. "Post-exilic" refers specifically to the period from the restoration, beginning at the end of the sixth century B.C.E., and extending for several centuries thereafter.

Prayer, The   See SHEMONEH ESREH.

Priesthood   (Hebrew: *kohanim*) The caste within the people of Israel designated by God to be in charge of the sacrificial service (see KOHEN). Aaron, brother of Moses, was consecrated as the first Israelite priest, and from him all Israelite priests trace their origin via the male line. Scripture holds that the priests are the tribe of Levi, one of the Israelite tribes. The Levites had no land assigned to them in the Land of Israel; they were counted separately in the census; they were supported by a tithe of the crop of the Land. The Levites were chosen for God's service by reason of their loyalty, when others strayed. This is the picture of Leviticus chapters 8–10. Priests were sanctified and had to keep purity laws and were restricted in whom they might marry; they could not

contract corpse uncleanness except for near of kin. They also gave instruction to the people, administered the Temple, and maintained its facilities.

Priestly Code   One of the sources that stands behind the Hebrew Bible, comprised of priestly narratives, found in the books of LEVITICUS and NUMBERS and parts of GENESIS and EXODUS. Often referred to as "P." Generally deemed to have come to closure after 586 B.C.E., drawing on materials prior to that date.

Promised Land   The Land of Israel, promised by God to the patriarchs, Abraham, Isaac, and Jacob, and delivered into the hands of the people, Israel, by Joshua, the successor of Moses.

Prophet   See NEBI'IM.

Prosbul   A legal formula developed by HILLEL to allow creditors to continue to collect on debts after the advent of the SABBATICAL YEAR, when, according to Deuteronomy 15:2, all debts are cancelled. By making payment of debts mandatory even during the seventh year, the prosbul responded to the problem of people's refusal to loan money to the needy as the Sabbatical approached.

Psalms, Book of   (Hebrew: *Tehillim*) A collection of poems of praise, supplication, and thanksgiving, 150 in all, divided into five books, Psalm 1–41, 42–72, 73–89, 90–106, 107–115. Many of the psalms were used for worship in Second Temple times, from 530 B.C.E. onward. Some of the psalms are called "royal" because in them the king is principal (2, 18, 20, 21, 28, 45, 61, 63, 72, 89, 101, 110, 132); he then represents the Lord to the community. Other psalms are devoted to the sacrificial offerings (47, 93, 96, 97, 98, 99), with the Lord as king. There are also Zion-Psalms (46, 48, 76, 114), celebrating God's presence in the Temple on Mount Zion and his defense of the holy mountain. Psalms are recited in the worship of synagogue and in personal piety.

Pseudepigrapha   "Writings with false attributions." Jewish and Christian writings of the third century B.C.E. through the sixth century C.E. allegedly written by a biblical figure, that rewrite sections of the Bible, or that otherwise resemble biblical texts. These works are not part of the biblical canon of Judaism or any branch of Christianity. The designation Pseudepigrapha was coined by nineteenth-century biblical scholarship.

Purification, Rites of   Chief among the media for the removal of the effects of death is water, which removes uncleanliness of diverse kinds from liquids, persons, and utensils. For water effectively to remove uncleanliness, it must collect naturally and not through human intervention. This defines the water collected in an immersion pool (*miqvah*), the use of which inaugurates the process of purification from uncleanliness. But there also is water that serves to remove corpse-uncleanliness itself, described at Numbers 19:1ff. While most other classifications of uncleanliness are overcome by still water, naturally collected, the water that removes corpse-uncleanliness must be gathered deliberately, in a useful vessel. Preparation of that water requires the highest degree of human alertness and intervention.

The principal medium for removing uncleanliness of other classifications than corpse-uncleanness is immersion in a pool of forty seahs of still water that has collected naturally, beyond the intervention of humanity. The immersion pool, in particular, is comprised of naturally collected rainwater runoff or water from equivalent, natural sources, e.g., seawater. It may not be drawn by human action, but by the indirect action of some person it may be led into the pool on its own, e.g., in a duct. The main point is that it must not be water drawn or in any way collected through human intervention. The immersion pool must be comprised of sufficient water to cover the entire body of a human being. Insufficient pools may be intermingled. One may further pipe valid water, e.g., a higher pool may be emptied into a lower pool to form the requisite volume, but one may not carry or draw the water. Still, drawn water may be used to augment the volume of a valid pool, meaning, a small quantity of drawn water is neutralized by, and fully integrated with, valid water. If water collects in jugs, one may break the jugs or turn them upside down, so the water flows naturally into the cistern, but the jugs may not be picked up and emptied into the cistern.

The point is that water, left in its natural condition, in sufficient volume, pouring down from heaven in the form of rain and collecting on its own upon the earth is God's medium for removing uncleanliness. Uncleanliness that comes about by any cause other than death thus is removed by God's own dispensation, not by humanity's intervention. But as to persons and objects that have contracted uncleanliness from death, nature on its own cannot produce the kind of water that removes that uncleanliness and restores the condition of nature. That can be done only by the highest level of human concentration, the most deliberate and focused action. The water is not still, but flowing water: living water overcoming death. And the water is kept alive, in constant motion, until it is stirred with the ash of the red heifer (Numbers 19:1ff, see PARAH). Any extrinsic action spoils the water; stopping to rest on a bench, doing any deed other than required for the rite itself disrupts the circle of sanctification within the world of uncleanness that the burning of the heifer has required.

Purim Festival commemorating the deliverance of Persian Jews from Haman's plot to destroy them in the fifth century B.C.E., recorded in the biblical book of ESTHER; celebrated on the fourteenth of Adar, generally in March. Purim is marked by reading of the Scroll of Esther (MEGILLAH), the use of noise-makers (ra'ashan) to drown out the name of the enemy Haman, through the exchange of gifts (*Mishloah manot*), and by the giving of charity. The celebratory atmosphere is enhanced by children's and adults' wearing of costumes and, especially in the modern period, by synagogues' or other Jewish institutions' hosting of carnivals. Alongside the merriment, the holiday presents a deep theological message. By recalling the potential danger of DIASPORA life to the Jews, Purim reflects upon the challenge of diaspora living and the danger of

Purim The Megillah (Scroll of Esther) read on Purim, surrounded by symbols of the holiday.

complacency. At the same time, it declares that because the ever-watchful God works quietly to make the right thing happen, the Jewish nation will outlive history. See MEGILLAH.

Q

Qabbalah (Hebrew: "received [knowledge]") A form of Jewish mysticism that originated in southern France (Provence) in the twelfth century and northern Spain in the thirteenth; an important movement in the medieval period, with continued significance within Hasidic Judaism today. The Qabbalah developed from systematic speculations about God's relationship to humanity and developed through new forms of commentary on Scripture that found hidden levels of meaning in the sacred text. Unique to Qabbalah is its theory of the existence of ten divine emanations—called *Sefirot*—which the Qabbalists see as spanning the void between the infinite God and the finite world.

The central document of the Qabbalah, the ZOHAR, was written by Moses de Leon in around 1280 C.E. but attributed to the Mishnaic authority YOHANAN BEN ZAKKAI. De Leon described God as both transcendent and immanent. God, that is, was a creator, separate from the created world and not subject to the forces of nature. At the same time, de Leon saw God as everywhere present and accessible in the form of the *Shekhinah*, a feminine, worldly manifestation of God. The Qabbalah thus rejected central tenets of medieval Jewish philosophy, which defined God as unitary and radically other. By contrast, the Qabbalists envisioned God as comprised of two distinct parts, one of them, the *Ein Sof* ("infinite"), an unknowable, unreachable, concealed aspect, and the other, the *Shekhinah*, a personification of God directly experienced by human beings.

The Qabbalah saw these two aspects of God as connected through the *Sefirot*, spiritual realities distinct from the *Ein Sof* but illuminated by the divine radiance that flows from the concealed part of God. Through these emanations, the essence and being of the *Ein Sof* becomes manifest in the world in which humans dwell. Since the earthly world thus is a visible representation of the upper world, worldly phenomena reveal the nature of the divine. In keeping with this thinking, the Qabbalah goes beyond the biblical conception that humans were created in God's image, recognizing an actual identification between the human and the divine. This identification is represented by the *Neshamah* (Hebrew: spirit), the highest part of the soul, which the Qabbalists understand to be derived directly from God and to be made up in part of the same stuff as God.

In Qabbalistic theory, prior to Adam's sin described at the beginning of the book of Genesis, there was no material world at all. Then the *Sefirot* interacted in perfect harmony. Only after the first sin did Adam take physical form and were the distinct male and female aspects of the *Sefirot* created. According to the Qabbalah, it has henceforth been people's task to restore the harmony in which the world was created. People accomplish this through ritual and moral activity. According to the Qabbalah, every proper deed contributes to the well being of God, reversing the impact of Adam's sin by 1) reuniting the aspects of God represented at the highest level of the *Sefirot* and 2) reestablishing the relationship between individual people and the *Sefirot* as a whole. The Qabbalah thus brought an entirely new function to the religious observances central in Rabbinic Judaism. According to the Qabbalah, such observances do not simply lead to a good and moral life or respond to God's command. Rather, they have cosmic repercussions, helping to reunite God and the *Shekhinah* and so to return the world to the perfect state in which God originally created it.

Qabbalist   Someone who experiences direct encounter with God's presence; a master of Qabbalistic texts. See QABBALAH.

Qaddish   A doxology recited in Aramaic (except for its final clause, which is in Hebrew), used to mark the close of individual sections of public worship services and on occasions when praise of God is appropriate. The Qaddish appears in four main forms: the full and half Qaddish, used as dividers within the liturgy; the mourners' Qaddish, recited by mourners to express their continued praise of God despite the loss they have experienced (see LEVAIAH); and the scholars' Qaddish, recited after the study of Jewish texts, in recognition of the greatness of God's revelation and to bring blessing upon those who study it. The Qaddish also expresses a powerful eschatological hope, with its prayer for the speedy coming of the MESSIAH and the establishment of God's kingdom on earth.

In light of its use by mourners, the Qaddish is today perhaps the best known and most evocative of Jewish prayers. The recognition of the power of this doxology is not however only modern. The Talmud states that recitation of the Qaddish by a son or grandson exerts a redeeming influence on behalf of the soul of a departed father or grandfather. Accordingly, it became the custom for the mourner to recite the Qaddish at each daily prayer service during the first year (in more recent times, eleven months) after death, during which time Judaism understands the soul of the departed to be subject to judgment. The Qaddish is again recited on behalf of the deceased on each subsequent anniversary of the death. The text of the Half Qaddish is as follows:

Leader: Magnified and sanctified be His great name in the world He has created according to His will. And may He establish His kingdom during your life and during your days and during the life of the whole household of Israel, speedily and in a near time! So say, "Amen!"

Response: Let His great name be blessed forever and unto all eternity!

Leader: Blessed, praised, and glorified, exalted, extolled, and honored, uplifted and lauded be the name of the Holy One, blessed be He, above all the blessings and hymns, the praises and consolations, which are uttered in the world. So say, "Amen!" May the prayers and supplications of all Israel be accepted by their Father, who is in Heaven! So say "Amen."

Qal veHomer   A principle of Scripture interpretation that maintains that what applies in a less important case will all the more so define the rule for the more important one; an argument *a fortiori*.

Qedushah   (Hebrew: "sanctification") The third of the Eighteen Benedictions (SHEMONEH ESREH), in which the congregation stands and imagines itself as the earthly embodiment of the heavenly host described in Ezekiel chapter 1. The text of the Qedushah for weekday mornings is as follows:

Leader: We proclaim Your holiness on earth as it is proclaimed in the heavens above. As it is written in Your prophet's vision, they called one to the other and said:

Response: Holy, holy, holy is the Lord

of hosts, the whole world is filled with His glory (Isaiah 6:3).

Leader: Heavenly voices respond with praise:

Response: Praised is the glory of the Lord from His place (Ezekiel 3:12).

Leader: And in Your holy psalms it is written:

Response: The Lord shall reign through all generations; your God, Zion, shall reign forever and ever. Halleluiah (Psalm 146:10).

Leader: We declare Your greatness through all generations, hallow Your holiness to all eternity. Your praise will never leave our lips, for You are God and ruler, great and holy.

The Qedushah is recited only in a quorum of ten. While its basic structure is always as recited on weekday mornings, on Sabbaths and festivals it is expanded to include two additional responses of the congregation, a declaration of the SHEMA (Deuteronomy 6:4), and a citation of God's statement, "I am the Lord your God" (Isaiah 43:4 and elsewhere).

Qehillah   The term used to refer to the organized Jewish community, standing for the institutions of Jewish self-government. Up to modern times, Judaism, like Islam, took for granted that it constituted an autonomous political entity and that its institutions would legitimately use force to effect the teachings of the Torah. On that basis, the Qehillah undertook to govern Jewry in all areas in which Jews were permitted to manage their own affairs, and, before modern times, these encompassed most aspects of everyday life.

Qehillah Qedoshah   (Hebrew: "The holy community") A term used to refer to the community of Judaism. See QEHILLAH.

Qeriyat Shema   (Hebrew: "Recitation

of the *Shema*," see SHEMA) Morning and night, the Jew recites the Shema as one of the principal parts of the liturgy, whether in a quorum of ten (*minyan*) or alone. The recital of the Shema is introduced by a celebration of God as Creator of the world. This is expressed in the morning as follows:

Praised are You, O Lord our God, King of the universe.

You fix the cycles of light and darkness;
You ordain the order of all creation
You cause light to shine over the earth;
Your radiant mercy is upon its inhabitants.
In Your goodness the work of creation
Is continually renewed day by day …
O cause a new light to shine on Zion;
May we all soon be worthy to behold its radiance.
Praised are You, O Lord, Creator of the heavenly bodies.*

The corresponding prayer in the evening refers to the setting of the sun:

Praised are You…
Your command brings on the dusk of evening.
Your wisdom opens the gates of heaven to a new day.
With understanding You order the cycles of time;
Your will determines the succession of seasons;
You order the stars in their heavenly courses.
You create day, and You create night,
Rolling away light before darkness …
Praised are You, O Lord, for the evening dusk.

The first statement of the creed,

*Translations: *Weekday Prayer Book,* ed. by the Rabbinical Assembly of American Prayerbook Committee, Rabbi Jules Harlow, Secretary (New York: Rabbinical Assembly, 1962).

therefore, holds that whatever happens in nature gives testimony to the sovereignty of the Creator.

In Judaism, God is a purposeful and rational Creator. The works of creation justify and testify to Torah, the revelation of Sinai. Torah is the mark not merely of divine sovereignty but of divine grace and love, source of life here and now and in eternity. So goes the second blessing prior to the recitation of the Shema:

Deep is Your love for us, O Lord our God;
Bounteous is Your compassion and tenderness.
You taught our fathers the laws of life,
And they trusted in You, Father and king,
For their sake be gracious to us, and teach us,
That we may learn Your laws and trust in You.
Father, merciful Father, have compassion upon us:
Endow us with discernment and understanding.
Grant us the will to study Your Torah,
To heed its words and to teach its precepts …
Enlighten our eyes in Your Torah,
Open our hearts to Your commandments …
Unite our thoughts with singleness of purpose
To hold You in reverence and in love …
You have drawn us close to You;
We praise You and thank You in truth.
With love do we thankfully proclaim Your unity.
And praise You who chose Your people Israel in love.

Of what does God's compassion consist? The ability to understand and the will to study the Torah. Israel, the holy people, sees itself as "chosen"—responsible to God—because of the Torah.

In the Shema, Torah—revelation— leads the holy community, Israel, to enunciate the chief teaching of revelation:

Hear, O Israel, the Lord Our God, the Lord is One.

This proclamation is followed by three Scriptural passages. The first is Deuteronomy 6:5–9:

You shall love the Lord your God with all your heart, with all your soul, with all your might.

And further, one must diligently teach one's children these words and talk of them everywhere and always, and place them on one's forehead, doorposts, and gates. The second Scripture is Deuteronomy 11:13–21, which emphasizes that if the holy community, Israel, keeps the commandments, they will enjoy worldly blessings; but that if they do not, they will be punished and disappear from the good land God gives them. The third is Numbers 15:37–41, the commandment to wear fringes on the corners of one's garments. The fringes are today attached to the prayer shawl worn at morning services by Conservative and Reform Jews, and worn on a separate undergarment for that purpose by Orthodox Jews, and they remind the faithful Jew of all the commandments of the Lord (see ṢIṢIT).

The proclamation of God's unity is completed and yet remains open, for having created humanity and revealed his will, God is not unaware of events since Sinai. God recognizes human failure and will redeem humanity from its present condition of un-redemption. God as Redeemer in time to come is the doctrine that concludes the twice-daily drama:

You are our King and our father's King,
Our redeemer and our father's redeemer.
You are our creator …
You have ever been our redeemer and deliverer

There can be no God but You …

You, O Lord our God, rescued us from Egypt;

You redeemed us from the house of bondage …

You split apart the waters of the Red Sea,

The faithful you rescued, the wicked drowned …

Then Your beloved sang hymns of thanksgiving …

They acclaimed the King, God on high,

Great and awesome source of all blessings,

The ever-living God, exalted in His majesty.

He humbles the proud and raises the lowly;

He helps the needy and answers His people's call …

Then Moses and all the children of Israel

Sang with great joy this song to the Lord:

Who is like You O Lord among the mighty?

Who is like You, so glorious in holiness?

So wondrous Your deeds, so worthy of praise!

The redeemed sang a new song to You;

They sang in chorus at the shore of the sea,

Acclaiming Your sovereignty with thanksgiving:

The Lord shall reign for ever and ever.

Rock of Israel, arise to Israel's defense!

Fulfill Your promise to deliver Judah and Israel.

Our redeemer is the Holy One of Israel,

The Lord of hosts is His name.

Praised are You, O Lord, redeemer of Israel.

Redemption is both in the past and in the future. That God not only creates but also redeems is attested by the redemption from Egyptian bondage. The congregation repeats the exultant song of Moses and the people at the Reed (Red) Sea, as participants in the salvation of old and of time to come. Then the people turn to the future and ask that Israel once more be redeemed.

The narratives of creation, of the Exodus from Egypt, and of the revelation of Torah at Sinai are repeated, not merely to tell the story of what once was, but rather to recreate out of the raw materials of everyday life the "true being"—life as it was, always is, and will be forever. In reciting the Shema, the faithful Israelite repeatedly refers to the crucial elements of the story that Judaism tells, thus uncovering the sacred, both in nature and in history.

Qibbuṣ Galuyyot   (Hebrew: "Gathering together of the exiles") The eschatological hope that all the people of Israel will be restored to Land of Israel by the Messiah at the end of days; in contemporary political terms, the gathering of Jews from the DIASPORA into the modern State of Israel.

Qiddush   (Hebrew: "Sanctification") The blessing, generally recited over wine, that proclaims the start of the Sabbath or a festival. For the Sabbath the text is as follows:

> Blessed are You, Lord our God, King of the world, who has sanctified us by Your commandments and have taken pleasure in us, and in love and grace have given us Your Holy Sabbath as an inheritance, a memorial of the creation, the first of the holy convocations, in memory of the Exodus from Egypt. For You have chosen us and sanctified us above all nations and in love and grace have given us Your Holy Sabbath as an inheritance. Blessed are You, Lord, who sanctifies the Sabbath.

Qiddush Cup   Cup used for holding the wine over which the prayer of sanctification of the Sabbath or festival QIDDUSH is recited.

Qiddush HaShem   Hebrew: "Sanctification of the name of God;" applies to conduct of Jews among non-Jews that brings esteem on Jews and Judaism; in medieval times the term came to refer especially to martyrdom.

Qiddushin   (Hebrew: "consecration") [1] The ritual that designates a woman as the future wife of a specific man, accomplished when, for a minor, a girl's father, or, for an adult, a woman accepts a token of betrothal worth a minimum sum of money; from that point, the woman is "consecrated" to that man and may not enter betrothal, or even more so, marriage, with any other; if she does, the offspring are *mamzerim*. [2] Mishnah tractate on the betrothal of a woman, sanctifying her to a particular man; more broadly, on the laws of transferring title and ownership of persons and property. The tractate presents a general account of rules of acquisition of persons and property (chap. 1); procedures of betrothal (chap. 2); stipulations in a betrothal, doubts (chap. 3); castes (priest, Levite, Israelite, and other) and who may marry whom (chaps. 3–4). See MAMZER.

Qinnim   Mishnah tractate made up of conundrums on how bird offerings of various classifications are confused and the way in which the confusions are to be resolved.

Qodashim   Fifth division of the Mishnah, devoted to Holy Things, Temple offerings on ordinary days, and the maintenance of the Temple building and the priesthood.

Qodesh   (Hebrew: "holy") Sanctified; antonym of *Hol* ("unsanctified;" "secular").

Qonam   Euphemistic way of saying "Qorban" ("Sacrifice!") the language of an oath. When someone says, "Qonam," it is a means of sanctifying to that person the thing to which reference is made, so that that person may not make common use of the object. See QORBAN.

Qorban   [1] an offering to God on the altar of the Jerusalem Temple; [2] "as an offering," the language of an oath, which assigns to the object subject to the oath the status of a Temple offering, hence makes the object forbidden for secular use by the person who has made the oath.

Qumran   See DEAD SEA SCROLLS.

R

Rabbi   (Hebrew: "my master") In classical Judaism, a master of the Torah with the knowledge necessary to render legal decisions based upon Jewish law. In modern times, the rabbi increasingly has become a synagogue functionary, charged with officiating at worship services, delivering sermons, teaching children and adults, performing pastoral counseling and, overall, serving as the executive officer of a synagogue. The primary requirement of the classical rabbi was knowledge of Talmudic law. The modern rabbi's interactions with secularly educated congregants as well as the role of representing Judaism to the non-Jewish world requires him and, in Reform and Conservative Judaism, her, to have a broad secular education and comprehension of general theology and philosophy in addition to a knowledge of Jewish history and practices.

Rabbinic Judaism   The form of Judaism developed by Jewish sages, called rabbis, in the aftermath of the Roman destruction of the Jerusalem Temple in 70 C.E. Articulated in the Mishnah, Midrashic literature, and in the Jerusalem and Babylonian Talmuds, this form of Judaism is the basis for all later forms of Judaism, which are direct descendants of Rabbinic theology and practice and which grow out of contemporary interpretations of Rabbinic documents.

Rabbinic Judaism emerged in a period in which Jews found their inherited religious ideologies—no less than themselves—under attack. Rome ruled over the Land of Israel, challenging the Bible's notion that the people of Israel would be sovereign in its own land; the destruction of the Jerusalem Temple meant the end of animal sacrifices, previously understood to be the only way the people could atone for their sins; and the disastrous Bar Kokhba revolt of 133–135 C.E. ended any expectation for the Temple's being rebuilt and Jewish life's return to the way it had been throughout the Second Temple period.

Judaism's rabbis responded to this situation by presenting a system of belief and practice that took into account the reality of their day. They developed a form of Judaism that could operate independently of the Temple and Temple priesthood, a Judaism that proclaimed that what mattered most to God was the commitment of each individual Jew, in his or her own home and at his or her own table, to observe the terms of the Sinaitic covenant. By following the divine will in matters of ethics and home ritual, the nation would encourage God to bring about redemption. Salvation, in this view, would come when each and every person correctly observed the Sabbath and the other laws of Judaism, not as the result of a messianic revolt, as had been attempted under Bar Kokhba.

The rabbis' delineation of the laws the people were to follow was based upon their idea that God's revelation to Moses at Sinai, described in the book of Exodus, contained two distinct parts. One component was the Written Torah, embodied in the text of the Pentateuch, which had always been transmitted in writing and made accessible to all of the people of Israel. The other part was the Oral Torah, which was formulated for memorization and transmitted orally by successive generations of sages, ultimately passing into the hands of Rabbinic authorities. In the Oral Torah, the rabbis claimed to possess an otherwise unknown component of God's revelation and so to be direct successors to Moses, whom they called "our Rabbi," thus designating him the first Rabbinic sage. According to this view, only under Rabbinic guidance could the Jewish people correctly observe God's will, since the written Scriptures alone do not provide all of the information needed properly to follow the law.

By the sixth century C.E., with the completion of the Babylonian Talmud, Rabbinic Judaism became the dominant form of Jewish practice and belief. It achieved this stature because of its compelling message, especially in the period of the ascent of Christianity, which claimed to embody a new covenant that replaced the one Jews understood to exist between themselves and God. Rabbinic ideology refocused the people's concerns from the events of political history, which are, after all, beyond the control of the individual, to events within the life and control of each person and family. Under the rabbis, what came to matter were the everyday details of life, the recurring actions that, day-in and day-out, defined who the people were and that demarcated what was truly important to them, namely, the way in which they related to family and community; the ethics by which they carried out their business dealings; the way in which they acknowledged their debt to God for the food they ate and for the wonders of nature. By making such aspects of life the central focus of Judaism, the rabbis assured that, as Scripture had proposed, the people would live as a nation of priests: eating their common food as though it were a sacrifice on the Temple's altar, seeing in their personal daily prayers and in their shared deeds of lovingkindness a

replacement for the sacrifices no longer offered.

Rabbinic Judaism remained messianic insofar as the people understood their religious observances to cause God to act on their behalf. But the Rabbinic system led them to expect no quick, spectacular response. A Messiah would come, but only in some distant future. In the meantime, the observance of the law and rituals of Judaism was its own reward. Creating a community based on the model defined by God through the Torah offered a taste of redemption and of a perfected world. This could be accomplished even though, within the bounds of real history, the Jews frequently had no control over their own destiny.

Those who created Rabbinic Judaism thus responded to the critical theological problem of their day. God's presence and love of the people had always been seen in the military victories that were understood to reflect God's protection of His people. Beginning in the first centuries, it appeared as though such protection no longer could be expected, let alone depended upon. The rabbis accordingly identified a new proof for the existence of God and a new explanation for how the people could be assured of God's support. It found this explanation in a new attitude toward God, which said that the people must create communities and lead their daily lives according to the exacting precepts expressed by God in the Torah. They would experience the presence of God through the perfection of their communities while, at the same time, laying the foundation for the moment when God would fulfill the messianic promise expressed in Scripture, ingathering the Jewish exiles and reestablishing the Israelite nation within its ancestral homeland, where it would be ruled by God through a messianic scion of the house of David.

Rabbinical Assembly   Association of Conservative rabbis worldwide. See CONSERVATIVE JUDAISM.

Rabbinical Council of America   The Rabbinical organization of the Union of Orthodox Jewish Congregations, founded in 1923. See ORTHODOX JUDAISM.

Rachel   Wife of Jacob, the biblical patriarch who succeeded Abraham and Isaac, and daughter of the brother of Jacob's mother, Laban. Jacob worked for his uncle, Laban, for seven years for the right to marry Rachel. Laban tricked him into marrying Rachel's sister, Leah. Jacob then worked another seven years for the right to marry Rachel. Rachel became the mother of Joseph and Benjamin. She died in childbirth, producing Benjamin.

Rahab   Prostitute in Jericho at the time of the Israelite siege conducted by Joshua as the Israelites entered the Promised Land after forty years of wandering in the desert, ca. 1200 B.C.E. She hid the spies that Joshua sent to the city (Joshua 2), because she believed in the power of the God of Israel. She made an agreement that she would protect the spies, and, when the Israelites conquered the city, they would protect her, which they did. She is represented by the later Talmudic Judaism as a virtuous woman and the mother of honorable descendants.

Rashi   Rabbi Solomon Isaac of Troyes, France, 1040–1105, the first letters of whose name yields the popular acronym. Rashi wrote the most influential commentaries in Judaism to the Hebrew Scriptures and the Babylonian TALMUD. His reading of these two foundation documents, the written and the oral Torah, respectively, forms the point of departure for all subsequent study. On the Hebrew Scriptures, his commentary is eclectic, gathering and arranging received comments into a collage of authoritative interpretation. On the Babylonian Talmud, the commentary is pedagogical and analytical, explaining the sense of words and the meaning of passages. Since Rashi's commentary on the Torah is the one thing Jews study along with Scripture, what Judaism teaches about the Pentateuch is mediated to the pious through Rashi's selection and arrangement of the received tradition. Since his commentary to the Babylonian Talmud is the primer that affords access to that document, here too what the pious learn about that authoritative document is defined by Rashi. He therefore may be said to have defined the religious world of Judaism from his time to the present.

Re'iyyah   (Hebrew: "Appearance offering") Offering presented on the pilgrim festivals of PASSOVER, SHABU'OT, and Tabernacles (see SUKKOT) by those who go up to the Temple of Jerusalem to be seen by God. On these occasions, families present the appearance offering and the festal offering, an obligatory burnt offering and peace offerings, respectively. The obligatory appearance offering is identified by the sages of Talmudic Judaism in Deuteronomy 16:14–17. The passages that refer to celebrating a festival (*ḥag*) are deemed to pertain to the festal offering (*ḥagigah*). Two matters then concern the law, first, the details of the pilgrims' offerings, second, the attainment, by pilgrims, of cultic cleanness to permit their participation in the cult and their eating their share of the Holy Things of the altar.

Rebbe   Title for a Hasidic master, also called a Ṣaddiq. While the term Rebbe is a variant of the more familiar title Rabbi, the two types of religious leaders are distinct. The Rebbe is a wonder-worker and holy man who functions as his disciples' spiritual mentor and guide and, through his prayers, is understood to be a particularly efficacious intermediary between man and God. This is different from the Rabbi, who in the classical tradition is viewed primarily as a legal scholar and arbiter of Jewish law. See ṢADDIQ.

Reconstructionist Judaism   A twentieth-century North American Jewish movement inspired by the teachings of Mordecai Kaplan (1881–1983), an Orthodox ordained rabbi who taught from 1909–1963 at the Conservative movement's Jewish Theological Seminary. Reconstructionism was formally organized in 1940 on the foundation of the Society for the Advancement of Judaism, which had been created by Kaplan in 1922. Its seminary, the Reconstructionst Rabbinical College, was founded in Philadelphia in 1968. Organized under the umbrella of the Federation of Reconstructionist Congregations and Ḥavurot, Reconstructionism is by far the smallest of North America's several Jewish movements.

Reconstructionism advances Kaplan's view that Judaism is a social rather than spiritual phenomenon. It rejects traditional theistic claims and notions of the supernatural, viewing God, rather, as a force that promotes justice, goodness, and truth. In line with this disavowal of the traditional notion of God, Reconstructionism also denies the concept of chosenness, so central in traditional Jewish theology. In place of concepts of God and chosenness, Reconstructionism focuses upon community as the center of Jewish life. It holds that all Jewish activity, including adherence to the law, which Kaplan affirmed, should be designed to promote the community of Judaism, which Kaplan referred to as a civilization, the people of which are the source of authority and of their own salvation.

Rejecting the concept of God as a sovereign creator, Reconstructionism adjures contemporary Jews to follow the practices of Jewish tradition for reasons that make sense now. Jewish practice, that is, is to be "reconstructed" so as to express values and meanings appropriate within the lives of Jews today. Prayer and ritual, in particular, are to be rethought in order to maximize the impact they have on the individual, not because they affect God. In light of Kaplan's understanding of the sociological nature of Judaism, he imagined the synagogue not just as a place of worship but as a community center, where study, art, drama, physical exercise, and a range of social activities could take their proper place as central aspects of the Jewish experience. This vision has been largely realized within the contemporary Reconstructionist movement.

Reform Judaism   Reform Judaism, also called Liberal or Progressive Judaism, sets forth a Judaic religious system that takes as its critical task the accommodation of Judaism to political changes in the status of the Jews from the late eighteenth century onward. These changes, particularly in Western Europe and the U.S.A., accorded to Jews the status of citizens like other citizens of the nations in which they lived. But they denied the Jews the status of a separate, holy people, living under its own laws and awaiting the Messiah to lead it back to the Holy Land at the end of history. Reform Judaism insisted that change in the religion, Judaism, in response to new challenges represented a valid continuation of that religion's long-term capacity to evolve. Reform Judaism thus denied that any version of the Torah enjoyed eternal validity. It affirmed that Jews should adopt the politics and culture of the countries in which they lived, preserving differences of only a religious character, narrowly construed.

The Reformers stated explicitly that

theirs would be a Judaism built on the facts of history. These would guide Jews to the definition of what was essential and what could be dropped. History then formed the court of appeal. CONSERVATIVE JUDAISM, also called the Historical School, took the same position, but reached different conclusions. History would show how change could be effected, and the principles of historical change would then govern. Orthodoxy met the issue in a different way, maintaining that Judaism was above history, not a matter of mere historical fact at all.

Reform Judaism grew beginning in the nineteenth century out of changes, called reforms, in minor aspects of public worship in the synagogue. Those who promoted these changes maintained that historical precedent legitimated change, and they rested their case on an appeal to the authoritative texts. Change, they thus argued, is legitimate, and their changes in particular wholly consonant with the law, or the tradition, or the inner dynamics of the faith, or the dictates of history, or whatever out of the past could justify their actions. The laymen who made the changes tried to demonstrate that the changes fit in with the law of Judaism. They took the trouble because Reform, even at the outset, claimed to restore, to continue, to persist in, the received pattern of the evolution of Judaism. The justification of change always invoked precedent. People who made changes had to show that the principle that guided what they did was not new, even though the specific things they did were. So to lay down a bridge between themselves and their past they laid out beams resting on deep-set piles. The foundation of change was formed of the bedrock of precedent. And more still: change restores, reverts to an unchanging ideal. So Reform claimed not to change at all but only to regain the correct state of

affairs, one that others, in the interval, themselves have changed. That forms the fundamental attitude of mind of the people who make changes and call the changes Reform. The appeal to history, a common mode of justification in the politics and theology of the nineteenth century, therefore defined the principal justification for the new Judaism: it was new because it renewed the old and enduring, the golden Judaism of a mythic age of perfection. Arguments on precedent drew the Reformers to the work of critical scholarship as they settled all questions by appeal to the facts of history.

Repentance   The Hebrew word is *teshubah*, from a root meaning "return," and the concept is generally understood to mean, "returning to God from a situation of estrangement." The turning is not only from sin, for sin serves as an indicator of a deeper pathology, which is utter estrangement from God. *Teshubah* thus involves not humiliation but reaffirmation of the self in God's image. It follows that repentance in Judaism forms a theological category encompassing moral issues of action and attitude, wrong action, arrogant attitude, in particular. Repentance forms a step in the path to God that starts with the estrangement represented by sin: doing what I want, instead of what God wants, thus rebellion and arrogance. Sin precipitates punishment, whether personal for individuals or historical for nations, punishment brings about repentance, which, in turn, leads to atonement and, it follows, reconciliation with God. That sequence of stages in the moral regeneration of sinful humanity, individual or collective, defines the context in which repentance finds its natural home.

The conception of repentance—regretting sin, determining not to repeat it, seeking forgiveness for it—defines the key to the moral life with God. No single component of the human condition takes higher priority in establishing right relationship with God, and none bears more profound implications for this-worldly attitudes and actions; the entire course of a human life, filled as it is with the natural propensity to sin, that is, to rebel against God but comprised also by the compelled requirement of confronting God's response, punishment for sin, takes its direction at the act of repentance, the first step in the regeneration of the human condition as it was meant to be. The concept takes on specificity when atonement comes to the fore: in the Temple, atonement involved correct offerings for sin; for the prophets, repentance would characterize the entire nation, Israel, come to its senses in the aftermath of God's punishment, and, in the Talmudic literature, repentance takes on a profoundly this-worldly, social sense. But in all statements of the matter, the single trait proves ubiquitous: repentance defines a stage in the relationship of humans and God, inclusive of repentance to one's fellow for sin against him or her.

There is no such thing as preemptive atonement, as Mishnah Yoma 8:9 states explicitly:

A He who says, "I shall sin and repent, sin and repent"—

B they give him no chance to do repentance.

C [If he said,] "I will sin and the Day of Atonement will atone"—the Day of Atonement does not atone.

D For transgressions done between man and the Omnipresent, the Day of Atonement atones.

E For transgressions between man and man, the Day of Atonement atones, only if the man will regain the good will of his friend.

The process of reconciliation with God encompasses a number of steps and components, not only repentance; and repentance, for its part, does not reach concrete definition in the formulation of the process. A sin offering in the Temple in Jerusalem, presented for unintentional sins, atones, and therein we find the beginning of the definition of repentance. It lies in the contrast between the sin offering at A, that is, atonement for unintentional sin, and those things that atone for intentional sin, which are two events, on the one side, and the expression of right attitude, *teshubah*, returning to God, on the other. The role of repentance emerges in the contrast with the sin offering; what atones for what is inadvertent has no bearing upon what is deliberate. The willful sin can be atoned for only if repentance has taken place: genuine regret, a turning away from the sin after the fact, therefore transforming the sin from one that is deliberate to one that is, if not unintentional beforehand, then, at least, unintentional afterward. Then death, on the one side, or the Day of Atonement, on the other, work their enchantment.

Forgiveness is available to all who repent, and the hand of God is continually stretched out to those who seek atonement (Babylonian Talmud Pesaḥim 119a). Moreover, recognizing the dramatic change of behavior and intense commitment to God's will that stand behind true repentance, Judaism praises those who have sinned and repented even beyond those who have never sinned: "In a place in which those who repent stand, those who are completely righteous cannot stand" (Babylonian Talmud Berakhot 34b).

In Jewish thought, repentance always is possible, even on the day of death. The only requirement is that the desire to repent be serious and that the individual forsake his or her sinful ways. Atonement is not achieved through the pronouncing of a linguistic formula or through simple participation in a rite of expiation. It depends, rather, upon a true commitment to changing one's life, turning from sin, and engaging in proper behavior before God.

Resurrection of the Dead   (Hebrew: *Tehiyat HaMetim*) In classical Judaism, an aspect of the future fulfillment of God's promises, to occur at the time God judges all human beings and initiates a messianic age. The doctrine of the resurrection of the dead emerged in Judaism as a produce of post-biblical Israelite and Greco-Roman thought. The Hebrew Bible expresses no such doctrine. It views God as the source of life and death, who may rescue a soul from deadly-danger (e.g., Psalms 49:15) but who does not actually revive people from death. The Rabbinic view, by contrast, depends upon the single biblical reference to resurrection (Daniel 12:2: "Many of those who sleep in the dust will awake"), and takes up an emerging post-biblical concern with this concept (see, e.g., 2 Maccabees 7:9; I Enoch 22, 90:33, 91:10, 92:3, and the probably later chapters 30–31). Based upon this foundation, the Rabbinic doctrine of resurrection took firm hold with the ascent of Pharisaism after the destruction of the Second Temple in 70 C.E., in particular with the decline of the Sadducees, who had rejected the notion of resurrection (see Acts 23:8, Matthew 22:23).

The centrality of resurrection in Jewish thought is indicated by Mishnah Sanhedrin 10:1, which lists as the first of those who have no portion in the world to come anyone who denies the origin in the Torah itself of belief in resurrection of the dead. Other sources dispute not the fact of resurrection but its mechanics. Babylonian Talmud Rosh Hashanah 16b–17a states that, on the day of judgment, three groups will arise: the thoroughly righteous, the thoroughly wicked, and those in the middle. The righteous immediately are sealed for eternal life, while the wicked are assigned to hell. The fate of those in the middle however is subject to dispute. Some authorities hold that they first are sent to hell, where they scream in prayer and are redeemed; others hold that, as a result of God's mercy, they share the fate of the thoroughly righteous. Elsewhere, the Talmud describes the process of resurrection as like the growth of a grain of wheat (Sanhedrin 90b, Ketubot 111b). Berakhot 60b describes resurrection as the reuniting of the soul with the dead body, and some sources hold that a small, incorruptible part of the body, or even a small amount of rotted flesh, will serve as the material from which a new body is fashioned.

The doctrine of resurrection has a prominent position in Jewish liturgy, forming the focus of the second benediction of the Amidah (see SHEMONEH ESREH), recited in all worship services. This prayer proclaims that God "causes death, gives life, and makes salvation spring forth; He makes the dead live and keeps faith with those who sleep in the dust." It concludes by praising God as one who resurrects the dead.

Reward and Punishment   Judaism holds that God's will is realized in the moral order of justice, involving reward and punishment. The principle is that all being conforms to rules, and that there is an exact punishment in response to each sin and a precise reward for each act of virtue. The Rabbinic sages thus deemed it a fact that humans live in a world in which good is rewarded and evil punished. Further, it was not enough to show that sin or crime provoke divine response, that God penalizes them. More than this, the penalty must fit the crime, measure must match measure, and the more exact the result to the cause, the more compelling the proof of immediate and concrete justice as the building block of world order that sages would put forth on the basis of Scripture.

The principle of commensurate reaction to each action extends also to God's response to Israel's atonement. Israel is punished for its sin. But when Israel repents and God forgives Israel and restores the holy people's fortunes, then that same principle that all things match takes over. This is to say that, when Israel sins, it is punished through that with which it sins, but, upon atonement, it also is comforted through that with which it has been punished. Here is a remarkably successful exposition in which sages assemble out of Scripture facts that, all together, demonstrate the moral order of reward and punishment, along with the merciful character of God and God's justice (Pesiqta deRab Kahana XVI:XI.1):

A "[Comfort, comfort my people, says your God.] Speak tenderly to the heart of Jerusalem and declare to her [that her warfare is ended, that her iniquity is pardoned, that she has received from the Lord's hand double for all her sins]" (Isaiah 40:1–2).

B When they sinned with the head, they were smitten at the head, but they were comforted through the head.

C When they sinned with the head: "Let us make a head and let us return to Egypt" (Numbers 14:4).

D ... they were smitten at the head: "The whole head is sick" (Isaiah 1:5).

E ... but they were comforted through the head: "Their king has passed before them and the Lord is at the head of them" (Micah 2:13).

The triplet of sin, punishment, and comfort is applied first to the head, and, in the continuation of the passage, to the other principal parts of the body. The point of the passage is to prove, through the exposition of God's exact response to human action, that immediate and concrete justice is the building block of world order.

Rosh Hakkeneset (Hebrew: "Head of the synagogue") In medieval through early modern Judaism, the individual responsible for the synagogue worship and maintenance of the building and communal affairs; collected charity funds and donations for Jews in the Holy Land.

Rosh Hashanah [1] The Jewish New Year, the first of Tishrei, marking the birthday of God's creation of the world. On this occasion, God asserts his sovereignty and judges the world for the coming year. The holiday is marked by synagogue worship and, in particular, the sounding of the SHOFAR, symbolically awakening the community to the need to atone for sin. The idea of God's sovereignty is expressed in this liturgical passage:

> Our God and God of our fathers, rule over the whole world in Your honor ... and appear in Your glorious might to all those who dwell in the civilization of Your world, so that everything made will know that You made it, and every creature discern that You have created him, so that all in whose nostrils is breath may say, "The Lord, the God of Israel is king, and His kingdom extends over all."

The concepts of divine sovereignty, divine memory, and divine disclosure correspond to creation, revelation, and redemption. That is, God created the world and rules, God is made self-manifest in the Torah, and God will redeem humanity in the end of days from the condition of sin and death, and accord eternal life to his dominion. Sovereignty is established by creation of the world. Judgment depends upon law: "From the beginning You made this, Your purpose known...." And, therefore, since people have been told what God requires of them, they are judged:

> On this day, sentence is passed upon countries, which to the sword and which to peace, which to famine and which to plenty, and each creature is judged today for life or death. Who is not judged on this day? For the remembrance of every creature comes before You, each man's deeds and destiny, words and way ....

As this story of judgment unfolds and people grow reflective, the Days of Awe seize the imagination: I live, I die, sooner or later it comes to all. The call for inner contemplation implicit in the mythic words elicits deep response.

The theme of revelation is further combined with redemption; the ram's horn, or shofar, which is sounded in the synagogue during daily worship for a month before the Rosh Hashanah festival, serves to unite the two:

> You did reveal Yourself in a cloud of glory.... Out of heaven You made them [Israel] hear Your voice ... Amid thunder and lightning You revealed Yourself to them, and while the Shofar sounded You shined forth upon them.... Our God and God of our fathers, sound the great Shofar for our freedom. Lift up the ensign to gather our exiles.... Lead us happily to Zion Your city, Jerusalem the place of Your sanctuary.

The complex themes of the New Year, the most theological of Jewish holy occasions, thus weave together the tapestry of a highly charged moment in a world subject to the personal scrutiny of a most active God.

[2] Rosh Hashanah is a Mishnah tractate on the celebration of the New Year; the designation of the new month through the year, testimony as to the appearance of the new moon (chaps. 1–3); the shofar, or ram's horn, sounded on the New Year (chaps. 3–4)

Rosh Ḥodesh   (Hebrew: "New Moon") The first day of the month, celebrated in the synagogue as a minor holiday, with the recitation of half-HALLEL, a special Torah reading, and the chanting of the MUSAF service (commemorating the additional sacrifices offered on Rosh Ḥodesh when the Jerusalem Temple stood). Its date was originally determined by an actual sighting of the new moon; since the first centuries, Rosh Ḥodesh has been established based upon a fixed calendar. It may be celebrated over one or two days, insofar as the lunar month is twenty-nine and a half days long.

Rosh Yeshivah   Head of a Talmudic academy.

Ruth, Book of   Biblical book about a gentile who becomes part of the people of Israel and accepts the dominion of the one God. Ruth was a Moabite who married a Judean resident in Moab. After her husband died, she remained loyal and, giving up her own people and land, moved to Judea with her mother-in-law, Naomi. She met and married Boaz, a kinsman of her deceased husband, and with him produced Obed, grandfather of David; hence she was the ancestress of the Messiah of the house of David. Some authorities claim that the book was designed as a slur on the ancestry of the House of David.

Ruth Rabbah   A Rabbinic commentary on the book of Ruth that makes the paramount points that [1] Israel's fate depends upon its proper conduct toward its leaders; [2] the leaders must not be arrogant; [3] the admission of the outsider depends upon the rules of the Torah; [4] the proselyte is accepted because the Torah makes it possible to do so, and the condition of acceptance is complete and total submission to the Torah; [5] those proselytes who are accepted are respected by God and are completely equal to all other Israelites; those who marry them are masters of the Torah, and their descendants are masters of the Torah; [6] what the proselyte accomplishes is to take shelter under the wings of God's presence, and the proselyte who does so stands in the royal line of David, Solomon, and the Messiah. Over and over again, the point is made that Ruth the Moabite, perceived by the ignorant as an outsider, enjoyed complete equality with all other Israelites, because she had accepted the yoke of the Torah, married a great sage, and, through her descendants, produced the sage king, David (see DAVID, KING).

S

Saadya ben Joseph Alfayumi (882–942) Born in Egypt, Saadya became the leader or "Gaon" of the Babylonian Jewish community. He issued virulent attacks against the powerful Karaite movement, which rejected the authority of Rabbinic Judaism. Saadya is reputed to be the first medieval philosopher to write monographs on topics of Jewish law and the first to write in Arabic. Saadya was also the first Jew to elaborate systematic and formal proofs for the existence of God. He took an interest in liturgy, grammar, and astrology. His theological and mystical writings on the *Shekhinah* (divine presence) and the *Ruah haQodesh* (spirit of God) influenced medieval HASIDISM and KABBALAH. He is best known for his major philosophical work, *The Book of Beliefs and Opinions*, for his systematic compilation of the prayer book, and for his liturgical poems.

Sabbateanism A seventeenth-century Judaic messianic movement organized around the figure of Shabbetai Zvi (1626–1676). The Sabbatean movement defined the Messiah not as a sage who kept and embodied the law but as the very *opposite*, as a holy man who violated the law in letter and in spirit. In positing a messiah in the mirror-image of the sage-messiah of Rabbinic Judaism, the Sabbatean movement, like KARAISM, paid its respects to the received system. To be sure, Shabbetai Zvi's followers depicted him as the embodiment of God and the fulfillment of the Torah. Faith in him was portrayed as faith in God incarnate, which is the essence or spirit of the law. But his enemies did not see matters that way. On this matter, Professor Elliot Wolfson states, "While there

is clearly an antinomian dimension to Sabbateanism, it seems more accurate to speak of his breaking of the law as the fuller expression of the law."

Born in Smyrna/Ismir, Shabbetai Zvi mastered Talmudic law and lore and enjoyed respect for his learning even among his opponents. A manic-depressive, during his manic periods he deliberately violated religious law, in actions called, in the doctrine of his movement, "strange or paradoxical actions." In depressed times he chose solitude "to wrestle with the demonic powers by which he felt attacked and partly overwhelmed." During a period of wanderings in Greece and Thrace, he placed himself in active opposition to Jewish law, declaring the commandments to be null and saying a benediction "to Him who allows what is forbidden." In this way he distinguished himself even before his meeting with the disciple who organized his movement, NATHAN OF GAZA. In 1665, the two met and Nathan announced to Shabbetai that the latter was the true Messiah. This independent confirmation of Shabbetai's own messianic dreams served, in Nathan's doctrine, to situate the Messiah's soul within the Qabbalistic doctrine. In May, 1665, Shabbetai announced himself as the Messiah, and various communities, hearing the news, split in their response to that claim. Leading rabbis opposed him, others took a more sympathetic view. Nathan proclaimed that the time of redemption had come. In 1666, the grand vizir offered Shabbetai the choice of accepting Islam or imprisonment and death. On September 15, 1666, Shabbetai converted to

Islam. Nathan of Gaza explained that the apostasy marked a descent of the Messiah to the realm of evil, outwardly to submit to its domination but actually to perform the last and most difficult part of his mission by conquering that realm from within.

The Messiah was engaged in a struggle with evil, just as, in his prior actions in violating the law, he undertook part of the labor of redemption. The apostate Messiah would then form the center of the messianic drama, meant to culminate, soon enough, in the triumph. Down to his death in 1672, Shabbetai Zvi carried out his duties as a Muslim and also observed Jewish ritual. He went through alternating periods of illumination and depression, and, in the former periods, founded new festivals and taught that accepting Islam involved "the Torah of grace," as against Judaism, "the Torah of truth." The Sabbatean heresy found its focus and definition in its opposition to the Rabbinic dogma that the Messiah would qualify as a great sage, in the model of Moses, called by sages, "our Rabbi." How better revolt against Rabbinic Judaism than at the very heart of its doctrine, by labeling the Messiah an anti-sage? But that attests to the power of Rabbinic Judaism to shape the imagination even of its foes.

Sabbath   The seventh day, sanctified as a day of rest, on which all work is prohibited. The Sabbath begins before sundown on Friday evening and continues until after sundown on Saturday night. Like all Jewish holy days, its onset is marked with the lighting of candles. The end of the Sabbath is marked by the HABDALAH ceremony, which praises God for the special blessings by which God has distinguished Israel from all other peoples and the Sabbath from all other days. Along with the prohibition against labor of any kind, including cooking, the Sabbath is

marked by special synagogue worship services. The Sabbath also involves a series of home rituals, revolving primarily around the family's participation in three festive meals. These comprise Friday night dinner, lunch on Saturday, and a third Sabbath meal (SEUDAH SHELISHIT) which takes place before the conclusion of the Sabbath on Saturday afternoon or evening. Along with special blessings, including the Sabbath Qiddush and, on Friday evening, parents' blessing of their children, these meals are marked as joyous celebrations through the singing of special Sabbath hymns (Zemirot).

According to Genesis 2:1–3, the Sabbath commemorates God's completion of the creation of a perfect world, on which occasion God himself rested. Exodus 20:8–11 states that, on this model, on the seventh day, all creation must rest. But Scripture also describes the Sabbath as a memorial to the Exodus from Egypt (Deuteronomy 5:12–15). Just as God released the people of Israel from Egyptian slavery, so the people, along with their own rest on the seventh day, must assure that all members of society, and

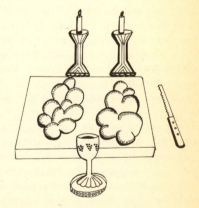

Sabbath   The Friday night Sabbath table featuring candlesticks, two loaves of ḥallah, and a qiddush cup.

even domesticated animals, are similarly released from work.

In theological terms, the Sabbath commemorates God's creation of a perfect world, in which God put Adam in Eden and asked only for his love, realized in obedience to a single commandment of restraint. But, through rebellion, Adam lost Eden. For its part, ancient ISRAEL, similarly, conquered the Land promised by God, so fulfilling the divine plan for the nation, but, through disobedience to God's commandments, the people of Israel also lost that Land. How are they to regain it and so to experience the fulfillment of God's convenantal promise? It is through the people's restoring the conditions that prevailed when God and Adam were last together, in Eden, at the completion of creation, when all existed exactly as God meant it to be. So the theology of the Sabbath intertwines an image of Adam and Eden with the history of the people of Israel and their Land. The story of Adam's yearning to recover Eden is embodied in Israel's re-creation of Paradise on the Sabbath day. It is Israel's task to restore the perfection of the world on that first Sabbath of Creation when God saw all that he had made and declared it "very good." With this model in mind, the people of Israel can work in concrete ways to restore the world to the moral and ethical perfection in which God meant it to exist. Thus they endeavor to bring about the fulfillment of God's promises under the covenant.

To ideally celebrate the Sabbath, all week long, through the six days of activity and creation, Jews look forward to the seventh day. Anticipation of the Sabbath thus enhances ordinary days of the week as well. By Friday afternoon, those who keep the Sabbath have bathed, put on their best garments, and set aside all thought of the affairs of the week. At home, the family

has cleaned, cooked, and arranged the finest table. After a brief Sabbath eve worship service in the synagogue, the family comes together to enjoy its best meal of the week, a meal at which particular Sabbath foods are served, including, in particular, egg bread made of fine white flour (ḤALLAH). In the morning, synagogue worship includes the public reading from the Torah and prophetic writings and an additional service in memory of the Temple sacrifices on Sabbaths of old. Then home for lunch and, very commonly, a Sabbath nap, the sweetest part of the day. As the day wanes, the synagogue calls for a late afternoon service, followed by Torah-study and a third meal. At the end of the Sabbath comes Habdalah, which, with spices, wine, and candlelight, marks the distinction between the holy time of the Sabbath and the ordinary time of weekday. Through the lingering smell of the spices, the Jew carries the ideals of the Sabbath into the coming week, striving to assure that the Sabbath's ideal of perfection marks all aspects of life in the workaday world as well.

Sabbatical Year   The final year of the seven-year agricultural cycle, when fields in the Land of Israel are to lie fallow and debts are to be remitted (Leviticus 25:1–7; Deuteronomy 15:9). In post-biblical times, economic problems caused by the remission of debts were resolved by Hillel's PROSBUL, a document that allowed debts to be collected even after the advent of the Sabbatical year. In the modern State of Israel, the Sabbatical year's agricultural restrictions are avoided through the temporary sale of fields to non-Jews. Rejecting this solution, the strictly observant follow the law literally and, during the Sabbatical year, do not purchase or consume food grown on the Land of Israel.

Ṣaddiq Righteous man; in HASIDISM, intermediary between man and God, master of a Hasidic circle. See also: REBBE.

Sadducees In the first century B.C.E. through the first century C.E., a sect of ancient Judaism, in competition with the PHARISEES. The Sadducees did not believe in a tradition of the fathers, that is, a teaching from God to Moses at Sinai preserved orally and not in writing, in addition to Scripture; the Pharisees did. They did not believe in the resurrection of the dead; the Pharisees did. No writings of the Sadducees survived, so we know about them mainly by what their opposition said; they stressed written Torah and the right of the priesthood to interpret it against Pharisaic claim that oral tradition held by Pharisees was a means of interpretation; they rejected belief in the resurrection of the dead, immortality of soul, angels, and divine providence.

Samuel [1] Eleventh century B.C.E., seer, priest, judge, prophet, and military leader. Samuel was born to his mother, HANNAH, in answer to her prayer (1 Samuel 2). He anointed Saul as king, then rejected Saul and anointed David in his place. [2] Principal Rabbinic authority in third century C.E. Babylonia, favored by the Persian emperor, Shahpur I.

Sanhedrin [1] Jewish legislative and administrative agency in Temple times, in charge of internal affairs of the Jewish community; based in the Jerusalem Temple.

[2] Mishnah tractate devoted to the organization of the government and court system and the punishments administered to those convicted by the courts of having committed various crimes. The court system is described at 1:1–5:5, which concerns various kinds of courts and their jurisdictions, the heads of the nation and of the courts, the procedures of the court system in property and capital cases. Then come rules on the death penalty (6:1–11:6), administered through stoning, burning, decapitation, and strangulation. How these penalties are administered is described, and the classifications of sins or crimes punished by each is specified. Extra-judicial penalties administered by Heaven are spelled out: all Israelites share in the world-to-come except those who deny that the Torah teaches the resurrection of the dead. Both versions of the Talmud devote important and lengthy expositions to this tractate.

Ṣara'at The skin ailment described at Leviticus 13–14; while often referred to as leprosy, affecting fabrics and wood and stone in the walls of houses as much as the skin of human beings, this is certainly not Hansen's disease. In Rabbinic interpretation, *sara'at* comes about by reason of gossip.

Sarah Wife of ABRAHAM and mother of ISAAC (Genesis 11, 12, 16), first of the matriarchs, that is, the wives of the patriarchs, or fathers, of the family that became the children of Israel. She was partner of Abraham in bringing belief in one God to humanity. She gave her servant Hagar to Abraham to produce a son for him when she believed she was infertile. Hagar gave birth to Ishmael. When her son, Isaac, was born, she insisted that Abraham send away Hagar and her son, Ishmael, so that he would not inherit alongside Isaac.

Saul, King Ca. 1020–1000 B.C.E., the first king of Israel; anointed by the prophet SAMUEL when the Israelites asked for a king to rule over them. He disappointed the prophet when he did not obey divine instructions to wipe out Israel's enemies, and Samuel rejected him as king and anointed David in his place. After a period of guerilla war, David succeeded to the throne when Saul and his son, Jonathan, were killed fighting Israel's enemies.

Scribes   See SOFERIM.

Scripture   The Bible; the holy books of ancient Israel, often referred to as the TANAKH (Torah, Prophets, Writings), and also known to Jews as the Written Torah (in contrast to the Oral Torah, embodied in the Talmudic literature); corresponds to the Christian "Old Testament."

Ṣedaqah   (Hebrew: "Righteousness") Term used for charity or philanthropy. Acts of righteousness in general were defined as help to the poor in particular; funds for the poor were called "funds for righteousness." The poor had a right to support, and everyone owed them proper assistance, with dignity and respect. A poor person could demand support using the words, "Acquire merit through me (*zakheh bi*)," meaning, carry out an act of righteousness through which you will personally be recognized as having done what the law does not require but does reward, an act of grace. Thus, giving ṣedaqah to the poor yields *zekhut*—merit—for the donor.

Seder   [1] Hebrew word for "order," referring particularly to the order of the Passover Seder, the banquet held in Jewish homes on the eve of PASSOVER, celebrating the Exodus of Israel from Egyptian bondage in the time of the Pharaohs under the leadership of Moses. The Passover Seder is celebrated through the use of certain symbols and the explanation of their meaning. In addition, the narrative of Israel in Egypt and Psalms of thanksgiving and praise are recited. See PASSOVER; HAGGADAH.

[2] A term that designates a large topical division of the Halakhah of the Mishnah, Tosefta, or Talmuds, of which there

Seder   Some of the symbols of the Passover Seder: three loaves of matzah, four cups of wine, the cup set aside for Elijah, harbinger of the Messiah, and, in the center, the Passover HAGGADAH which contains the liturgy of the Seder.

are six: Zeraim, Moed, Nashim, Neziqin, Qodoshim, and Tohorot. See MISHNAH.

Sefer HaEmunot veHaDe'ot   (Hebrew: "Book of Beliefs and Opinions") The Hebrew title of the major philosophical work of SAADYA BEN JOSEPH ALFAYUMI (882–942), the great scholar and leader of the Babylonian Jewish community. The work was composed in Arabic and translated into Hebrew by Judah ibn Tibbon. A philosophical defense of Rabbinic Judaism, the book details the postulates of Judaism ("beliefs") alongside the truths that are ascertainable through philosophical reflection ("opinions"), which Saadya sees as strengthening, rather than undermining, religious faith. Thus, Saadya identifies two paths to religious truth: revelation, necessary because not everyone is capable of philosophical thought; and empirical reflection, since, without it, superstition and incorrect claims regarding the content of revealed religion will multiply over time.

Sefer Torah (Hebrew: "Scroll of Torah") The parchment scroll on which the Pentateuch is written by hand and from which the Scriptural lection is read during synagogue worship. The scroll is treated with great reverence. It is kept in a special ark in the prominent position in the synagogue and is taken out, read, and returned to the ark with ceremony and procession.

Selah A musical direction in the biblical book of Psalms the meaning of which is uncertain.

Seliḥot (Hebrew: "Forgivenesses") A collection of medieval poems on the subject of forgiveness, recited on fast days and when special intercession by God is desired. As an aspect of the individual's spiritual preparation for YOM KIPPUR, with its central themes of penance and God's forgiveness, Seliḥot prayers are recited daily from the Saturday night prior to ROSH HASHANAH until the Day of Atonement itself.

Semikhah (Hebrew: "laying on of hands") The traditional ritual of Rabbinic ordination, through the laying on of hands.

Sephardim Jews descended from a family-line originating in Spain, Portugal, or Islamic Mediterranean countries, as distinct from those of German or Polish ancestry, called ASHKENAZIM. The name Sepharad is found in Obadiah 1:20 and came to apply to Spain. Sephardic Jewry originated in Spain and Portugal. After the Jews' expulsion from Spain (1492) and Portugal (1497), they settled in North Africa and the Middle East as well, so that the term Sephardic came to apply also to Jews living in these lands.

Se'udah Shel Miṣvah A banquet held in fulfillment of a religious duty, e.g., as part of the marriage-rite, in celebration of a wedding.

Shabbat (Hebrew: "Sabbath") Mishnah tractate on the observance of the Sabbath. The tractate discusses: general principles of Sabbath observance (chap. 1); preparing for the Sabbath, with special reference to light, food, clothing (chaps. 2–6); prohibited acts of labor on the Sabbath (chaps. 7–15); other taboos associated with the Sabbath, e.g., fire; circumcision on the Sabbath, permitted procedures in connection with food for human beings and beasts, seemly and unseemly behavior on the Sabbath (chaps. 16–24). This material is amplified in the Tosefta and expounded in the Babylonian and Jerusalem versions of the Talmud. See SABBATH.

Shabbat Bereshit (Hebrew: "The Sabbath of Genesis") The first Sabbath following the festival of SUKKOT, on which the annual reading of the Torah commences anew with the first chapters of the book of Genesis.

Shabbat HaGadol (Hebrew: "The Great Sabbath") The Sabbath preceding the beginning of PASSOVER. The designation "great" is probably a reference to Malachi 4:5, read as part of the day's prophetic portion, which refers to the return of the prophet Elijah on "the *great* and terrible day of the Lord."

Shabbat HaḤodesh (Hebrew: "The Sabbath of the month") The Sabbath preceding or coinciding with the first day of Nisan, the month in which PASSOVER falls, deemed the month of redemption. Shabbat HaḤodesh is marked by the reading of Exodus 12:1–20, which contains God's instructions to Moses concerning preparation for the Exodus.

Shabbat Ḥazon (Hebrew: "Sabbath of

the Vision") The Sabbath preceding the fast of the Ninth of Ab. The title Shabbat Ḥazon refers to the day's prophetic reading, Isaiah 1:1–27, which depicts Isaiah's vision of the sin and corruption of the people Israel, which led to the sorrow and grief mourned on the Ninth of Ab itself (see AB, NINTH OF).

Shabbat Ḥol HaMoʻed   The Sabbath that falls during the middle days of Passover or Sukkot, marked by special Torah readings and, on Passover, the chanting of the Song of Songs and, on Sukkot, the chanting of Ecclesiastes.

Shabbat Mevarekim   The Sabbath immediately preceding the week in which a new month begins. In Ashkenazic congregations, a prayer for a blessed month is recited, and the month's name and the day of the week on which it will begin is announced.

Shabbat Naḥamu   (Hebrew: "Sabbath of Consolation") The Sabbath immediately following the Ninth of Ab, the theme of which is consolation and which is named for the opening words of the day's prophetic portion, taken from Isaiah 40: "Comfort (naḥamu), comfort my people, says your God." See AB, NINTH OF.

Shabbat Parah   (Hebrew: "Sabbath of the Heifer") The Sabbath preceding SHABBAT HAHODESH, on which Numbers 19:1–22, concerning the ritual of the red heifer, is read as an addition to the week's Torah portion. This is a reminder of the need to purify oneself in anticipation of the coming PASSOVER celebration. See PARAH.

Shabbat Rosh Ḥodesh   (Hebrew: "The Sabbath of the New Moon") A Sabbath that coincides with the beginning of the new Jewish month, marked in the synagogue by the additional reading of the

Torah portion for the new month and a special prophetic lection (Isaiah 66:1–24).

Shabbat Sheqalim   The Sabbath preceding the week in which the month of Adar begins, on which Exodus 30:11–16, on the collection of the Sheqel offering in support of the Temple, is added to the Torah service.

Shabbat Shirah   (Hebrew: "Sabbath of the Song") The Sabbath on which the Song at the Sea (Exodus 14–17) comprises the Torah reading.

Shabbat Shuvah   (Hebrew: "The Sabbath of Repentance") The Sabbath that falls between ROSH HASHANAH and YOM KIPPUR, so named because of the first word—Shuvah—of the prophet passage read in the synagogue on that day: "Return, [O Israel, to the Lord your God, for you have stumbled because of your iniquity] (Hosea 14:1). Shabbat Shuvah is also marked by congregational rabbis' sermons on the theme of repentance, appropriate to the High Holiday season.

Shabbat Zakhor   (Hebrew: "Sabbath of Remembrance") The Sabbath preceding PURIM, on which Deuteronomy 25:17–19 is read in addition to the regular weekly Torah portion. The added passage exhorts the people of Israel to remember the cruelty showed them by the Amalekites. The theme of vigilance against anti-semitism is appropriate to Purim, which commemorates the Jews' victory over their enemies.

Shabuʻot   (Hebrew: "Weeks," "Pentecost") Called "The Season of the Giving of the Torah," the pilgrimage festival that follows seven weeks after PASSOVER. Shabuʻot celebrates God's giving and Israel's receiving the Torah at Sinai. It is also called Pentecost ("fifty") because it comes fifty days after Passover, celebrating the Exodus, for "in the third month after the children of Israel had gone forth from the land of Egypt, on that same day they came into the wilderness of Sinai" (Exodus 19:1). The Feast of Weeks adds its own quite distinctive message. For if "ISRAEL" encompasses all those who stand at Sinai, then the community of Israel finds place for anyone who chooses to accept the Torah at Sinai—by choice, not only by birth. In the natural calendar of the Holy Land, Shabuʻot marks the end of the barley harvest and the beginning of the wheat harvest, so that another name for it is Ḥag HaBikkinim, the Festival of First Fruits.

Shabuʻot is celebrated primarily in public worship in the synagogue, in the declamation of the Torah and the study of the Torah. The stage is set by the custom of the faithful to spend the entire night of the festival, from the sundown that marks the beginning, to sunrise, in community Torah-study under synagogue auspices (*Tiqqun Leil Shabuʻot*). That is followed by morning services. So the congregation has reenacted Israel's action at Sinai, receiving and meditating on the revealed Torah. But at the morning worship, the congregation then is given a jarring message, a reminder that Israel is Israel not by reason of inheritance alone but by an act of choice. Scripture records that a "mixed multitude" assembled for the Exodus and presented themselves at Sinai. That means people not at Sinai by birth choose to become Israel by accepting the Torah. How is that message made articulate? It is not by what is said in so many words but by a portion of the Torah that is added to the obligatory declamation of the Pentateuch and the prophets. And that is the book of Ruth, which tells the story of how a woman deriving from Moab, which abused Israel at they wandered in the wilderness, and the male heirs of which are excluded from Israel by reason of its churlishness, chose to make herself part of Israel by accepting the yoke of the Torah and the dominion of God.

The chanting of the book of Ruth in celebration of the Festival of the Giving of the Torah, defines what Shabuʻot contributes to the definition of the Jewish people. The message of the book of Ruth contains the critical point of insistence: "Israel" is defined by other-than-this-worldly, ethnic facts. Someone of ethnically-dubious origin, from outside Israel-by-birth, by accepting the Torah, not only adheres to Israel but becomes the ancestress of the Messiah. In the patriarchal and genealogical framework of the narrative, privileging men and favoring family ties, one cannot identify an outsider more sharply than as gentile, woman, and widow. The message of Shabuʻot conveyed by the climactic inclusion of the book of Ruth is, Israel is Israel by reason of the Torah, and Israel will be saved at the end of time by the Messiah of the house of David, the grandson of the outsider on two counts, the Moabite woman, Ruth.

Shaḥarit   The morning worship service, consisting of Psalms read from day to day, the SHEMA and its benedictions, the Prayer of Eighteen Benedictions, and ALENU (see SHEMONEH ESTREH). During public worship on Monday and Thursday morning, as well as on Sabbaths and festivals, the Torah is read.

Shaliaḥ Ṣibbur   (Hebrew: "Agent of the Community") In synagogue worship, an individual who leads the congregation in prayer. In traditional Judaism, the prayers of the Shaliaḥ Ṣibbur, especially in the repetition of the Amidah (see SHEMONEH ESREH), are understood to fulfill the obligation to pray of members of the congregation who do not themselves know the correct words. As an agent who prays on behalf of the community, the Shaliaḥ Ṣibbur is expected to embody traits of personal piety. A Shaliaḥ Ṣibbur is distinguished from a Ḥazzan (cantor), in that, unlike the latter, the Shaliaḥ Ṣibbur is not necessarily recognized for the quality of his singing voice or for his mastery of liturgical music.

Shammai   Colleague of HILLEL, first-century Pharisaic sage. Founder of one of the two great schools of the Halakhah of the first two centuries C.E.

Shaqla veTarya   See TALMUDIC DIA-LECTICS.

Sheba' Berakhot   (Hebrew   "Seven Blessings")   The   seven   benedictions recited over a cup of wine at a wedding ceremony and by relatives of the couple who visit them for a week thereafter. They are: [1] Praised are You, O Lord our God, King of the universe, Creator of the fruit of the vine. [2] Praised are You, O Lord our God, King of the universe, who created all things for Your glory. [3] Praised are You, O Lord our God, King of the universe, Creator of Adam. [4] Praised are You, O Lord our God, King of the universe, who created man and woman in His image, fashioning woman from man as his mate, that together they might perpetuate life. Praised are You, O Lord, Creator of man. [5] May Zion rejoice as her children are restored to her in joy. Praised are You, O Lord, who causes Zion to rejoice at her children's return. [6] Grant perfect joy to these loving companions, as You did to the first man and woman in the Garden of Eden. Praised are You, O Lord, who grants the joy of bride and groom. [7] Praised are You, O Lord our God, King of the universe, who created joy and gladness, bride and groom, mirth, song, delight and rejoicing, love and harmony, peace and companionship. O

Lord our God, may there ever be heard in the cities of Judah and in the streets of Jerusalem voices of joy and gladness, voices of bride and groom, the jubilant voices of those joined in marriage under the bridal canopy, the voices of young people feasting and singing. Praised are You, O Lord, who causes the groom to rejoice with his bride. See ḤUPPAH.

Shebat   Eleventh month of the Jewish calendar,   January-February.   See TU BISHEBAT.

Shebi'it   (Hebrew: seventh) Mishnah tractate on conduct of farming before, during, and after the SABBATICAL YEAR; the sixth year of the Sabbatical cycle (chap. 1–2); the sabbatical year itself (chaps. 3–9): field labor that may or may not be done, permitted and forbidden uses of produce grown in the Sabbatical year; the release of debts at the end of the Sab-batical year, and the PROSBUL, the docu-ment that allows the lender to assign his debts to the court and so to avoid remit-ting them in the Sabbatical year (chap. 10).

Shebu'ot   (Hebrew: "Oaths") Mish-nah tractate elucidating the issues of Leviticus 5–6: those who are liable to present a guilt offering, uncleanness of the cult and its Holy Things and the guilt offerings (chaps. 1–2); oaths (chaps. 3–8), treated in the following topical divi-sions: oaths in general (chap. 3); the rash oath and the vain oath (chap. 3); the oath of testimony (Leviticus 5:1; chap. 4); the oath of bailment (Leviticus 6:2ff; chap. 5); the oath imposed by the judges (chaps. 6–7); oaths and bailments (chap. 8).

Sheḥitah   (Hebrew: "ritual slaugh-ter")   The act of slaughtering an animal for meat, a process of particular concern within the Jewish dietary laws (kashrut). The rules of sheḥitah are designed to assure that the animal is killed quickly and painlessly, that it has no internal defects, and that no blood will be consumed. The slaughterer uses a sharp knife to sever the animal's esophagus and trachea in one swift cut, without chopping or tearing the flesh. After slaughter, the cut and all of the animal's organs are examined for defects such as perforations, blisters, cysts, swelling, and other blemishes. Such defects render the meat impermissible for consumption by Jews. See DIETARY LAWS.

Shekhinah   The worldly manifestation of God, as the deity is experienced by humankind, especially in contexts of revelation or in the perceived sanctification of specific objects, people, or locations. Derived from the Hebrew root signifying "to dwell," the Shekhinah is often described as God's indwelling presence, that is, the aspect of God experienced as residing in earthly contexts.

First appearing in early post-biblical texts, the term Shekhinah corresponds roughly to the "Logos" or "Holy Spirit" of early Christian thought. In Aramaic translations of the Hebrew Bible, the term translates expressions such as "face of God" and "glory of God." The Targums (see TARGUM) thus avoid attributing blatantly anthropomorphic features directly to God. In Rabbinic texts, Shekhinah is used more broadly, both to designate the physical manifestation of God and, on occasion, simply as another word for God.

Talmudic rabbis understood the term Shekhinah metaphorically and did not view the Shekhinah as a real, physical aspect of God. The Talmudic literature presents descriptions of conversations between God and the Shekhinah and images of the Shekhinah's presence within this world, especially in the form of light (e.g., Exodus Rabbah 32:4). But such passages often are introduced with the caveat "as if it could be," making explicit their metaphorical sense.

Medieval Jewish philosophers avoided all possibility of anthropomorphism by describing the Shekhinah not as a physical representation of God or as an aspect of God's essence but as an independent entity created by God. Saadyah Gaon (see SAADYA BEN JOSEPH ALFAYUMI) followed by MAIMONIDES, describes the Shekhinah as the intermediary between God and humans that accounts for prophetic visions. Following this same view, JUDAH HALEVI holds that the Shekhinah and not God appeared in prophetic visions. According to Halevi, this same visible aspect of the Shekhinah dwelled in the Temple in Jerusalem. A different, unseen, spiritual Shekhinah dwells with every righteous Israelite.

Qabbalists defined the Shekhinah as the sphere closest to the empirical world, of which it is the sustaining force. Representing the feminine principal, the Shekhinah has no light of its own but receives divine light from the other spheres. In the mystics' view, through prayer and following the commandments, Jews assist in reuniting the Shekhinah with the heavenly masculine principle. Jews thus work to restore the original unity of God, which was destroyed by the people's sins, by evil powers, and as a result of the Jews' exile. See also QABBALAH.

Shelamim   Votive offerings in the Temple, which yield meat for the priest and the person who presents the offering.

Shema   The statement: "Hear, O Israel, the Lord our God, the Lord is One." This creed takes the form of a climactic proclamation in the liturgy of morning and evening prayer, weekdays and holy days alike. Then the faithful Israelite proclaims the unity and uniqueness of God, in the context of the doctrines of God as creator of the world, source of the Torah, and redeemer of ISRAEL. The entire set of doctrines forms the creed of Judaism. See QERIYAT SHEMA.

Shemini Atzeret (Hebrew: "Eighth day of convocation") The eighth and final day of the festival of SUKKOT (Leviticus 23:34–36), understood within post-biblical Judaism to be a separate festival unto itself. In the synagogue, a special prayer that abundant rain will fall in the Land of Israel is said, and, as on the final day of all festivals, memorial prayers are recited. In the Land of Israel, Shemini Atzeret coincides with the festival of SIMḤAT TORAH; in the diaspora, Simḥat Torah falls on the following day.

Shemoneh Esreh (Hebrew: "Eighteen") The Eighteen Benedictions, the central prayer of the Jewish liturgy, known also as the Amidah ("Standing Prayer," since it is recited while standing) and, in the Talmudic literature, simply as HaTefillah ("The Prayer" *par excellence*). The Shemoneh Esreh occurs in all Jewish worship services in a variety of formulations appropriate to the specific weekday, Sabbath, or holiday.

Originally comprised of eighteen benedictions, in Talmudic times a nineteenth was introduced, a malediction against heretics. These nineteen, recited during all daily worship services, include statements of God's power and prayers requesting that God grant to people understanding, forgive sin, heal the sick, ingather the Jewish people, humble the arrogant, rebuild Jerusalem, and bring the Messiah. On Sabbaths and festivals, the Shemoneh Esreh contains a smaller number of benedictions, with the requests found in the daily prayers replaced with a section that concerns the specific themes of the Sabbath or festival.

During day-time prayer services, the Shemoneh Esreh is first recited silently by the congregation and then repeated by the prayer-leader. During this repetition, the congregation joins with the leader in reciting the QEDUSHAH. If an individual prays alone, or if the required quorum of ten is not present, the Shemoneh Esreh is not repeated aloud, and the Qedushah is not recited at all.

As recited in its weekday formulation, the Shemoneh Esreh defines the human situation of Israel: what the faithful should and do ask of God, the teaching concerning God's rule in the everyday life of humanity. From what people beseech, we gain a picture of how they conceive of God in their everyday lives. These, on ordinary days, are the words that the community of Israel says in direct address to God, with the topics summarized in italics at each paragraph:

Wisdom—Repentance
You graciously endow man with
   intelligence;
You teach him knowledge and
   understanding.
Grant us knowledge, discernment, and
   wisdom.
Praised are You, O Lord, for the gift of
   knowledge.

Our Father, bring us back to Your Torah
Our King, draw us near to Your service;
Lead us back to you truly repentant.
Praised are You, O Lord who welcomes
   repentance.

Forgiveness—Redemption
Our Father, forgive us, for we have
   sinned;
Our King, pardon us, for we have
   transgressed;
You forgive sin and pardon transgression.
Praised are You, gracious and forgiving
   Lord.

Behold our affliction and deliver us.

Redeem us soon for the sake of Your name,

For You are the mighty Redeemer.

Praised are You, O Lord, Redeemer of Israel.

Heal Us—Bless Our Years

Heal us, O Lord, and we shall be healed;

Help us and save us, for You are our glory.

Grant perfect healing for all our afflictions,

O faithful and merciful God of healing.

Praised are You, O Lord, Healer of His people.

O Lord our God! Make this a blessed year;

May its varied produce bring us happiness.

Bring blessing upon the whole earth.

Bless the year with Your abounding goodness.

Praised are You, O Lord, who blesses our years.

Gather Our Exiles—Reign Over Us

South the great shofar to herald [our] freedom;

Raise high the banner to gather all exiles;

Gather the dispersed from the corners of the earth.

Praised are You, O Lord, who gathers our exiles.

Restore our judges as in days of old;

Restore our counselors as in former times;

Remove from us sorrow and anguish.

Reign over us alone with loving kindness;

With justice and mercy sustain our cause.

Praised are You, O Lord, King who loves justice.

Humble the Arrogant—Sustain the Righteous

Frustrate the hopes of those who malign us;

Let all evil very soon disappear;

Let all Your enemies be speedily destroyed.

May You quickly uproot and crush the arrogant;

May You subdue and humble them in our time.

Praised are You, O Lord, who humbles the arrogant.

Let Your tender mercies, O Lord God, be stirred

For the righteous, the pious, the leaders of Israel,

Toward devoted scholars and faithful proselytes.

Be merciful to us of the house of Israel;

Reward all who trust in You;

Cast our lot with those who are faithful to You.

May we never come to despair, for our trust is in You.

Praised are You, O Lord, who sustains the righteous.

Favor Your City and Your People

Have mercy, O Lord, and return to Jerusalem, Your city;

May Your Presence dwell there as You promised.

Rebuild it now, in our days and for all time;

Re-establish there the majesty of David, Your servant.

Praised are You, O Lord, who rebuilds Jerusalem.

Bring to flower the shoot of Your servant David.

Hasten the advent of the messianic redemption;

Each and every day we hope for Your deliverance.

Praised are You, O Lord, who assures our deliverance.

O Lord, our God, hear our cry!

Have compassion upon us and pity us;

Accept our prayer with loving favor.

You, O God, listen to entreaty and prayer.

O King, do not turn us away unanswered,

For You mercifully heed Your people's supplication.

Praised are You, O Lord, who is attentive to prayer.

O Lord, Our God, favor Your people Israel;

Accept with love Israel's offering of prayer;

May our worship be ever acceptable to You.

May our eyes witness Your return in mercy to Zion.

Praised are You, O Lord, whose Presence returns to Zion.

Our Thankfulness

We thank You, O Lord our God and God of our fathers,

Defender of our lives, Shield of our safety;

Through all generations we thank You and praise You.

Our lives are in Your hands, our souls in Your charge.

We thank You for the miracles which daily attend us,

For Your wonders and favor morning, noon, and night.

You are beneficent with boundless mercy and love.

From of old we have always placed our hope in You.

For all these blessings, O our King,

We shall ever praise and exalt You.

Every living creature thanks You, and praises You in truth.

O God, You are our deliverance and our help. Selah!

Praised are You, O Lord. for Your goodness and Your glory.

Peace and well-being

Grant peace and well-being to the whole house of Israel;

Give us of Your grace, Your love, and Your mercy.

Bless us all, O our Father, with the light of Your presence.

It is Your light that revealed to us Your life-giving Torah,

And taught us love and tenderness, justice, mercy, and peace.

May it please You to bless Your people in every season,

To bless them at all times with Your light of peace.

Praised are You, O Lord, who blesses Israel with peace.*

*Translation: *Weekday Prayer Book*, ed. by the Rabbinical Assembly of America Prayerbook Committee, Rabbi Jules Harlow, Secretary (New York: Rabbinical Assembly, 1962).

Shemot   (Hebrew: "Names") The Hebrew title of the second book of the Pentateuch, Exodus, derived from that book's first words: "These are the *names* of the sons of Israel who came to Egypt with Jacob, each with his household." See EXODUS, BOOK OF.

Sheol   The underworld; the abode of the dead. It is a land of dust, darkness, forgetfulness, where the shades of the dead gather (Isaiah 14:8–20, Psalm 88:3–12). The word in the Pseudepigraphic book called 1 Enoch 22 speaks of a place where the righteous and wicked are separated, with punishment assigned to the wicked.

Sheqalim   Mishnah tractate on collecting and using the half-sheqel collected from all Israelites to support the daily whole offerings for collective atonement presented in the Temple in Jerusalem; collecting the sheqel (chaps. 1–2); using the sheqel for Temple offerings for the altar (chaps. 3–4); the Temple administration and its procedures (chaps. 5–8).

Sheqel   A coin. A half-sheqel coin was collected from all adult male Israelites to support the daily Whole Offering of the Temple, which is presented morning and evening to atone for the collective sins of Israel.

Shiva   (Hebrew: "seven") The period of mourning that lasts for seven days after the funeral. During this time, close relatives of the deceased remain at home, where daily prayer services are held and where visitors are received to offer condolences. Observance of this ritual is referred to as "sitting Shiva."

In the home in which Shiva is observed, mirrors are covered, a symbol of turning away from human vanity. A candle is kept burning, the light symbolizing the soul. Observing an ancient sign of mourning, the mourners sit on low stools or the floor. Except under the constraint of severe financial loss, mourners of the immediate family of the deceased are prohibited from conducting business and similarly do not engage in housework, which is performed by other family members, or other temporal matters. They also refrain from luxuries, including wearing leather shoes and bathing or engaging in other activities solely for pleasure. In contemporary practice, members of the Conservative and especially the Reform movements do not invariably observe all of these traditions and frequently sit Shiva for fewer than the traditionally mandated seven days.

Shiva ʿAsar BeTammuz (Hebrew: "Seventeenth of Tammuz") Fast day commemorating five catastrophes: the first tablets of the Torah were broken by Moses; the daily whole offering was cancelled, the city wall of Jerusalem was breached by the Romans; Apostemos burned the Torah, and set up an idol in the Temple.

Shoah (Hebrew: "Holocaust") The mass murder, in death factories erected for that purpose, of more than five million Jews in Europe by Germany and its allies from 1933, when the German National Socialist Workers Party ("Nazis") came to power, to 1945, when the Allies vanquished Germany. See HOLOCAUST AND REDEMPTION, JUDAISM OF.

Shofar Ram's horn, sounded during high holy day period, from the beginning of Elul, the lunar month before Tishre and the advent of ROSH HASHANAH, the New Year, until the end of YOM KIPPUR, the Day of Atonement; elicits strong emotions of remorse for sin.

Shofarot *Shofar*-verses, concerning revelation, read in the New Year Additional Service. See MALKHUYOT, ZIKHRONOT.

Shoḥet (Hebrew: "Ritual slaughterer") One who is qualified properly to slaughter an animal, knowledgeable concerning the defects in certain parts of the animal that disqualify use of the meat, e.g., in the brain, windpipe, esophagus, heart, lungs, intestines, because the animal would have died naturally of these defects. See SHEḤITAH.

Shulḥan Arukh (Hebrew: "a table properly set") A code of Jewish law by Joseph Karo (see KARO, JOSEPH), published in 1565. The work covers [1] ritual obligations of every day life from dawn to dusk; blessings, prayers, and observances of Sabbaths and festivals (*oraḥ ḥayyim*); [2] laws governing the conduct of life and life passages, dietary laws, mourning, ethics, piety, and religious virtues, respect for parents, charity (*yoreh deah*); [3] laws of

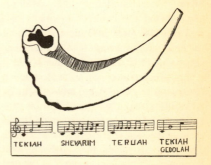

Shofar   A shofar (ram's horn) with its musical sounds.

marriage, divorce, and other questions of personal status (*even haezer*); [4] civil law and institutions of the community of Judaism (*ḥoshen mishpat*). The Shulḥan Arukh has been translated into all the languages in which Jews live and continues today to be consulted for everyday guidance. See also ARBA'AH TURIM.

Shushan Purim   The celebration of Purim on 15 Adar in cities that have been walled since the time of the biblical leader Joshua (e.g., Jerusalem), commemorating the Jews of Shushan's successful thwarting of Haman's plan to exterminate them on that day. Shushan Purim falls the day after the celebration of Purim in unwalled cities.

Ṣidduk HaDin   (Hebrew: "Justification of the judgment") The prayer recited by a dying person.

Siddur   In Ashkenazi Judaism, the term for the prayer book used on all days of the year except the high holy days. The Siddur (from the Hebrew word "order") contains the order of worship for the morning, afternoon, and evening services for weekdays, the Sabbath, and festivals, and frequently also contains rites of home and family, including Grace after Meals, the wedding service, and other liturgies.

Sifra   A compilation of Midrash exegeses on the book of Leviticus that makes a systematic statement concerning the definition of the MISHNAH in relationship to Scripture. Unlike the other Midrash compilations that concern the Pentateuch (the two Sifres (see SIFRE) and MEKHILTA ATTRIBUTED TO R. ISHMAEL), Sifra is programmatically cogent in its sustained treatment of the issues defined by the Mishnah. The relationship of the Mishnah with Scripture—in mythic language, of the oral to the written part of the Torah—required definition. The authorship of Sifra

composed the one document to accomplish the union of Scripture and the Mishnah. This was achieved not merely formally by provision of proof texts from Scripture for statements of the Mishnah—as are found in the two versions of the Talmud—but through a profound analysis of the interior structure of thought. It was by means of the critique of practical logic and the rehabilitation of the probative logic of hierarchical classification in particular that the authorship of Sifra accomplished this remarkable feat of intellect. That authorship achieved the (re-)union of the two Torahs into a single cogent statement within the framework of the written Torah by penetrating into the deep composition of logic that underlay the creation of the world in its correct components, rightly classified, and in its right order, as portrayed by the Torah.

This was done in two ways. Specifically, it involved, first of all, systematically demolishing the logic that sustains an autonomous Mishnah, which appeals to the intrinsic traits of things to accomplish classification and hierarchization. Secondly, it was done by demonstrating the dependency, for the identification of the correct classification of things, not upon the traits of things viewed in the abstract, but upon the classification of things by Scripture in particular. The framers of Sifra recast the two parts of the Torah into a single coherent statement through unitary and cogent discourse. So in choosing, as to structure, a book of the Pentateuch, and, as to form, the exegetical form involving paraphrase and amplification of a phrase of a base-text of Scripture, the authorship of Sifra made its entire statement in a nutshell. Then by composing a document that for very long stretches simply cannot have been put together without the Mishnah and at the same time subjecting the generative logical principles of the Mishnah to devastating critique, that same authorship took up its position. The destruction of the Mishnah as an autonomous and freestanding statement, based upon its own logic, is followed by the reconstruction of large tracts of the Mishnah as a statement wholly within, and in accordance with, the logic and program of the written Torah in Leviticus. That is what defines Sifra, the one genuinely cogent and sustained statement among the four Midrashic compilations that present exegetical discourse on the Pentateuch.

The dominant approach to uniting the two Torahs, oral and written, into a single cogent statement, involved reading the written Torah into the oral. In form, this was done through inserting into the Mishnah (that is, the oral Torah) a long sequence of proof texts. The other solution required reading the oral Torah into the written one, by inserting into the written Torah citations and allusions to the oral one, and, as a matter of fact, also by demonstrating, on both philosophical and theological grounds, the utter subordination and dependency of the oral Torah, the Mishnah, to the written Torah — while at the same time defending and vindicating that same oral Torah. Sifra, followed unsystematically to be sure by the two Sifres, did just that. Sifra's authorship attempted to set forth the dual Torah as a single, cogent statement, doing so by reading the Mishnah into Scripture not merely for proposition but for expression of proposition. On the surface, that decision represented a literary, not merely a theological, judgment. But within the deep structure of thought, it was far more than a mere matter of how to select and organize propositions.

That judgment upon the Mishnah forms part of the polemic of Sifra's authorship— but only part of it. Sifra's authorship conducts a sustained polemic against the failure of the Mishnah to cite Scripture very much or systematically to link its ideas to Scripture through the medium of formal demonstration by exegesis. Sifra's rhetorical exegesis follows a standard redactional form. Scripture will be cited. Then a statement will be made about its meaning, or a statement of law correlative to that Scripture will be given. That statement sometimes cites the Mishnah, often verbatim. Finally, the author of Sifra invariably states, "Now is that not (merely) logical?" And the point of that statement will be, Can this position not be gained through the working of mere logic, based upon facts supplied (to be sure) by Scripture?

Sifre   (Aramaic: "Books") An early Halakhic midrash on the biblical books of Numbers and Deuteronomy, written as a line-by-line and often word-by-word commentary on the biblical texts. See SIFRE TO DEUTERONOMY, SIFRE TO NUMBERS.

Sifre to Deuteronomy   Rabbinic commentary yielding a philosophical reading of the book of Deuteronomy. Since in the book of Deuteronomy, Moses explicitly sets forth a vision of Israel's future history, sages in Sifre to Deuteronomy examined that vision to uncover the rules that explain what happens to Israel. Like Sifra, Sifre to Deuteronomy pursues a diverse topical program in order to demonstrate a few fundamental propositions. Distinctive to Sifre to Deuteronomy is its systematic mode of methodical analysis, in which it takes the details of cases and carefully re-frames them into rules pertaining to all cases. The authorship thus asks those questions of susceptibility to generalization that first-class philosophical minds raise.

Four principal topics encompass the

document's propositions, of which the first three correspond to the three relationships into which Israel entered: with Heaven, on earth, and within. These yield systematic statements that concern the relationships between ISRAEL and God, with special reference to the covenant, the Torah, and the Land; Israel and the nations, with interest in Israel's history, past, present, and future, and how that cyclic is to be known; Israel on its own terms, with focus upon Israel's distinctive leadership. The fourth rubric encompasses non-specific *ad hoc* propositions, which form aggregates of proofs of large truths, but, rather, prevailing modes of thought, demonstrating the inner structure of intellect and yielding the formation, out of the cases of Scripture, of encompassing rules.

Sifre to Numbers A midrashic commentary to most of the book of Numbers. While the document follows no uniform topical program, it exhibits a recurrent effort to prove a two correlated points: [1] reason unaided by Scripture produces uncertain propositions; and [2] reason operating within the limits of Scripture produces truth. These two principles are implicit in a systematic reading of most of the book of Numbers, verse by verse. The exegetical forms stand for a single proposition: the human mind joins God's mind when humanity receives and sets forth the Torah. The Torah opens the road into the mind of God, and our minds can lead us on that road, because our mind and God's mind are comparable. We share a common rationality.

Sim Shalom Sabbath, festival, and weekday prayer book of the Conservative movement of American Judaism, produced by the movement's Rabbinical Assembly. First published in 1985, a new, completely revised edition, omitting the service for weekdays, appeared in 1997.

Alongside a generally new design, the second edition offers an alternative text of the Amidah (see SHEMONEH ESREH) that includes reference to the biblical matriarchs, alongside the patriarchs. It also contains alternative passages for the MUSAF Amidah that eliminate reference to Temple sacrifices.

Simḥat Bat (Hebrew: "Rejoicing for a Daughter") In contemporary Judaism, a ceremony that marks the entry of a new born baby girl into the covenant; parallel in function to the BERIT MILAH (circumcision) ceremony performed upon the birth of a boy. Solely the creation of contemporary Judaism, the Simḥat Bat has no fixed formula or content but is comprised of blessings and other readings that reflect upon the significance of the new birth and the parents' hopes for the child's future within the Jewish community. As in the Berit Milah ceremony, at this time a Hebrew name is assigned. While no ritual similar to circumcision itself is available, contemporary practice has included candle lightings, washing of the baby's feet, and other ritual acts to mark the occasion.

Simḥat Torah (Hebrew: "Rejoicing of the Torah") The last day of the festival of SUKKOT, when, in the synagogue, the annual reading of the Torah is completed and recommenced. The worship service on Simḥat Torah is marked by singing and dancing with the Torah scrolls, which are carried around the sanctuary in seven processions. Customarily, each participant in the worship is called for an ALIYAH, with passages from the day's Torah reading repeated as many times as is necessary to accommodate all in attendance. The greatest honor is reserved for the individual who recites the blessings before and after the reading of the final passage of the book of Deuteronomy, who is referred to as the Bridegroom of the Torah (*Ḥatan Torah*), and for the one who recites the blessings for the beginning of the book of Genesis, who is called the Bridegroom of Genesis (*Ḥatan Bereshit*). In the diaspora, where Sukkot is celebrated for nine days, Simḥat Torah falls on day nine and so is distinct from SHEMINI ATZERET, the eighth day. In the Land of Israel, where Sukkot is celebrated for eight days, Simhat Torah coincides with Shemini Atzeret.

Sin   (Hebrew: *Ḥet*) Defined in the model of the first sin, the one committed by Adam and Eve in Eden, sin is an act of rebellion against God. Rebellion takes two forms. As a gesture of omission sin embodies the failure to carry out one's obligation to God set forth in the Torah. As one of commission, it constitutes an act of defiance. In both cases, sin comes about by reason of a person's intention to reject the will of God, set forth in the Torah. However accomplished, whether through omission or commission, an act becomes sinful because of the attitude that accompanies it. That is why a person is responsible for sin, answerable to God in particular, who may be said to take the matter personally, just as it is meant. The consequence of sin is death for the individual, exile and estrangement for the people of Israel, and disruption for the world. That is why sin accounts for much of the flaw of creation.

Why do people rebel against God? The answer is arrogance, and that has to be accounted for. Specifically, they become arrogant when they are prosperous; then they trust in themselves and take for granted that their own power has secured abundance. They forget that it is God who, by His act of will, has given them what they have gotten. Prosperity and success bear their own threatening consequence in the change of humanity's attitude. So arrogance comes from an excess of good fortune, but it is the absence of humility that accounts for the wrong attitude.

How is it that people's will does not correspond with, but rebels against, the will of God? Here humanity's free will requires clarification. Humans and God both are possessed of free will. But humanity's free will encompasses the capacity to rebel against God, and that comes about because innate in the human will is the impulse to do evil, *yeṣer hara'* in Hebrew. So humans correspond to God but are complex, comprised by conflicting impulses, where God is one and unconflicted.

That impulse to do evil struggles with the impulse to do good, *yeṣer hatob*. The struggle between the two impulses then corresponds with the cosmic struggle between humanity's will and God's word. But creation bears within itself the forces that ultimately will resolve the struggle. That struggle will come to an end in the world-to-come, which will come about by an act of divine response to human regeneration. Then the impulse to do evil, having perished in the regeneration brought about by man, will be finally slain by God, leading to an end to sin.

Sinai   The mountain, in the wilderness between Egypt and the Land of Israel, on which God revealed the Torah to MOSES. Mount Sinai is also identified with Mount Horeb.

Sinai Desert   The wilderness between Egypt and the Land of Israel where the Israelites wandered for forty years, from the Exodus until the entire generation of the Exodus had died out. A mountain located in that wilderness, called Mount Sinai, is thought to be the mountain of God, near "the wilderness of Ṣin" (Exodus 16:1).

Şişit Knotted fringes affixed in accordance with Numbers 15:38 to the four corners (*arba kanfot*) of a shawl or garment, especially of a TALLIT, signifying the commandments one is to practice through the day.

Sivan The third month of Jewish year, June-July.

Soferim (Hebrew: "Scribes") A professional class responsible for the preparation of legal documents in ancient Israel. The scribes furthermore interpreted the Torah and served as the clerks of the Israelite court system. In the first century, they were village officials and teachers. In later Rabbinic Judaism, they are cited as the authorities behind various early rulings and as interpreters of Scripture. "Words of the scribes" refer to teachings of oral tradition written down by the rabbis in the MISHNAH and related documents.

Solomon, King The third king of Israel in Jerusalem, son of King David. Solomon ruled for forty years in the mid-tenth century B.C.E. He built the Temple of Jerusalem and other important buildings and developed international relations. The narrative of 1 Kings 1–11 records the principal events of his reign. He entered into marriages for political purposes. When he died, the northern tribes rejected the rule of the Davidic dynasty. He is credited with wisdom, administrative skill, wide knowledge, mastery of proverbs, and the wit to solve riddles.

Song of Songs Known also as the Song of Solomon, a collection of love songs that Judaism and Christianity have taken to portray the love between God and ISRAEL or God and the Church, respectively. These sensuous poems, alternatively speaking for a man and a woman, are treated as richly allegorical. The Song of Songs is read in synagogue worship on PASSOVER.

Song of Songs Rabbah The Song of Songs appears in the Torah because this collection of love-songs is understood to speak about the relationship between God and ISRAEL. The compilers of the midrashic Song of Songs Rabbah intend to justify that reading. They do this by turning to everyday experience—the love of husband and wife—for a metaphor of God's love for Israel and Israel's love for God. Thus, when Solomon's song says, "O that you would kiss me with the kisses of your mouth! For your love is better than wine" (Song 1:2), Judaic sages think of how God kissed Israel. The sages thus read the Song of Songs as a sequence of statements of urgent love between God and Israel.

In reading the Song of Songs in this manner, sages identify implicit meanings that are always few and invariably self-evident; no serious effort goes into demonstrating the fact that God speaks, or Israel speaks; the point of departure, rather, is the message and meaning either God or Israel is understood to mean to convey. To take one instance, time and again we are told that a certain expression of love is God's speaking to Israel about the Sea, Sinai, and the world to come; or the first redemption, from Egypt; the second redemption, from Babylonia; and the third redemption, at the end of days. The repertoire of symbols covers Temple and schoolhouse, personal piety and public worship, and other matched pairs and sequences of coherent matters, all of them seen as embedded within the poetry. Here is Scripture's poetry read as metaphor. So Israel's holy life is metaphorized through the poetry of love and beloved, Lover and Israel.

Sotah [1] The wife accused of adultery, Numbers 5; [2] Mishnah tractate on the ordeal inflicted upon the wife accused of adultery; invoking the ordeal (chap. 1); narrative of the ordeal (chaps. 1–3); rules of imposing the ordeal, exemptions, testimony (chaps. 4–6); rites conducted in Hebrew in addition to that involving the accused wife (chaps. 7–9); the anointed for battle and draft exempts (Deuteronomy 20:1–9; chap. 8); the rite of breaking the heifer's neck in connection with the neglected corpse (Deuteronomy 21:1–9; chap. 9). See PARAH.

Sukkah [1] Booth, tabernacle, used on the festival of Sukkot in accordance with Leviticus 23:33–43. [2] Mishnah tractate devoted to the festival of Tabernacles; objects used in celebrating the festival, the Sukkah, the lulab, and etrog (chaps. 1–3); rites and offerings on the Festival (chaps. 4–5). See SUKKOT.

Sukkot One of Judaism's three pilgrimage festivals (alongside PASSOVER and SHABU'OT), celebrated on the first full moon after the autumnal equinox. Called in English "Tabernacles," Sukkot is celebrated as "The Season of Our Rejoicing." It forms the climax of the autumnal holy day season, which begins with ROSH HASHANAH and YOM KIPPUR and concerns sin, forgiveness, and rejoicing.

Lasting for three weeks, the autumnal festival cycle commences with the first day of the lunar month in which the autumnal equinox takes place. That is the first of Tishrei, which is Rosh Hashanah, the New Year of Judaism. It commemorates the creation of the world and is the day on which God recalls the deeds of the year past and judges Israel. Ten days later, on the tenth of Tishrei, comes Yom Kippur, the Day of Atonement, which completes the judgment. Five days later, the fifteenth of Tishre, the full moon after the autumnal equinox, is Sukkot, celebrated for seven days, like Passover. (In the diaspora,

Passover and Sukkot last for eight days, in the State of Israel, as Scripture requires, seven.) Sukkot depicts the people of Israel as pilgrims, wandering in the wilderness, expiating the sin of a generation that rebelled against God through the sin of the Golden Calf (Exodus 32).

Sukkot places Israel after the Exodus from Egypt, beyond the Sea and Sinai, wandering about in the wilderness, where, by reason of rebellion against God, they wandered for forty years. Israel then is reminded that it is a people that has sinned, but that God can and does forgive. There they remained until the entire generation of the wilderness had died out, and Israel was ready to enter the Promised Land. Passover places Israel's freedom into the context of the affirmation of life beyond sin; Sukkot returns Israel to the fragility of abiding in the wilderness. Leviticus 23:33–43 defines the festival:

> And the Lord said to Moses, "Say to the people of Israel, On the fifteenth day of this seventh month and for seven days is the feast of huts to the Lord.... You shall dwell in huts for seven days; all that are native in Israel shall dwell in huts, that your generations may know that I made the people of Israel dwell in huts when I brought them out of the land of Egypt; I am the Lord your God."

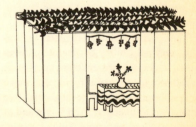

Sukkah The Sukkah used on the festival of Sukkot.

The principal observance of the festival is the construction of a frail hut or booth, for temporary use. In it, Israel lives once more in the condition of that sinful generation, eating meals and (where the climate permits) sleeping out-of-doors. What defines the hut is the roofing, which must cast more shade than light, but not be fully covered over. Roofing of branches, leaves, fruit, and flowers allows light to show through, and, at night, the stars. At this time of harvest bounty it is good to be reminded of our travail and dependence upon heavenly succor. The hut is an abode that cannot serve in the rainy season that is coming, announced by the new moon that occasions the festival. Israel is to take shelter, in reverting to the wilderness, in any random, ramshackle hut, covered with what nature has provided but in form and in purpose what people otherwise do not value.

The temporary abode of the Israelite, the Sukkah in its transience matches Israel's condition in the wilderness, wandering between Egypt and the Land, death and eternal life. Just as Passover marks the differentiation of Israel from Egypt, so Sukkot addresses the condition of Israel. The story concerns the generation that must die out before Israel can enter the Land. So entering the Sukkah reminds Israel not only of the fragility of its condition but also—in the aftermath of the penitential season—of its actuality: yet sinful, yet awaiting death, so that a new generation will be ready for the Land.

The festival of Sukkot registers the fragility and culpability of liberated, covenanted Israel. The present tense takes over, for the people of Israel is required to make its residence a temporary hut. Jews see themselves as liberated from Egypt and as present at Sinai, and, now, Sukkot continues the pattern of living in the presence of the past. See ETROG, LULAB.

Superstition   Folk customs and practices not accepted by a religion's elite, who determine the religion's official content. In Judaism, as in other religions, superstitions are often related to extra-religious powers or to spiritual experience and frequently are associated with magic and medicine. Insofar as Judaism distinguishes folk practices (*minhag*) from required behaviors (*halakhah*), the designation "superstition" is most likely to be attached to the former and may, as such, include even such accepted Jewish practices as covering mirrors in a house of mourning, breaking a glass at a wedding ceremony, or eating sweet foods at ROSH HASHANAH to ensure a sweet new year. Notably, there is a frequent lack of clarity in Jewish law regarding which behaviors belong in the category of *minhag* and which are required, and, similarly, practices that start as *minhag* often become accepted by the religious elite and come to be viewed as obligatory. This suggests the extent to which a practice's categorization as superstition may depend as much upon the community's attitude as it reflects the objective character of the behavior under consideration.

Synagogue   (Hebrew: *Beit HaKnesset*) A place set aside for Jewish communal worship. Unlike a temple, which is conceived as a residence of God and is administered by a priesthood, the synagogue is a community institution, a place of meeting and prayer, administered by a lay leadership, in particular, the rabbi and cantor. In modern times, synagogues are built and maintained by groups of Jews who voluntarily band together to create such institutions. While, in the United States and in Western Europe, synagogues frequently are affiliated with, and pay dues to, the Orthodox, Conservative, or Reform movements, they are financially and administratively independent, hiring and firing personnel and determining the content and nature of their programs, according to the needs and desires of their particular membership.

Following the destruction of the Jerusalem Temple in 70 C.E., the synagogue became the preeminent institutional center of Jewish religion and culture. The growth of the synagogue in the medieval period led to the creation of specific administrative posts, the cantor, responsible for leading worship, and the sexton, charged with maintenance of the building. Only in the nineteenth century, in Western Europe, did the rabbi, previously an employee of the Jewish community and primarily responsible for adjudicating matters of law, become a synagogue employee, charged with synagogue administration, leadership of worship, and pastoral duties. Since that time, especially in the United States, synagogues have increasingly become large, multi-purpose institutions, housing not only sanctuaries for worship but also schools, social halls, and other meeting facilities.

Judaism has few set rules for synagogue architecture, so that synagogues normally are built according to the esthetic demands of the particular community. In the western hemisphere, the sanctuary almost always faces east, toward Jerusalem, and it has as its focal point the ark in which the Torah scrolls are kept. In traditional sanctuaries, women have a separate seating area, either behind a partition (*meḥitzah*) or in a balcony.

In modern times, especially in REFORM JUDAISM, the synagogue is often referred to as a temple. This reflects the Reform movement's break from the traditional Jewish yearning for the rebuilding of the Jerusalem Temple and the reinstitution of the sacrificial cult that took place there.

Early reformers in the U.S.A. took the name "temple" for their places of worship, arguing that their sanctuaries were comparable to the original Temple and that they had no desire for a return to the Jewish ancestral homeland or for the recreation of the earlier, priest-centered form of divine worship.

Since Jewish prayer may take place in almost any location (excluding such obviously inappropriate places as a privy), what ultimately comprises the synagogue must be defined more as what goes on in the building than the architectural character of the space in question. A synagogue is not contained space of a particular design but the presence of a community of Jews assembled for the conduct of certain specific activities, in particular liturgical rites. The essence of the synagogue thus is embodied in the prayer quorum that meets there, not in the building. But the physical building, once sanctified for use as a synagogue, is deemed holier than a space that has not been set aside to this purpose. So the synagogue finds its definition in its function. It is a place in which Jews meet to carry out the holy purposes of prayer and so to form a Jewish community. A synagogue is any location in which this function is carried out, and that is without regard to the location of the Jews or the character of the space, if any, that contains them.

Szold, Henrietta One of the earliest and most effective leaders in the movement to redefine the role of women in Judaism; founder of the Women's Zionist Movement (*Hadassah*), who formed it into the single most important organization in American and world Zionism. Her philosophy is expressed in a particular incident. When her mother died, she insisted on saying the memorial prayer (*Qaddish*) in her mother's memory and refused the offer of a well-meaning male to say it on her behalf. This is what she replied in her letter:

> It is impossible for me to find words in which to tell you how deeply I was touched by your offer to act as *"Qaddish"* for my dear mother. I cannot even thank you—it is something that goes beyond thanks. It is beautiful, what you have offered to do—I shall never forget it.
>
> You will wonder, then, that I cannot accept your offer. Perhaps it would be best form not to try to explain to you in writing, but to wait until I see you to tell you why it is so. I know well, and appreciate what you say about, the Jewish custom; and Jewish custom is very dear and sacred to me. And yet I cannot ask you to say *Qaddish* after my mother. The *Qaddish* means to me that the survivor publicly and markedly manifests his wish and intention to assume the relation to the Jewish community which his parent had, and that so the chain of tradition remains unbroken from generation to generation, each adding its own link. You can do that for the generations of your family, I must do that for the generations of my family.
>
> I believe that the elimination of women from such duties was never intended by our law and custom— women were freed from positive duties when they could not perform them, but not when they could. It was never intended that, if they could perform them, their performance of them should not be considered as valuable and valid as when one of the male sex performed them. And of the *Qaddish* I feel sure this is particularly true.
>
> My mother had eight daughters and no son; and yet never did I hear a word of regret pass the lips of either my mother or my father that one of us was not a son. When my father died, my mother would not permit others to take her daughters' place in saying the *Qaddish,* and so I am sure I am acting in her spirit when I am moved to decline your offer. But beautiful your offer remains nevertheless, and, I repeat, I know full well that it is much more in consonance with the generally accepted Jewish tradition than is my or my family's tradition. You understand me, don't you?
>
> ("The Jewish Woman: An Anthology," *Response* 1973, 18:76.)

This statement represents the first recorded assertion of a woman's liturgical rights in the history of Judaism in the English-speaking world.

T

Ta'anit [1] Minor fasts, lasting from dawn to dusk, generally in times of trouble or drought; [2] Mishnah tractate devoted to fasts that are called in order to pray for rain; the sequence of fasts for rain (chap. 1); liturgy of the community for a fast day (chap. 2); rules about public fasts (chap. 2); using the shofar as an alarm, besides to call fast days (chap. 3); the delegation (*ma'amad*): Israelite participation in the cult (chap. 4). (See FAST DAYS.)

Ta'anit Esther Fast of Esther, which takes place on the 13th of Adar, the day prior to Purim, in commemoration of Esther's own fast, recorded at Esther 4:16: "Go, gather all the Jews to be found in Susa, and hold a fast on my behalf, and neither eat nor drink for three days, night or day. I and my maids will also fast as you do. Then I will go to the king, though it is against the law; and if I perish, I perish."

Tabernacles See SUKKOT.

Tahanun (Hebrew: "Supplication") A confession of sin and petition for God's forgiveness, recited in the daily morning and afternoon prayers following the cantor's repetition of the Amidah (see SHEMONEH ESREH). Tahanun is not recited on joyous occasions or in a house of mourning.

Tallit Prayer shawl, four-cornered cloth with fringes (Numbers 15:38) worn by adult males during morning worship. See SISIT.

Tallit Qatan (Hebrew: "Small Tallit") A rectangular garment with fringes on its four corners, worn by observant men under their shirt during the entire day, thus fulfilling the commandment of Numbers 15:38. (See SISIT).

Talmid Hakham Disciple of the wise; a sage, master of the Torah.

Talmud Either of two vast commentaries to the MISHNAH, one created in the Land of Israel (c. 400 C.E.) and called the Jerusalem Talmud (Hebrew: *Yerushalmi*), and the other composed in Babylonia (c. 600 C.E.), called the Babylonian Talmud (Hebrew: *Bavli*). Both Talmuds are comprised of two separate parts, the Mishnah, which is the underlying text subject to analysis, and the Gemara, comprising the Rabbinic commentary on the Mishnah. Generally when the term Talmud is used, reference is to the Gemara, that is, to the Talmudic interpretation of the Mishnah.

The Babylonian Talmud contains explanations of thirty-seven of the Mishnah's sixty-three tractates. Excluded are the tractates devoted to agricultural tithes, which are not paid from produce grown outside of the Land of Israel, and Temple

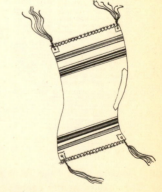

Tallit (prayer shawl)

sacrifices, which were no longer offered in the period of the Talmud's formulation. The Talmud of the Land of Israel comments on thirty-nine of the Mishnah's tractates, including those on tithing, a topic pertinent to the rabbis of the Land of Israel who created this document.

The Babylonian is the larger Talmud, containing a significant amount of Midrashic material as well as commentary on the Mishnah. Because of its size and later date of composition, Judaism holds the Babylonian Talmud to be the consummate text of Rabbinic Judaism, melding together the various prior strains of material into one conclusive statement. The Babylonian Talmud therefore has stood at the foundation of all later theological and legal developments within Judaism from the time of its completion and until the present day.

As for the nature of their commentary on the Mishnah, both versions of the Talmud comprise sustained, systematic amplifications and analyses of passages of the Mishnah and other teachings alongside

Talmud Drawing of a page from the Talmud. The text is in the center surrounded by commentaries.

the Mishnah, including the Tosefta, that are accorded the status of Tannaitic authority. Both the Jerusalem and Babylonian versions of the Talmud consist of commentaries on some of the same passages of the Mishnah (tractates in the divisions of Appointed Times, Women, and Damages, but not in Agriculture or Holy Things; neither Talmud discusses Purities, except for the tractate NIDDAH). Both are laid out in the same way, that is, as ad hoc treatments of phrases or even whole paragraphs of the Mishnah. The two versions of the Talmud thus are identical in form. Both also exhibit definitive traits in common. Specifically, they share the program of harmonizing one rule or principle with another. Both, furthermore, propose to uncover the scriptural foundation of the Mishnah's rules. In common, therefore, they undertake the sustained demonstration of the theology of the Torah: its perfection, on the one side, its unity (oral and written), on the other.

Both versions of the Talmud take up a few sentences of the prior text and paraphrase and analyze them. Both ask the same questions, e.g., clarifying the language of the Mishnah, identifying the scriptural foundations of the Mishnah's rules, comparing the Mishnah's rules with those of the Tosefta or other texts of Tannaitic status. They furthermore are comparable because they organize their materials in the same way. They moreover take up pretty much the same topical agenda, in common selecting some divisions of the Mishnah and ignoring others, agreeing in particular to treat the matters of everyday practice, as distinct from theory, covered by the Mishnah's divisions of Appointed Times, Women, and Damages. In both, moreover, we find not only the same received document, the Mishnah, but occasionally also citations of, and allusions to, the same supplementary collection to the Mishnah, the Tosefta, and also a further kind of saying, one bearing the marks of formalization and memorization that serve to classify it as authoritative ("Tannaitic") but external to the composition of the Mishnah and the compilation of the Tosefta.

Both versions of the Talmud invariably do to the Mishnah one of these four things, and each of these procedures will ordinarily be expressed in patterned language:

1 text criticism;
2 exegesis of the meaning of the Mishnah, including glosses and amplifications;
3 addition of Scriptural prooftexts of the Mishnah's central propositions; and
4 harmonization of one Mishnah passage with another such passage or with a statement of Tosefta.

Each of these types of compositions follows a well-defined form, so that, if we were given only an account in abstract terms of the arrangement of subject and predicate or a simple account of the selection of citation language (e.g., "as it is said," "our rabbis have taught,") we could readily predict the purpose of the composition. Formal literary traits thus accompany the purpose of the commentaries and permit differentiation of one type from another.

The writers of the Mishnah created a coherent document, with a topical program formed in accord with the logical order dictated by the characteristics of a given topic, and with a set of highly distinctive formulary and formal traits as well. But these are obscured when the document is taken apart and reconstituted in the way in which the versions of the Talmud do. The re-definition of the Torah accomplished by the two versions of the Talmud therefore represented a vast revision of the initial writing down of the oral component of the Torah—a point at which hermeneutics shaded into a profoundly theological activity.

Talmud Torah [1] (Hebrew: "Torah Study") Study of the Torah is a principal action of Judaism, because Judaism maintains that humanity finds God in books, through the act of learning. Torah study brings about an encounter with God that differs from the meeting with God at prayer. The difference is captured in the phrase, "When I pray, I speak to God. When I study the Torah, God speaks to me." Talmud Torah recapitulates the people of Israel's encounter with God at Sinai. That is meant concretely: when Israel assembles for the study of the Torah, God is present. Talmud Torah thus is not to be confused with an academic exercise of intellectual enlightenment. It is not simply a quest for information. Learning itself, rather, constitutes an act of worship, so that knowledge of a particular order, acquired for the purpose of knowing God's will and word for Israel, sanctifies the person who has attained that knowledge. That conception of the act of study is particular to Judaism obviously quite different from the attitude toward study found in the secular setting of purely academic study. [2] Also: a school where Torah is studied, usually an elementary school.

Talmudic Dialectics Characteristic of the Talmud of Babylonia and commonplace in medieval and modern Judaic exegesis of legal texts, *shaqla vetarya*, give and take, sustains a dialectical argument. Dialectics provides for a moving exchange, in which parties to the argument counter one another's arguments in a progression of exchanges (often, in what seems like an infinite progress to an indeterminate conclusion). The dialectical argument addresses not the problem and the solution alone but the problem and the various ways by which a solution may be reached. It is not a set-piece of two positions, with an analysis of each, such as formal dialogue exposes with elegance; it is, rather, an unfolding analytical argument, explaining why this, not that, then why not that but rather this; and onward to the other thing and the thing beyond that (see PILPUL).

When we follow not only what the sages of the Talmud say but how they express themselves, their modes of critical thought, we encounter a massive, concrete instance of the power of intellect to purify and refine. For the sages of the Talmud, alongside the great masters of Greek philosophy and their Christian and Muslim continuators, exercise the power of rational and systematic inquiry, tenacious criticism, the exchange of not only opinion but reason for opinion, argument and evidence. They provide a model of how intellectuals take up the tasks of social criticism and pursue the disciplines of the mind in the service of the social order.

Tamid [1] Daily whole offering; [2] Mishnah tractate that narrates how the daily whole offering is presented: priests prepare the altar (chaps. 1–2); select the lamb (chap. 3); clear the ashes from the altar (chap. 3); slaughter the lamb (chap. 4); bless the congregation, place the limbs on the altar (chap. 5); clear the ashes (chaps. 5–6).

Tammuz Fourth month of the Jewish calendar, June-July.

TaNaKH Acronym for the Hebrew Scriptures (Old Testament), comprised by Torah (Pentateuch), Nebi'im (Prophets), and Ketubim (Writings).

Tanna [1] An authority of Jewish law

who flourished in the first two centuries C.E., whose words are cited in the Mishnah; also one who studies and teaches; a Rabbinical master mentioned in the Mishnah is called a *Tanna*. [2] A professional memorizer of authoritative rules, whether found in the Mishnah or of the same status as those that are in that document.

Tannaitic Adjective deriving from the noun Tanna, which indicates that the referenced tradition or document has the authority of the earliest Rabbinic masters. Thus, "Tannaitic literature" means, literature produced by authorities of Tannaitic status; this includes the MISHNAH, TOSEFTA, and baraitot (traditions preserved outside of finished compilations but assigned Tannaitic standing and authority).

Taqqanah Decree, ordinance issued by a Rabbinic authority. Exemplified by the special decrees issued by Rabban YOHANAN BEN ZAKKAI at Yavneh after the destruction of the Temple in 70 C.E., when it was necessary to take account, in the celebration of festivals, of the cessation of the Temple rites.

Targum (Hebrew: "Translation") Ancient translation of Scripture into Aramaic, the international language that most Jews knew. The Rabbinic period saw the composition of a number of *Targumim* (Targums), including Targum Onkelos (2nd–3rd century C.E.), Targum Jonathan (on the prophets; completed 7th century C.E.), and Targum Yerushalmi (on the Pentateuch; 7th–8th century C.E.). To judge by the range of Targums we now possess, the Pentateuch received the most interest, but the prophetic books were all translated into Aramaic, as were most of the books of the Writings. A certain amount of commentary is included in the translations.

Tebet Tenth month of the Jewish year, December-January.

Tebul Yom (Hebrew: "One who has immersed on that same day") [1] A person who was ritually impure, who immersed on the same day, and who awaits the setting of the sun, which marks the completion of the process of purification (Leviticus 22:5–7).

[2] Mishnah tractate on the uncleanliness assigned to one who has immersed and is waiting for sunset to complete the purification process; the tractate discusses the rules for connections between one thing and someone else, e.g., liquids touching what he has touched, or solid food touching what he has touched (chaps. 1–3) and the uncleanness affecting the Tebul Yom (chaps. 3–4)

Tefillat HaDerekh (Hebrew: "Prayer for the Road") A prayer recited by travelers as they embark upon a journey. The prayer requests that God sustain and protect the traveler from harm, bless the work of his or her hands, and allow him or her to return home safely.

Tefillin Phylacteries, small leather cases containing four passages from the Hebrew Scriptures, Exodus 13:1–10, 11–16, Deuteronomy 6:4–9 and 11:13–21, written on parchment. The cases are affixed with leather straps on the left arm

Tefillin A man wearing tefillin.

and forehead of adult males during the weekday morning worship, literally fulfilling the commandment at Exodus 13:9, that one should make God's words a sign on one's hand and a memorial between one's eyes.

Temurah (Hebrew: exchange, substitution) Mishnah Tractate on the rules for substituting one animal for another within the cult, in line with Leviticus 27:14: who may make a statement substituting one beast that has been consecrated for another; how it is done (chaps. 1–2); the status of the offspring of substitutes (chaps. 3–4); language used in effecting an act of substitution (chaps. 5–6).

Ten Commandments (Hebrew: *'Aseret HaDibrot*) Revealed by God to Moses at Sinai, the Ten Commandments (Exodus 20:1–14, Deuteronomy 5:6–18) are as follows: [1] I am the Lord your God who brought you out of the Land of Egypt; you shall have no other gods besides Me. [2] You shall not make yourself a sculptured image. [3] You shall not swear falsely by the name of the Lord your God. [4] Remember the Sabbath day to keep it holy. [5] Honor your father and your mother. [6] You shall not murder. [7] You shall not commit adultery. [8] You shall not steal. [9] You shall not bear false witness against your neighbor. [10] You shall not covet. The Ten Commandments in Judaism are regarded as a key summary of the requirements of the Torah.

Ten Days of Repentance (Hebrew: *'Aserat Yemei Teshuvah*) The ten days between ROSH HASHANAH and YOM KIPPUR, considered a period in which God is particularly open to accepting REPENTANCE. During this period, the prayer Avinu Malkenu (Hebrew: "Our Father, Our King"), a compilation of requests and needs, and penitential prayers (SELIḤOT) are recited daily (except on the Sabbath).

Ten Tribes of Northern Israel   The ten tribes that separated from the Davidic monarchy of Jerusalem after the death of Solomon, David's son, and formed a king-dom of their own. They are the children of Jacob other than Judah and Benjamin. In 701 B.C.E., they were conquered by the Assyrians and exiled from the Land of Israel. Their present location and identity have been subjected to much speculation, but no one knows who their contemporary heirs are. See TWELVE TRIBES OF ISRAEL.

Teqiʻah   Alarm sound produced by the sounding of a *shofar*, on New Year and other occasions when the Shofar is used.

Tequfah   (Hebrew: "circuit") In the Jewish calendar, a season, demarcated as follows: *Tequfat Nisan*, the mean sun at the vernal equinox point; *Tequfat Tammuz*, the summer solstice point; *Tequfat Tishrei*, the autumnal equinox point; *Tequfat Tebet*, the winter solstice point.

Teref, Terefah   Hebrew: "Torn," and by extension, "carrion" in line with Exo-dus 32:31: "You shall not eat any flesh that is torn by beasts in the field." This passage is taken to prohibit consumption of any beast that dies due to physical defects or injuries rather than through a proper act of ritual slaughter. The term Teref is extended to refer generally to any unko-sher food.

Terumot   [1] Priestly rations; the por-tion of the crop in the Land of Israel that is raised up for the priest (hence the usual translation: "heave offering"); this is the first agricultural gift separated from pro-duce, given to the priests, who are to eat it in a state of cultic cleanness.

[2] Mishnah tractate devoted to heave offering, which is separated by farmers and handed over to the priesthood at the harvest; how heave offering is separated (chaps. 1–4); heave offering that has been separated but still is in the domain of the householder (chaps. 4–10); consumption of heave offering by a non-priest and the penalties thereof (chaps. 6–8); seed grain in the status of heave offering that has been planted (chap. 9); heave offering cooked or prepared with unconsecrated produce (chap. 10); the disposition of heave offering in the hands of the priest, proper preparation of food in the status of heave offering (chap. 11).

Tetragrammaton   Name of God rep-resented by four Hebrew letters: Y/H/W/H, generally translated as "Lord." Pro-nounced only by the High Priest in the Holy of Holies on the Day of Atonement. When encountered in the liturgical read-ing of the Torah, the term is pronounced *Adonai*. See ELOHIM.

Tiqqun Leil Shabuʼot   The practice of community study of Torah, often the book of Ruth, during the entire night of the festival of SHABUʻOT, which com-memorates God's giving of the Torah to the people of Israel at Sinai. In this way, the community reenacts what is under-stood to be Israel's action at Sinai, receiv-ing and then immediately meditating on the revealed Torah.

Tisha beAb   See AB, NINTH OF.

Tishrei   The seventh month of the Jew-ish year (counting from Nisan, in which Passover falls), the lunar month in which the first full moon after the autumnal equinox occurs, September-October. The first day of Tishre is the New Year (Rosh Hashanah), the tenth is the Day of Atone-ment (Yom Kippur), the fifteenth is the first day of Tabernacles (SUKKOT).

Tohorot   [1] Sixth division of the

Mishnah, devoted to rules of cultic cleanness that govern in the Temple; also rules of cultic cleanness observed in the homes of those who wish to eat their everyday food in accordance with the laws governing the Temple priests' meals in the holy place.

[2] Mishnah tractate devoted to the susceptibility to uncleanliness of food, ordinarily at home; susceptibility to uncleanliness of Holy Things, heave offering, and unconsecrated food (chaps. 1–3); doubts in matters of uncleanliness (chaps. 3–6); the relationship of the observant and non-observant Israelite in connection with preserving the cultic cleanliness of food and drink (chaps. 7–8); special liquids, olive oil, and wine (chaps. 9–10).

Torah (Hebrew: "Instruction," "revelation," "teaching") Derived from the Hebrew root meaning "instruction," the term Torah refers to the sum total of the revelation of God to humankind, encompassing the written (*Torah shebikhtab*) and oral (*Torah shebe'al peh*) laws. The former includes the books of the Hebrew Bible, said to have been transmitted by God to Moses in writing; the latter is represented in the Talmudic literature, understood to comprise teachings that God instructed Moses orally and that were

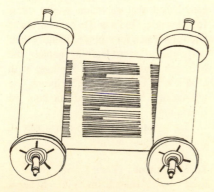

Torah An open Torah scroll.

handed down through the generations, until, beginning in the first centuries C.E., they were written down to prevent them from being lost. Having the sense of "revelation" and understood to define exactly what God expects of the Jews, the concept of Torah is central in Jewish practice and belief.

The term Torah used with the definite article ("The Torah") refers to the Pentateuch, the Five Books of Moses, often signifying in particular the handwritten scroll of the Pentateuch used in the synagogue; by extension, the term is taken to signify the whole of the Hebrew Scriptures or Old Testament. Beyond this, the term may have the sense of the "whole Torah," written and oral, and so may stand for the entire content of Judaism itself. Thus, by the end of Judaism's formative period, in the fifth and sixth centuries C.E., the word Torah lost its capital T, becoming simply "torah," meaning, "that which is in the status of The Torah," hence, anything that is authoritative as God's will for the people of Israel. What for nearly a millennium had been a particular scroll or book came to serve as a symbol of an entire system. When a rabbi spoke of "torah," he no longer meant only a particular object, a scroll and its contents. Now the word encompassed a distinctive and well-defined world view and way of life, defined by the religion of Judaism.

Beginning in the Rabbinical literature of late antiquity, therefore, the word Torah connotes a broad range of distinct categories. "Torah," referring to the rabbis who study it and the community that accepts its teachings, connotes a social status and a social group, a type of social relationship. It further denotes a legal status and differentiates among legal norms. As symbolic abstraction, the word encompasses actions and status, points of social differentiation and legal and normative standing as well as "revealed truth." If people wanted to explain how they would be saved, they would use the word "torah." If they wished to sort out their relationships with gentiles, they would use the world "torah." Torah stood for salvation and accounted for Israel's this-worldly condition and the hope of life in the world to come.

The most important initiative in so broadening the meaning of the word "torah" occurred in Mishnah Tractate ABOT, ca. 250 C.E.. There, the meaning of "the Torah" as a particular book of revelation is joined by a second sense. In Abot, Torah is instrumental. The figure of the sage, his ideals and conduct, form the goal, focus, and center. Tractate Abot regards study of torah as what a sage does. The substance of torah is that a sage says, whether or not the saying relates directly to scriptural revelation. The sages in tractate Abot usually do not quote verses of Scripture and explain them, nor do they speak in God's name. Yet, it is clear, sages talk torah. It follows that whatever a sage says falls into the classification of torah. Accordingly, Abot treats torah-learning as an indicator of the status of the sage. Tractate Abot stands as the first document of the doctrine that the sage embodies the torah and is a holy man. The beginning is to claim that a sage's saying falls into the category of torah. The end is to view the sage himself as torah incarnate.

The next major step in the expansion of the meaning of the word "torah" is found in the Jerusalem Talmud, which treats the Mishnah as equivalent to Scripture. Once the Mishnah entered the status of Scripture, it would take but a short step to a theory of the Mishnah as part of the revelation at Sinai—hence, oral torah. The Mishnah now is claimed to contain statements made by God to Moses. Here emerges a clear and unmistakable expression of the distinction between two forms in which a single torah was revealed at Mount Sinai, part in writing, part orally. In that same document, it is held that because people observed the rules of the torah, they expected to be saved. And if they did not observe them, they accepted their punishment. The torah thus comes to stand for something more than revelation and a life of study, and the sage now appears as a holy, not merely a learned, man. In this way, the word "torah" forms the centerpiece of a theory of Israel's history, on the one side, and future, on the other. Torah has ceased to constitute a specific thing when stories about studying the torah yield not a judgment as to status (i.e., praise for the learned man) but a promise of supernatural blessing now and salvation in time to come.

To the rabbis, the principal way to salvation was to "study torah," which meant memorizing passages from the torah and engaging in profound analytic inquiry into their meaning. Mastery of torah transformed the person engaged in torah study into a supernatural figure who could do things ordinary folk could not do. The category of "torah" had vastly expanded from something concrete into a symbol. Now, once the principle had been established that salvation would come from keeping God's will in general, it was but a small step for rabbis to identify their particular corpus of learning, namely, the Mishnah and associated sayings, with God's will expressed in Scripture, the universally acknowledged medium of revelation.

See TALMUD TORAH, TORAH SHEBE'AL PEH, TORAH SHEBIKHTAB.

Torah Mantel   The fabric covering used by Ashkenazim and Spanish Sephardic communities to cover a Torah scroll when it is not in use. The mantel is often made of velvet or other heavy fabric and is elaborately decorated with appropriate motifs, such as the Tree of Life, the lion that represents the tribe of Judah, or a crown, symbolizing the Torah's majestic sovereignty. Among Jews from the Middle East, the scrolls are kept in a rigid case.

Torah SheBe'al Peh (Hebrew: "Oral Torah") The Torah that was orally formulated and orally transmitted; now recorded in the MISHNAH, TOSEFTA, the Jerusalem and Babylonian versions of the TALMUD and the various Midrashic compilations of late antiquity. Tractate Abot 1:1 begins with the declaration, "Moses received Torah at Sinai and handed it on to Joshua...." The document thus boldly expresses the claim that Judaism is comprised by "Torah" revealed at Sinai both in writing and the in memory, that is, in oral tradition. See also CANON.

Torah SheBiKhtab (Hebrew: "Written Torah") The Torah, as written down in the Five Books of Moses.

Tosafot (Hebrew: "additions") Novellae on the Talmud, additions generally to the commentary of Rashi. The Tosafists, authorities who produced Tosafot, flourished during the twelfth to fourteenth centuries in northern France.

Tosefta (Hebrew: "supplement") A Rabbinic supplement to, commentary on, and amplification of the MISHNAH. Compiled at the beginning of the fourth century C.E., the Tosefta, like the Mishnah, contains material presumably preserved from the preceding centuries. But since the Tosefta is understood within the circles of traditional Judaism to contain materials excluded from the Mishnah itself, it does not have a significant place in the determination of Jewish law. Within classical Judaism, it accordingly has been the least

studied legal document of early Rabbinic Judaism.

Four times larger than the document it amplifies, the Tosefta is wholly depending upon the Mishnah for its rhetoric, topical program, and logic of coherent discourse. It has no structure of its own but most commonly cites and glosses a passage of the Mishnah, not differentiating its forms and wording of sentences from those of the cited passage. Only seldom—for somewhat under a sixth of the whole of its volume—does the Tosefta present a statement that may be interpreted entirely independently of the Mishnah's counterpart (if any). The Tosefta covers nearly the whole of the Mishnah's program but has none of its own.

While the Tosefta serves as the Mishnah's first commentary, first amplification, and first extension, this does not mean it is a very accessible document. The opposite is the case, and the reason derives from the Tosefta's very character as a document of mediation, expansion, and extension of another piece of writing. The Tosefta makes sense only in relationship to the Mishnah. That is so not only for its program and order, which are defined by the Mishnah, but also for its individual compositions. Each completed unit of thought of the Tosefta is to be understood in relationship with the Mishnah: is it a citation of and commentary to the Mishnah passage that forms its counterpart? Is the passage fully to be comprehended on its own or only in relationship to a counterpart passage of the Mishnah? Or is the passage freestanding? The answers to these three questions define the first step in making any sense at all of a passage of the Tosefta.

The Tosefta stands, almost in its entirety, within the circle of the Mishnah's interests, only rarely asking questions about topics omitted altogether by the Mishnah's authors, always following the topical decisions on what to discuss as laid down by the founders of the whole. One cannot write about the Tosefta's theology or law as though these constitute a system susceptible of description and interpretation independent of the Mishnah's system. At the same time, the exegetes of the Mishnah, in the Tosefta, and in the two Talmuds, stand apart from, and later than, the authors of the Mishnah itself. Accordingly, the exegetes systematically say whatever they wish to say by attaching their ideas to a document earlier than their own, and by making the principal document say what they wish to contribute. The system of expressing ideas through reframing those of predecessors preserves the continuity of tradition and establishes a deep stability and order upon the culture framed by that tradition.

Tractate   See MASSEKHET.

Tu BiShebat   (Hebrew: "the fifteenth of Shebat") The New Year for trees, regarded for liturgical purposes as a minor festival (see Mishnah Rosh Hashanah 1:1). In the modern state of Israel, Tu BiShebat is celebrated as Arbor Day, marked by tree-planting ceremonies.

Twelve Tribes of Israel   The children of the patriarch Jacob, his wives Leah and Rachel, and his concubines are the progenitors of the Israelite tribes, among whom the Land of Israel was divided after it was conquered by Joshua. These are treated in Genesis 49 in the blessing of Jacob as he lay dying: Reuben, Simeon, Levi, Judah, Zebulun, Issachar, Dan, Gad, Asher, Naphtali, Joseph, and Benjamin. When reference is made to "twelve tribes," it generally means, the whole of corporate Israel. See TEN TRIBES OF NORTHERN ISRAEL.

U

Uqsin Mishnah tractate on connections between different parts of food, e.g., the twig and the apple, the husk and the nut; susceptibility to uncleanness and joining together of distinct parts of the same piece of fruit (chaps. 1–2); connection in food (chap. 2); susceptibility to uncleanness of food (chap. 3).

Usury See NESHEKH.

Uzziah King of the nation of Judah in 785–734 B.C.E., the time of the prophet Isaiah, a prophet of Jerusalem. Uzziah successfully battled the Philistines and received tribute from the Ammonites. 2 Kings 15:5 reports that he was stricken with leprosy, at which point his son Jotham took on the role of co-regent.

V

Vidui (Hebrew: "confession") A confession of sin made at the onset of death. In line with the view that death effects atonement for sins, the dying Jew states:

My God and God of my fathers, accept my prayer….

Forgive me for all the sins I have committed in my lifetime….

Accept my pain and suffering as atonement and forgive my wrong-doing for against You alone have I sinned….

I acknowledge that my life and recovery depend on You.

May it be Your will to heal me.

Yet if You have decreed that I shall die of this affliction,

May my death atone for all sins and transgressions I have committed before You.

Shelter me in the shadow of Your wings.

Grant me a share in the world-to-come.

Father of orphans and Guardian of widows, protect my beloved family….

Into Your hand I commit my soul. You redeem me, O Lord God of truth.

Then comes the declaration of the faith:

Hear O Israel, the Lord is our God, the Lord alone.

The Lord He is God.

The Lord He is God.

The Vidui prepares the way for the entry of the dying person into the life of the world-to-come.

Virtue (Hebrew: *middot*) For Judaism the virtuous person (*ba'al middot*) imitates the virtue of God. God's traits of justice and equity, love and compassion, form the model for God's creatures. The virtues that Judaism teaches are supposed to characterize the individual and the community. Both are to conduct themselves in God's image: "Just as I am merciful and long-suffering, so you must be merciful and long-suffering," says the Talmud. The doctrine of virtue, which yields ethical teachings for right conduct, finds its context in the scriptural narrative. Virtue begins in an attitude of voluntary obedience to, and vice commences in an attitude of rebellion against, God.

Virtue and practical ethics stand for those traits that bring about reconciliation between the children of Adam and Eve and God, and for traits or activities that disrupt the relationship. So the Torah finds its dynamic in the struggle between God's plan for creation—to create a perfect world of justice—and the free will of humanity. All virtuous traits then find their place within an encompassing vision that explains who we are by telling the story of creation. In Judaism, "we"—humanity—are Adam and Eve, fallen from Eden, and, when possessed of the Torah, able to regain Eden. All virtue is defined in that context. In the Torah, the Rabbinic sages find that arrogance is a vice and causes sin, while humility is a virtue, and there they learn the reason why: virtue begins in our relationship to God.

W

Wiesel, Elie (1928–) Noted Holocaust survivor and novelist, winner in 1986 of the Nobel Peace Prize. A leading representative of survivors of Nazi concentration camps and a champion in the fight against oppression and racism. Wiesel has spent his life describing the horrors of World War II and struggling with the human and religious issues that the Holocaust raises.

Born in Sighet, Romania, during World War II, Wiesel was held in the concentration camps at Auschwitz and Buchenwald, where his parents and a sister died. After the war, he studied philosophy at the University of Paris, became a journalist, and moved to the United States where, since 1976, he has been a professor of humanities at Boston University.

Wiesel's first and perhaps most famous book, *Night* (1958), is a memoir of his experiences in the concentration camps. It forms a trilogy with *Dawn* (1960) and *The Accident* (1961), which concern the lives of survivors. Rather than a positive theological response to the horror of the Holocaust—an affirmation of God in the face of evil—in these works Wiesel portrays the evolution of his despair, beginning, in *Night*, with his transition from youthful belief to disillusionment and erosion of faith. Wiesel's point is not that there is no God, or even that God has abandoned His people (though this theme does appear). Rather, Wiesel focuses upon God's apparent complicity in the horrors. The Holocaust can happen only because God wills it, even if that "will" is recognized only in God's silence. Contrary to the classical Jewish perspective, in Wiesel's view, God is indifferent to suffering and human history. Wiesel thus paints a tragic vision of a void in which God is absent.

Wiesel's attitude means that there should come an end to prayer and thanksgiving, there apparently being nothing for which to thank God. In Wiesel's thought, though, the rejection of religion runs alongside a desire to continue in belief and practice, to return to the age of innocent faith and sense of God's protection. Two important themes emerge from this dichotomy. One is the concept of struggle with God and the appropriateness of humankind's crying out to God for explanations. The other is the obligation for people themselves to take responsibility for the world in which they live, to fight, as Wiesel himself has, for what is right and proper.

Wiesel's other books include *The Jews of Silence*, *A Beggar in Jerusalem*, *The Testament*, *Town Beyond the Wall*, *The Gates of the Forest*, *The Oath*, and *All Rivers run to the Sea: Memoirs*.

Wissenschaft des Judentums (German: Science of Judaism); scientific study, using scholarly methods of philology, history, and philosophy, of Jewish religion, literature, and history; founded in nineteenth-century Germany. The academic tradition of the study of Judaism in secular universities and seminaries in the U.S.A. and western Europe originates in this original scientific study of Judaism.

Women In the law of classical Judaism, men are the principal active force while women are acted upon, an arena for concern in particular when they represent points of danger, e.g., when their status is unclear, specifically, when a woman is betrothed and married; when the marriage comes to an end; and at similar turning points. The principal focus of a social vision framed by men, such as that of the MISHNAH, not only encompasses, but focuses upon, woman, who is perceived as the indicative abnormality in a world in which men are the norm.

The principal point of interest is the time at which a women changes hands. That is, she becomes, and ceases to be, holy to a particular man, enters and leaves the marital union. These are the dangerous and disorderly points in the relationship of woman to man, therefore to society. Notably, five of the seven tractates of the Mishnah that pertain to women and family are devoted to the transfer of women, the formation and dissolution of the marital bond. Of them, three treat what by man is done here on earth, that is, formation of a marital bond through betrothal and marriage contract and dissolution through divorce and its consequences: QIDDUSHIN, KETUBOT, and GITTIN. One of them is devoted to the problem of adultery, that is, to what by woman is done here on earth: SOTAH. YEBAMOT, greatest of the seven in size and in formal and substantive brilliance, deals with the corresponding heavenly intervention in the formation and dissolution of marriage: the affect of death upon the marital bond, and the dissolution, through death, of that bond. The other two tractates, NEDARIM and NAZIR, draw into one of the two realms of reality, Heaven and earth, as they work out the effects of vows—generally taken by married women and subject to the confirmation or abrogation of the husband—to Heaven. These vows make a deep impact upon the marital relationship of the woman who has taken such a vow.

Written Torah See TORAH SHEBIKHTAB.

Y

Yabam (Hebrew: "Levir") In line with Deuteronomy 25:1–5, the surviving brother of a childless, deceased man; required either to marry his sister-in-law, that is, levirate marriage; or undertake the rite of removing the shoe. See ḤALIṢAH.

Yadayim Mishnah tractate on washing the hands to remove cultic uncleanliness; washing hands (chaps. 1–2); the status of uncleanliness imputed to hands (chap. 3); the status of uncleanliness imputed to sacred Scriptures (chaps. 3–4).

Yahrzeit (Yiddish: "Anniversary") Anniversary of death of a close relative. Observed by the recitation of QADDISH and by kindling a twenty-four hour memorial light.

Yahweh The Hebrew letters for the name of God (YHWH), represented in Roman characters and supplied with vowels. The term is ordinarily translated as "the Lord," as distinct from the Hebrew word *Elohim*, translated as "God," or "the divinity." The term "*Yahweh Elohim*" then is represented in English as "Lord God." See JEHOVAH. Not normally used by Jews but often used by non-Jews to indicate the Israelite God.

Yamim Noraim (Hebrew: "The Days of Awe") The first ten days of the lunar month of Tishrei in the fall, comprising the New Year (Rosh Hashanah) and the Day of Atonement (Yom Kippur), days of solemn penitence. These days mark the start of the fall season in connection with the autumnal equinox, marking, in the Land of Israel, the end of the dry season and the commencement of the fall rains. Israel's collective life in the Land is in the balance; without rain, the summer season of death extends itself, and drought brings famine. With rain, life is renewed. One should expect the religious ideology of this season to concern all ISRAEL, and so the story realized in the holy season of the Ten Days of Awe concerns the individual Israelite in the setting of all of humanity. It tells that the New Year commemorates the creation of the world, and that, on the New Year, every creature comes before God to be judged for deeds performed in the past year. Then, ten days later, the decree is sealed. But that day, the Day of Atonement, on its own, has the power to atone for sin. Thus the judgment of the New Year is mitigated or even set aside. Leviticus 16:32–34 is clear that this day on its own brings forgiveness:

> It shall be a statute for you forever that in the seventh month, on the tenth day of the month, you shall afflict yourself and shall do no work, either the native or the stranger who sojourns among you; for on this day shall atonement be made for you, to cleanse you, from all your sins you shall be clean before the Lord.… And this shall be an everlasting statute for you, that atonement may be made for the people of Israel once in the year because of their sins.

See ROSH HASHANAH, YOM KIPPUR.

Yavneh Town beside the Mediterranean coast of the Land of Israel at which, after the destruction of the Temple in 70 C.E., sages assembled and conducted schools and courts; center of the master-disciple circle of YOHANAN BEN ZAKKAI.

Yebamot Mishnah tractate devoted to

levirate marriage (Deuteronomy 25:1–5), which discusses establishing the levirate marital bond, or severing the levirate bond through the rite of removing the shoe (chaps. 1–5); the special marital bond, marriage into the priesthood: when a woman may eat heave offering (see chap. 6); who may eat heave offering (see TERUMOT) (chaps. 7–8); severing the marital bond (chaps. 10–16); marital bonds subject to doubt (chaps. 10–11); severing the levirate bond through the rite of removing the shoe (chap. 12); severing the marital bond of a minor, the right of refusal (chap. 13); the infirm marital bond of a deaf mute (chap. 14); severing the marital bond through the death of the husband (chaps. 15–16).

Yerushalmi   The Jerusalem TALMUD, also known as the Talmud of the Land of Israel, produced in the Land of Israel, ca. 400 C.E., in Tiberias and Caesarea, as a commentary to the Mishnah's first, second, third, and fourth divisions; made up mostly of amplification and extension of passages of the Mishnah. Approximately 90 percent of the document comprises commentary on the Mishnah. The Yerushalmi invariably does to the Mishnah one of four things: (1) text criticism; (2) exegesis of the meaning of the Mishnah, including glosses and amplifications; (3) addition of Scriptural proof texts of the Mishnah's central propositions; and (4) harmonization of one Mishnah passage with another such passage or with a statement of TOSEFTA. The first two of these four procedures remain wholly within the narrow framework of the Mishnah passage under discussion. The second pair take an essentially independent stance *vis-a-vis* the Mishnah pericope at hand. The Mishnah is read by the Yerushalmi as a composite of discrete and essentially autonomous rules, a set of atoms, not an integrated

molecule; the most striking formal traits of the Mishnah are obliterated. The Mishnah as a whole and complete statement of a viewpoint no longer exists.

The Yerushalmi provides some indication of effort at establishing the correct text of various passages of the Mishnah. This nearly always is in the context of deciding the law. It is not a random search for a "perfect" text. It rather represents a deliberate and principled inquiry into the law as revealed by the phrasing of a passage. That is why, in the bulk of these passages, the legal consequences of one reading as opposed to another are carefully articulated, sometimes even tied to a range of other points subject to dispute. The Mishnah rarely finds it necessary to cite a Scriptural proof text for its propositions. The Yerushalmi, by contrast, does so whenever possible.

Yeṣer HaRa', Yeṣer HaTob   (Hebrew: "Evil inclination, good inclination"). People and God are possessed of free will. But our free will encompasses the capacity to rebel against God, and that comes about because innate in our will is the impulse to do evil (*yeṣer hara'*). The impulse within people to do evil struggles with their impulse to do good (*yeṣer hatob*). But creation bears within itself the forces that ultimately will resolve the struggle. That struggle will come to an end in the world-to-come, which itself comes about by an act of divine response to human regeneration. The individual Israelite struggles with the impulse to do evil, which, with God's help, through application to Torah study, he overcomes. That the impulse to do evil is localized in sexuality is expressed in the attached composition, which leaves no doubt of sages' definition of the prime seat of the impulse (Babylonian Talmud Sukkah 52a):

A   Said R. Yohanan, "There is in man a

small organ, which makes him feel hungry when he is sated,

B "and makes him feel sated when he is hungry,

C "as it is said, 'When they were starved, they became full' (Hosea 13:6)."

In a variety of ways, the impulse to do evil finds its opposite and complement in Torah study. The impulse to do evil can be overcome, specifically through Torah study (Genesis Rabbah LIV:I.1):

H "At that time Abimelech and Phicol the commander of his army said to Abraham, 'God is with you in all that you do'" (Genesis 21:22).

I R. Joshua b. Levi said, "The cited verse refers to the impulse to do evil.

J "Under ordinary circumstances if someone grows up with a fellow for two or three years, he develops a close tie with him. But the impulse to do evil grows with someone from youth to old age, and, if possible, a person strikes down the impulse to do evil even when he is seventy or eighty.

K "So did David say, 'All my bones shall say, "Lord, who is like unto you, who delivers the poor from him who is too strong for him, yes, the poor and the needy from him who spoils him"' (Psalm 35:10)."

Now the antidote is made explicit:

L Said R. Aha, "And is there a greater thief than this one? And Solomon said, 'If your enemy be hungry, give him bread to eat' (Proverbs 25:21). The meaning is, the bread of the Torah [which will help a person resist the enemy that is the impulse to do evil], as it is said, 'Come, eat of my bread' (Proverbs 9:5).

M "'If he is thirsty give him water to drink' (Proverbs 25:21), that is, the water of the Torah, as it is said, 'Ho, everyone who is thirsty come for water' (Isaiah 55:1)."

N R. Berekhiah said, "The verse says, '...also his enemies' (Proverbs 16:7), with the word 'also' encompassing the insects of the house, vermin, flies and the like.'"

Sometimes Torah study is treated in concrete terms, with an explanation of precisely how the Torah serves as antidote to sin, and sometimes, as here, in symbolic terms. Torah study teaches the lesson of humility, the powerful antidote to the cause of sin, which is arrogance. This is how Torah study brings about victory over sin. What one learns, in specific terms, persuades humans not to sin but to exercise humility in light of what they know about themselves.

Yeshiva Talmudic academy, also called BET MIDRASH.

Yiddish Once the Jewish vernacular of central and eastern Europe, now used in United States, Israel, Argentina, Brazil and Mexico, in addition to the natural language; originally a Judeo-German dialect, containing a number of Hebrew and Slavic words. A principal medium for the expression of Judaism, the Yiddish language contains numerous theological words from the Rabbinic canon and assigns them important everyday meanings.

Yigdal Synagogue hymn that contains the thirteen principles of faith formulated by MAIMONIDES; sung at the end of synagogue worship as the creed of Judaism. These principles are as follows: (1) existence of God; (2) God's unity; (3) God's incorporeality; (4) God's eternity; (5) the obligation to worship God alone; (6) prophecy; (7) Moses as the greatest of the prophets; (8) the divine origin of Torah; (9) the eternal validity of Torah; (10)

God's knowledge of man's deeds; (12) God's promise to send a Messiah; and (13) God's promise to resurrect the dead

Yiḥud (Hebrew: "isolation, seclusion") Isolation of a woman and a man, for purposes of sexual relations, as part of the marriage rite.

Yissurin (Hebrew: "Sickness and Suffering") Suffering, for example, sickness, old age, and death, is integral to God's plan. Yissurin represents an occasion to atone for sin in this world, leaving the way open to eternal life in the world-to-come after death. But the Rabbinic sages did not regard sickness, old age, and death as necessarily representing a punishment. These components of the human condition not only do not form challenges to the logic of God's just governance of the world, but express that very benevolence that infuses justice. So the patriarchs themselves initially beseeched God to bestow the blessings of old age, suffering, and sickness, each for its rational purpose (Genesis Rabbah LXV:IX.1).

A "When Isaac was old, and his eyes were dim, so that he could not see, he called Esau his older son, and said to him, 'My son,' and he answered, 'Here I am'" (Genesis 27:1):

B Said R. Judah bar Simon, "Abraham sought [the physical traits of] old age [so that from his appearance, people would know that he was old]. He said before him, 'Lord of all ages, when a man and his son enter somewhere, no one knows whom to honor. If you crown a man with the traits of old age, people will know whom to honor.'

C "Said to him the Holy One, blessed be He, 'By your life, this is a good thing that you have asked for, and it will begin with you.'

D "From the beginning of the book of Genesis to this passage, there is no reference to old age. But when Abraham our father came along, the traits of old age were given to him, as it is said, 'And Abraham was old' (Genesis 24:1)."

So much for old age, but what about what goes with it, the suffering of infirmities? Here Isaac makes his contribution, now being credited with that very conception that explains the justice of human suffering:

E "Isaac asked God for suffering. He said before him, 'Lord of the age, if someone dies without suffering, the measure of strict justice is stretched out against him. But if you bring suffering on him, the measure of strict justice will not be stretched out against him. [Suffering will help counter the man's sins, and the measure of strict justice will be mitigated through suffering by the measure of mercy.]'

F "Said to him the Holy One, blessed be He, 'By your life, this is a good thing that you have asked for, and it will begin with you.'

G "From the beginning of the book of Genesis to this passage, there is no reference to suffering. But when Isaac came along, suffering was given to him: his eyes were dim."

Finally, what of sickness, the third in the components of man's fate? That is Jacob's contribution, and the wisdom and good will of God come once more to full articulation in suffering:

H "Jacob asked for sickness. He said before him, 'Lord of all ages, if a person dies without illness, he will not settle his affairs for his children. If he is sick for two or three days, he will settle his affairs with his children.'

I   "Said to him the Holy One, blessed be He, 'By your life, this is a good thing that you have asked for, and it will begin with you.'

J   "That is in line with this verse: 'And someone said to Joseph, "Behold, your father is sick"' (Genesis 48:1)."

K   Said R. Levi, "Abraham introduced the innovation of old age, Isaac introduced the innovation of suffering, Jacob introduced the innovation of sickness."

We proceed now to a further case of the same classification, now chronic illness and its origin in the wisdom of the saints, now Hezekiah:

L   "Hezekiah introduced the innovation of chronic illness. He said to him, 'You have kept a man in good condition until the day he dies. But if someone is sick and gets better, is sick and gets better, he will carry out a complete and sincere act of repentance for his sins.'

M   "Said to him the Holy One, blessed be He, 'By your life, this is a good thing that you have asked for, and it will begin with you.'

N   "'The writing of Hezekiah, king of Judah, when he had been sick and recovered of his sickness' (Isaiah 38:9)."

O   Said R. Samuel b. Nahman, "On the basis of that verse we know that between one illness and another there was an illness more serious than either one."

Old age, suffering, and sickness do not represent flaws in creation but things to be desired. Each serves a good purpose. All form acts of divine mercy. The mode of explanation appeals to reason and practical considerations attached thereto.

Still, matters do not come out even; all die, but not everyone suffers premature death or sickness. Much more galling: sometimes wicked people live long, healthy and prosperous lives, happily making everyone around them miserable, then die peacefully in their sleep at a ripe old age. And—then or now one need not visit a cancer ward to find misery afflicting genuinely good and pious people. So while the doctrine of the benevolence expressed by sickness, suffering, and old age, serves, it hardly constitutes a universal and sufficient justification. And, however reasonable suffering may be shown to be, in the end reason hardly suffices in the face of the raw agony of incurable illness. But Judaism invokes God's own plan. Specifically, when the righteous suffer, it is God who is testing them (Genesis Rabbah LV:II.1f):

A   "The Lord tries the righteous, but the wicked and him who loves violence his soul hates" (Psalms 11:5):

B   Said R. Jonathan, "A potter does not test a weak utensil, for if he hits it just once, he will break it. What does the potter test? He tests the strong ones, for even if he strikes them repeatedly, they will not break. So the Holy One, blessed be He, does not try the wicked but the righteous: 'The Lord tries the righteous' (Psalms 11:5)."

C   Said R. Yossi bar Haninah, "When a linen maker knows that the flax is in good shape, then the more he beats it, the more it will improve and glisten. When it is not of good quality, if he beats it just once, he will split it. So the Holy One, blessed be He, does not try the wicked but the righteous: 'The Lord tries the righteous' (Psalms 11:5)."

The suffering of the righteous pays tribute to their strength and is a mark of their virtue. That is shown by appeal to both analogies (potter, flax-maker) and Scripture. Suffering then shows God's favor for the one who suffers, indicating that such a one is worthy of God's attention and special interest.

One is obligated to say a blessing over evil as one blesses over the good, as it is said, "And you shall love the Lord your God with all your heart, with all your soul, and with all your might" (Deuteronomy 6:5). "With all your heart"—with both of your inclinations, with the good inclination and with the evil inclination. "And with all your soul"—even if He takes your soul. "And with all your might"— with all of your money (Mishnah Berakhot 9:4A-E). Accordingly, the correct attitude toward suffering entails grateful acknowledgement that what God metes out is just and merciful.

Yizkor (Hebrew: "May He remember...") The memorial worship service, recited during community prayer on the festivals of PASSOVER, SHABU'OT, SUKKOT, and on YOM KIPPUR. During the Yizkor prayers, individuals memorialize deceased relatives and martyrs of the Jewish people. Alongside the memorial prayer proper, which begins with the word *Yizkor*, the service includes a recitation of Psalm 23 and ends with the reading of the mourners QADDISH.

Yohanan ben Zakkai   Principal Rabbinic authority of the first century C.E., head of the sages at Yavneh after the destruction of the Temple. He instructed the leading sages of the late first and early second century and laid the foundations of the Mishnah. In 68 C.E., assisted by his disciples, Eliezer and Joshua, Yohanan was smuggled out of besieged Jerusalem in a coffin and went over to the Romans. He was allowed to continue his Torah study and laid the foundations for the rebuilding of Judaism after the destruction of the Second Temple. His key-saying in the Sayings of the Fathers (see ABOT) is, "If you have done much in study of the Torah, do not take pride in that fact, for to that end you were created."

Yom Kippur   (Hebrew: "Day   of Atonement") The most personal, solemn, and moving of the Days of Awe, the Day of Atonement, the Sabbath of Sabbaths, is marked by fasting and continuous prayer. It is the single most widely observed rite of Judaism. On the Day of Atonement it is forbidden to (1) eat, (2) drink, (3) bathe, (4) put on any sort of oil, (5) put on a sandal, (6) or engage in sexual relations (Mishnah Yoma 8:1). The holy day begins with a public remission of vows (see KOL NIDREI), so that the congregants may appear before God unencumbered by vows they, thoughtlessly, take to God:

> All vows and oaths we take, all promises and obligations we make between this Day of Atonement and the next we hereby publicly retract in the event that we should forget them and hereby declare our intention to be absolved of them.

Sung on at sunset on the eve of the Day of Atonement, the formula called Kol Nidrei, for the opening words, moves masses of Jews to come to synagogue who otherwise scarcely find their way there. In the synagogue, the Jew then makes confession:

> Our God and God of our fathers, may our prayer come before You. Do not hide Yourself from our supplication, for we are not so arrogant or stiffnecked as to say before You ... We are righteous and have not sinned. But we have sinned.
> We are guilt laden, we have been faithless, we have robbed....
> We have committed iniquity, caused unrighteousness, have been presumptuous...

We have counseled evil, scoffed, revolted,
blasphemed....

The Hebrew confession is built upon an
alphabetical acrostic, as if by making certain every letter is represented, God, who
knows human secrets, will combine them
into appropriate words. The very alphabet
bears witness against us before God.

A further list of sins follows, also built
on alphabetical lines. Prayers to be spoken
by the congregation are all in the plural:
"For the sin which we have sinned against
You with the utterance of the lips.... For
the sin which we have sinned before You
openly and secretly...." The community
takes upon itself responsibility for what is
done in it. All Israel is part of one community, one body, and all are responsible for
the acts of each. The sins confessed are
mostly against society, against one's fellow men; few pertain to ritual laws. At the
end comes a final word:

> O my God, before I was formed, I was
> nothing. Not that I have been formed, it
> is as though I had not been formed, for I
> am dust in my life, more so after death.
> Behold I am before You like a vessel
> filled with shame and confusion. May it
> be Your will ... that I may no more sin,
> and forgive the sins I have already com-
> mitted in Your abundant compassion.

While much of the liturgy speaks of
"we," the individual focus dominates,
beginning to end. The Days of Awe speak
to the heart of the individual, telling a
story of judgment and atonement. So the
individual Jew stands before God: possessing no merits, yet hopeful of God's
love and compassion.

The Day of Atonement represents one
medium of atonement that the Torah sets
forth, others of which are offerings of various kinds and death. Thus: a sin offering
and an unconditional guilt offering atone.
Death and the Day of Atonement atone
when joined with repentance. Repentance
atones for minor transgressions of positive and negative commandments. And as
to serious transgressions, [repentance]
suspends the punishment until the Day of
Atonement comes along and atones
(Mishnah Yoma 8:8). But there is no such
thing as preemptive repentance: He who
says, "I shall sin and repent, sin and
repent"—they give him no chance to do
repentance. [If he said,] "I will sin and the
Day of Atonement will atone"—the Day
of Atonement does not atone (Mishnah
Yoma 8:9A-B).

Yoma   Mishnah tractate devoted to the
Day of Atonement, especially dealing
with Temple rites for that day, in line with
Leviticus 16: conduct of the rites on the
Day of Atonement (chaps. 1–7); the laws
of the Day of Atonement (chap. 8): not
eating, not drinking; atonement: what the
Day atones for, what repentance and rec-
onciliation must accomplish. See
KIPPURIM.

Z

Zab/ah A male/female afflicted with the uncleanness of flux described at Leviticus 15.

Zabim Mishnah tractate on the uncleanliness described at Leviticus 15; becoming a Zab (chaps. 1–2); transferring the uncleanliness affecting the Zab to other objects (chaps. 2–5), through pressure (chaps. 2–4).

Zebaḥim (Hebrew: "Animal offerings") Mishnah tractate devoted to rules of everyday animal sacrifice in the Temple; improper intention on the part of the priest and how it invalidates the act of sacrifice (chaps. 1–4); rules for the sacrifice of animals and fowl ((chaps. 5–7); rules of the altar (chaps. 8–12), e.g., disposing of sacrificial portions or blood that have been confused with portions or blood from another offering (chap. 8); the altar sanctifies what is appropriate but not what is not (chap. 9); precedence in the use of the altar (chap. 10); blood of the sin offering that spurts onto a garment (exposition of Leviticus 6:27–28; chap. 11); dividing hides of animals among eligible priests (chap. 12); proper location of the altar (Jerusalem alone) and the act of sacrifice (chaps. 13–14).

Zechariah One of the twelve minor prophets of the Hebrew Scriptures. Chapters 1–8 contain prophecies of Zechariah, 9–14 belong to two other, unnamed prophets (9–11, 12–14, respectively). Zechariah flourished ca. 520–518 B.C.E., a contemporary of Ḥaggai in the early part of the Persian period. He prophesied concerning the rebuilding of the Temple, which he believed was required for the coming of the end-of-days, which he thought was imminent. Eight night-visions (1:7–6:8) portray the coming of the end of the world and the organization of life in the community at the end of times. These visions reflect his combination of priestly and prophetic gifts. The second and third parts of the book elaborate on the themes of the end of time that characterize Zechariah's prophecy.

Zera'im First division of the Mishnah, devoted to the rules governing agriculture in the Holy Land, with special reference to God's share in the crops, the Sabbatical Year, and tithing and gifts to the priesthood. Comprised by the tractates Berakhot (Blessings), Peah (Corner of the field), Demai (doubtfully-tithed produce), Kilayim (mixed seeds), Terumot (priestly rations, heave offering), Ma'aserot (tithes), Ma'aser Sheni (second tithe), Ḥallah (dough offering), Orlah (produce of a fruit tree in the fourth year after its planting), and Bikkurim (first fruits). The YERUSHALMI supplies a commentary for all the tractates of Zeraim, the Babylonian TALMUD only for Berakhot.

Zikhronot Remembrances, prayers on theme of God's remembering his mercy, covenant, found in the ROSH HASHANAH MUSAF worship service.

Zion The highest point in Jerusalem, the location of the Temple of Jerusalem. In poetic writings of the Hebrew Bible, the term often refers to the whole of Jerusalem or to the Jewish people. See ZIONISM.

Zionism The modern belief that the Jews should have a homeland, made concrete in the nineteenth and twentieth century program of developing the Land of Israel (the biblical Zion) as a Jewish state. While the idea that the Jews will have Zion as their homeland goes back to the original promise of God to the patriarch Abraham, modern political Zionism dates only to the nineteenth century. Under the leadership of Theodor Herzl, in 1878 the Zionist Organization was organized in Basel, and European and American Jews began to work for the creation of a Jewish state in what was then the province of the Ottoman Empire known as Palestine. The Zionist cause was boosted in 1917 when the British assumed control of Palestine and issued the Balfour Declaration, which supported the establishment there of a Jewish homeland. Between 1917 and 1947, hundreds of thousands of Jews settled in Palestine. From 1933 to 1945, however, the Jews in Europe, facing persecution by the Germans, were officially prohibited from entering the country in sizable numbers due to pressure put on the British mandatory power by the Arab population. In the aftermath of World War II, many of the Jews who had survived wanted to go to Palestine. In 1947, the United Nations voted to create a Jewish and an Arab state on the land. In 1948, the Jewish state declared independence and survived invasion by its Arab neighbors, thus fulfilling the dream of modern Zionism. Since then, Zionists inside and outside Israel have worked to assure the safety and stability of the Jewish state and to promote worldwide Jewish immigration to Israel.

Zohar   (Hebrew: "The   book   of

Splendor, Radiance, Enlightenment") Medieval Qabbalistic book of immense proportions and commensurate influence, completed by the fourteenth century in Spain; a mystical commentary on biblical passages; stories of the mystical life of the early Rabbinic authority Simeon b. Yohai; the principal document for conveying Judaism's story in mystical form. The work is a multi-layered commentary on the Pentateuch and the Five Scrolls (Esther, Ruth, Song of Songs, Qohelet (Ecclesiastes) and Lamentation s). It is an anthology of texts composed and revised over a long period of time, from the latter part of the thirteenth century into the fourteenth century. The main, but not the sole, author was Moses de Leon, who worked in Spain between 1281 and 1286. We can speak of a completed book of the Zohar only from the sixteenth century, when Qabbalists began to prepare the manuscripts for printing.

The Zohar speaks in the name of important second-century rabbis. This is because the mystics took for granted that their doctrines were tradition, part of the Torah, and derived from the same authorities who gave them the MISHNAH and other parts of the Oral Torah. In the Zohar, hidden meanings of Scripture are spelled out. These meanings contain the story of the creation and the cosmos that unfolds in the structure of the ten emanations (*sefirot*) of God. These provide the paradigmatic plan for all that unfolds from the supreme deity, called the "*En Sof*," or infinity. See QABBALAH.